C

Aspects
of
Reading
Acquisition

Previous volumes based on the annual Hyman Blumberg
Symposia on Research in Early Childhood Education
(available in both paperbound and clothbound editions)

Julian C. Stanley, general series editor

I. *Preschool Programs for the Disadvantaged: Five Experimental
Approaches to Early Childhood Education*, pp. ix + 204, 1972.
Edited by Julian C. Stanley.

II. *Compensatory Education for Children, Ages 2 to 8: Recent Studies
of Educational Intervention*, pp. viii + 213, 1973.
Edited by Julian C. Stanley.

III. *Mathematical Talent: Discovery, Description, and Development*,
pp. xvii + 215, 1974.
Edited by Julian C. Stanley, Daniel P. Keating, and Lynn H. Fox.

IV. Manuscript under consideration.

V. *Aspects of Reading Acquisition*, pp. xviii + 217, 1976.
Edited by John T. Guthrie.

VI. Intellectual Talent: Research and Development, pp. xviii + 348, 1976.
Edited by Daniel P. Keating.

The Blumberg Series is published by The Johns Hopkins University
Press, Baltimore, Maryland 21218.

Aspects of Reading Acquisition

Proceedings of the Fifth Annual
Hyman Blumberg Symposium
on Research in Early Childhood Education

Edited by John T. Guthrie

The Johns Hopkins University Press
Baltimore and London

The Johns Hopkins University Press, Baltimore, Maryland 21218
The Johns Hopkins University Press Ltd., London

Library of Congress Catalog Card Number 75-36956
ISBN 0-8018-1800-1 (clothbound edition)
ISBN 0-8018-1801-X (paperbound edition)

Library of Congress Cataloging in Publication Data

Hyman Blumberg Symposium on Research in Early Childhood
    Education, 5th, Johns Hopkins University, 1974.
    Aspects of reading acquisition.

    Includes index.
    1. Reading—Congresses. I. Guthrie, John T.
II. Title.
LB1049.95.H93   1974   372.4   75-36956
ISBN 0-8018-1800-1
ISBN 0-8018-1801-X pbk.

*To my colleagues
in Pediatrics, Education, and Psychology
at The Johns Hopkins University*

Contents

TABLES

FIGURES

Contributors

Isabel L. Beck, Ph.D., Research Associate and Director of Reading Curriculum Development, Learning Research and Development Center; Assistant Professor of Education, Department of Reading and Language Arts, University of Pittsburgh, Pittsburgh, Pennsylvania.

D. Frank Benson, M.D., Director, Neurobehavioral Center, Veterans Administration Hospital, Boston, Massachusetts.

Doris R. Entwisle, Professor of Social Relations and Engineering Science, The Johns Hopkins University, Baltimore, Maryland.

Janette Friel, Associate in Clinical Psychology, Department of Clinical Psychology, University of Florida, Gainesville, Florida.

Marcel Kinsbourne, B.M., B.CH., D.M., M.R.C.P., The Hospital For Sick Children, Toronto, Ontario, Canada.

Paula Menyuk, Professor, School of Education, Boston University, Boston, Massachusetts.

Lauren B. Resnick, Associate Director, Learning Research and Development Center, University of Pittsburgh, Pittsburgh, Pennsylvania.

Fran Rudegeair, Research Assistant, Department of Clinical Psychology, University of Florida, Gainesville, Florida.

S. Jay Samuels, Professor of Educational Psychology; Director, Minnesota Reading Research Project, University of Minnesota, Minneapolis, Minnesota.

Paul Satz, Ph.D., Professor of Psychology, Departments of Psychology and Clinical Psychology, Director, Neuropsychology Laboratory, Shands Teaching Hospital and Clinics, University of Florida, Gainesville, Florida.

Joanna Williams, Editor, *Journal of Educational Psychology*; Visiting Professor, Teachers College, Columbia University, New York, New York.

Preface

These papers were presented at the Fifth Annual Blumberg Symposium on Research in Early Childhood Education. The conference was held at Johns Hopkins University November 13 and 14, 1974. There were ninety-two registrants who attended the meetings, which does not include about fifteen persons who participated in only one of the sessions. There were two lectures in the morning and two in the afternoon on each day. Following each address the audience gathered in an adjoining concourse for coffee and conversation with the speakers, who located themselves at designated discussion posts. To gauge the reactions of the audience, questionnaires were distributed to forty-three of the registrants who attended the final session, which was a critique of the symposium.

The first five items on the questionnaire recorded the backgrounds of the participants. From this information two groups were readily distinguished. One group consisted of twelve college or university teaching faculty and researchers who held PhDs. One member had a Masters degree plus ninety credits. The other group contained thirty-one practitioners. All except six had a Masters degree and classified themselves as reading specialists or school psychologists.

The next sections of the questionnaire contained twenty-four statements about the symposium. The participants were asked to respond to the statements on a four-point scale: (1) strongly agree, (2) agree, (3) disagree, and (4) strongly disagree. It was intended that eight statements would pertain to the information that was learned. For example: "The lectures brought me up-to-date on new information in the field." Another set of items related to the applicability of the information to the professional activities of the respondents. For instance: "The concepts I learned will be applicable in some of my daily work." The third set of items addressed the issue of integration among the multidisciplinary presentations. An example of this set was: "Reading was a solid link that held the different speeches together." Items from these three sets were listed in random order. Half of them were phrased positively, like the examples, and half were phrased negatively to reduce response bias.

Results of the questionnaire portray an intriguing reaction. The scores for each person on each subset were placed on a 0–24 scale to accommodate the negatively phrased statements. On the scale, 0 is an extremely negative response, 12 is neutral, and 24 is extremely positive. Outcomes for the reading practitioners and researchers on the three subjects are displayed in the figure below:

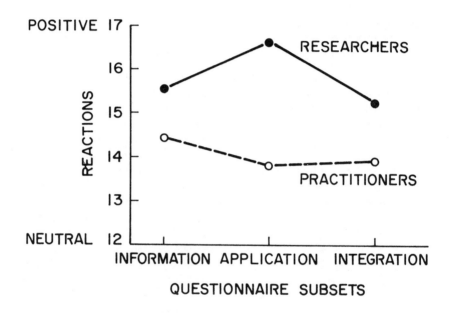

The figure shows that both groups found the presentations highly informative, substantially useful in their professional endeavors, and rather well integrated. Researchers were significantly ($t=2.04$, $df=41$, $p<.025$) more favorable than the practitioners on the total questionnaire (with all three subsets combined).

It is of interest to examine whether the three subsets were qualitatively different, i.e., measuring distinct reactions, or whether they were all measures of one generalized attitude. Did people who felt that the symposium was informative also find it applicable; and did people who found it informative also find it well integrated? To examine these issues, reliabilities (KR21) for each subset and the total were computed for the groups combined: Information = .45, Application = .77, Integration = .61, and Total = .86. Correlations among the subjects were also calculated for the whole group. The information subset and the application subset correlated at a level of .61; application and integration correlated at .70. Individuals who found the presentations informative were likely to find them applicable. This relationship coincides with commonsense. Not so apparent is the reason for the high association between the perceived practical utility and the integration among the presentations. Perhaps individuals who can generate implications of the material for their own work can also generate interconnections among the topics that were discussed.

The third correlation, between informational and integrational qualities of the talks was lower (0.37) than the others. Seeing the presentations as informative and integrated were relatively independent operations. It is useful to note that the pattern of correlations for the two groups separately was similar to the pattern for the total.

Reactions from the participants suggest that symposia of this genre may play a key role in the dissemination of research findings, the incorporation of contemporary thinking into practice, and communication across disciplinary boundaries. It is worth emphasizing that the practitioners perceived the material as applicable to their work, although little attempt was made by the speakers to provide explicit implications for practice. An unpredicted outcome was that the diverse addresses were viewed as well-connected. Both researchers and practitioners believed that subject matters ranging from curriculum design to neuropathology to social psychology are relevant to reading acquisition.

Perhaps the favorable reaction of the participants in this conference foretells the readiness of scholars and practitioners alike for new forms of interdisciplinary interaction in reading.

The present volume resulted from the Fifth Annual Hyman Blumberg Symposium on Research in Early Childhood Education. The coordinator of these symposia, Professor Julian C. Stanley, who invited me to organize the fifth session, was extremely generous with his time, counsel, and latitude in supporting this conference. Also instrumental in the project was the International Reading Association, which provided released time for three staff members, and lent professional assistance.

Grateful appreciation is extended to Janice Hiester for ably managing the organizational details and communications with the speakers. Mary Seifert assisted as a host and resource person, as did Jane Tyler, Irwin Kirsch, Malcolm Preston, and Joan Finucci. William George and Ron Allen facilitated the financial arrangements. We have a debt of acknowledgment to the speakers who, for the most part, submitted written drafts promptly and conscientiously revised their manuscripts before submitting them for publication. We also wish to thank The Spencer Foundation for its partial support of the publication of this book.

Aspects
of
Reading
Acquisition

John T. Guthrie

Introduction

The phenomenon of reading first attracted scholarly attention when Plato proclaimed that learning to read is "distinguishing the separate letters both by the eye and by the ear, in order that, when you hear them spoken or see them written you will not be confused by their position" (Jowett 1937, p. 212). By the turn of the twentieth century about thirty studies on reading had been reported in English. To this collection were added about one hundred investigations per year from 1930 to 1970. In the 1970s the pace of inquiry has accelerated by about 75% every year (Smith & Otto 1973).

A broad diversity of disciplines has nourished this growing body of knowledge. In 1925 at the University of Chicago, William S. Gray commenced an annual review of reading research that was divided into the four sections of physiology, sociology, psychology, and teaching. Without intending to contribute to a hardening of the categories, the papers included in the Fifth Blumberg Symposium may be grouped into roughly the same headings. First, the neurological.

A cogent model of the acquisition of reading implies that reading failures can be accounted for. According to many clinicians, some children who have not learned to read have neurological impairments, such as lag of development, insult, or poor lateralization. But, before we can completely determine the neurological impediments to reading acquisition, we need to identify the neurological operations that are needed for normal reading processes. Probably a critical step in identifying these operations is to locate where, in the brain, reading activities are centralized. In this volume Benson outlines a model of the locus of neurological operations that control reading. What is the nature of his evidence?

Since reading is part of language, the neurology of reading may be amenable to the same methods of inquiry as the neurology of language. Geschwind (1972) says that "virtually everything we know of how the functions of language are organized in the human brain has been learned

1

from abnormal conditions or under abnormal circumstances: brain damage, brain surgery, electrical stimulation of brains exposed during surgery, and the effects of drugs on the brain. Of these the most fruitful has been the study of language disorders, followed by postmortem analysis of the brain, in patients who have suffered brain damage. From these studies has emerged a model of how language areas of the brain are interconnected and what each area does" (p. 76). In the present symposium, Benson, one of Geschwind's close associates, has taken this approach to reading. He pieces together pathological cases to develop a model of how reading occurs neurologically.

Benson's model is derived from studies of adults, but it probably has implications about the growth of reading in children. Indeed, electro-neurophysiological measurement on children confirms Benson's view-point that the angular gyrus is one of the critical loci of reading and may be impaired in children who are poor readers (Preston, Guthrie, & Childs 1974). While these measurements are too primitive to generate scientific laws with educational implications now, they are a crack in the ice obscuring individual differences in neurological development. Like individual differences in cognitive and affective traits, knowl-edge of individual differences in neurological growth should prove use-ful in future educational planning and intervention.

Second, the affective aspects of reading. Learning to read is some-thing that happens within a person. Programming a machine to read is not the same as teaching a child who has a sociopersonal history that he brings to the task. A cogent developmental perspective of reading acquisition has been offered by Athey (1970). She reminds us that in the preschool years children are required to contend with a host of demands and tasks posed by the culture. In response to these demands, children learn problem-solving strategies and coping mechanisms. Perceptions of themselves are shaped by these experiences. She proposes that read-ing is another cultural demand imposed on children, and their accom-plishment of this task is likely to be a function of their strategies de-rived from previous encounters with the adult world.

Coinciding with this conjectural model is evidence that children who fail to learn to read often manifest anomalies of sociopersonal develop-ment. There have been recent confirmations of the early evidence from Gates in 1941 and Robinson in 1946 that children who are poor readers at nine or ten years of age are often emotionally unstable. Among poor readers the traits of self-confidence, self-reliance, perseverance in tasks, and realistic perceptions of others are underdeveloped. Robin-son (1946) speculated that emotional stability and reading achievement are circular. Poor reading at the early stages leads to a deterioration of self-concept that leads to poor reading in a continuous cycle. However, evidence about the direction of causation in the relationship between self-concept and reading achievement has been notably absent.

In the present symposium Entwisle lays some of the first stones in the foundation of a causal analysis of these factors. She illustrates, with certain qualifications, that reading achievement, in terms of grades, seeks the level of the child's expectation for himself in terms of grades. If the child's expectations for himself are viewed as a reflection of his past problem-solving strategies, it follows from Athey's developmental model that these expectations should serve as a link to future achievement.

Third, the psychological aspects. Just as the child brings a self-concept, he brings language competencies to the challenge of learning to read. While his language system is not completely mature at age five or six (Chomsky 1969), his rules of grammar and store of words are sufficient to process an infinite array of messages by listening and speaking. The written language obeys the same rules and contains samples of the same store of words as the spoken language. The primary difference is that script is composed from glyphs and the speech is composed from phonemes. The fact that the rules of correspondence between speech and script are complicated in English (Venezky 1967) is a historical accident rather than an inherent limitation of the mapping system. For example, Finnish has such a simple fit between script and sound that children at the end of first grade can read nearly all words in the language (Venezky 1973).

To grasp the correspondence between the speech code that he knows and the written code that he is required to learn, the child must perform several operations: (1) learn to recognize letters; (2) learn rules for the combinations of letters into syllables and words; (3) learn rules of correspondence between the written and spoken forms of letters, syllables, and words; and (4) learn how to derive meaning from printed words and sentences, which may not follow automatically from the application of language operations. In this symposium Menyuk relates the child's acquisition and knowledge of the sound system of the language to his acquisition of our written system. In addition, she compares successful and unsuccessful readers in terms of their mastery of phonological and orthographic aspects of the language to elucidate the learning processes involved in relating the two codes.

To this point three classes of variables have been forwarded as pertinent to reading acquisition: neurological, affective, and linguistic. One of the ways this knowledge (or extensions of this knowledge) can be used in education is through the development of prediction power. A problem for educators is how to assist children who do not learn readily from procedures that appear to be adequate for most. One strategy is to prevent the occurrence of learning failures by detecting high-risk children before they enter school and scheduling them for special interventions. In his contribution to this meeting Satz reports a collaborative effort to develop a detection system. From a theory of reading disability he constructed a test battery that was administered longitudinally from kindergarten to fourth grade. His accuracy in forecasting the extremely low and high achieving students is substantial and his battery may provide a starting point for improvements in programs for prevention of reading problems.

Regardless of how well or poorly a child is predicted to perform, effective teaching will be based on knowledge about the skills that children pick up during the acquisition process. The processes that occur in skilled reading have been outlined by Jane Mackworth (1972). She proposes that a mature reader engages in: (1) visual reception of about one to two words, which takes about 250 msecs; (2) iconic storage of the sensory trace from this stimulus, which may last for about one second; (3) acoustic input, which consists of bestowing sounds on the visual inputs held in iconic storage; (4) storing the sound units in short-term memory, which may last for several seconds but is eradicated by incoming material; and (5) deriving meaning from the material in short-term memory and storing the meaings permanently in long-term memory. The model is, at once, complicated and oversimplified.

How is such a network of operations learned by children? Kinsbourne proposes a model of acquisition in his offering to this symposium. His framework contains visual processes, auditory processes, and cross-modal association. These components are included in the early stages of Mackworth's dynamic time-series model. Kinsbourne reports that an empirical test of his model renders a moderate degree of confirmation and a substantial amount of unexplained variance in reading ability. Whether this variance will be accounted for in the future by more precise measurement of Kinsbourne's components, by the addition of memory and meaning to his acquisition model or by noncognitive variables, is an open issue.

Fourth, the teaching challenge. For as long as reading has existed it has been taught. That the most suitable procedures for teaching are not self-evident is reflected by the fact that about one-third of all the articles published between 1962–1973 on reading, as reviewed in the *Journal of Educational Research*, were devoted to teaching. Of 2,011 studies, 765 addressed the dilemma of instruction.

Controversies in the United States about methods have raged since schools were built in early New England. In 1683 *The New England Primer* was released and swept into wide popularity. Its atomistic approach consisted of teaching the following elements in sequence: alphabet, vowels, consonants, double letters, italics, capitals, two-letter syllables, and gradually reaching six-syllable words. To avoid the "irksome and vexatious" labor of learning letters, Josiah Bumstead published *My Little Primer* in 1840, which was based on the whole-word approach. The relative merits of these approaches have been argued heatedly for decades (Smith 1965). In this symposium Samuels presents the controversy as it exists today, contrasting methods derived from a psycholinguistic model of reading with procedures drawn from a learning hierarchy paradigm. He concludes that an updated version of the atomistic approach is advised.

The business of constructing a reading curriculum is besieged by a swarm of practical and theoretical problems. As Resnick and Beck recount in their contribution to the symposium, we do not have a sufficiently comprehensive and precise model of reading acquisition from which to deduce instructional practices. Probably such a deduction is impossible anyway. Their intriguing suggestion is that good theory about reading acquisition and good practice of teaching may need to be grown simultaneously in the same laboratory. Fortunately for both psychologists and educators, the old notion that educational challenges can be met by direct application of psychological theory is now being recognized as a mirage.

REFERENCES

Athey, I. 1970. "Affective factors in reading," in Singer, H. and Ruddell, R. (eds.), *Theoretical models and processes in reading*, Newark, Delaware: International Reading Association.

Chomsky, C. 1969. *The acquisition of syntax in children from 5 to 10*. Cambridge, Massachusetts: M.I.T. Press.

Gates, A. I. 1941. The role of personality adjustment in reading disability. *Journal of Genetic Psychology* 59: 77–83.

Geschwind, N. 1972. Language and the brain. *Scientific American* 226: 76–84.

Jowett, B. 1937. *The Dialogues of Plato*, New York: Random House.

Mackworth, J. 1972. Some models of the reading process: Learners and skilled readers. *Reading Research Quarterly* 7: 701–33.

Preston, M., Guthrie, J. T. and Childs, B. 1974. Visual evoked responses in normal and disabled readers. *Psychophysiology* 11: 452–57.

Robinson, H. M. 1946. *Why pupils fail in reading*. Chicago: University of Chicago Press.

Smith, K. M. and Otto, W. 1973. A review of the summary and review of investigations related to reading after forty-one years. *Journal of Educational Research* 66: 363–68.

Smith, N. B. 1965. *American reading instruction*. Newark, Delaware: International Reading Association.

Venezky, R. L. 1967. English orthography: Its graphic structure and relation to sound. *Reading Research Quarterly* 2: 75–106.

———. 1973. Letter-sound generalizations of first, second and third grade Finnish children. *Journal of Educational Psychology* 64: 288–92.

1

D. Frank Benson

Alexia

INTRODUCTION

Language is certainly one of the most complex functions that has been acquired by the human, and under present circumstances it is virtually impossible to understand how this function is performed. In simple outline, three methods are presently used in attempting to analyze language. One is the study of mature language function, either by means of introspection or through elegant psychometric studies of normal subjects. At best this approach is very difficult and demands construction of erudite models of linguistic function, an unknown with multiple variables. The problem is not dissimilar to the old adage of the blind man studying an elephant with a micrometer. The other two methods of analyzing language utilize incomplete or abnormal language. One is the study of the development of language in the child. A great deal of research has been and still is being performed in developmental studies of language. These studies probe the incompletely acquired language function seen at various stages of childhood. Most of our knowledge of the acquisition of language must be sought in this manner, including the acquisition of reading.

The final method of studying language function is to analyze diseased language. While such a method of study does not offer direct answers to the problem of acquisition of language or reading skills, it can provide some useful guidelines. Demonstration of variations in acquired reading disturbances offers suggestions about attributes necessary for reading. Also information concerning the cerebral substrate necessary for language function can be implied. With this in mind I have attempted to collate much of the information accumulated over the past hundred years in the neurological studies of acquired reading disorders and, in

---

This report was supported, in part, by grant #NS02609 from the National Institutes of Health to Boston University School of Medicine.

particular, to outline anatomical correlates for reading from the study of acquired reading disorders.

While it must be recognized that the information base for this study is limited, a sufficient number of clinical-pathological correlations have been accumulated to allow us to discuss the location of pathological processes occurring in cases of reading disturbance. Our information is incomplete, however, and only concerns the gross anatomical substrate; we have almost no information about the cellular activity taking place during mental processes such as reading.

Finally, please remember that the correlations that I will outline do not necessarily represent the anatomical substrate of reading. Instead they demonstrate the neuroanatomical areas where damage is frequently accompanied by a change in the ability to read. With these limitations in mind, let us proceed to a discussion of acquired reading disturbances.

DEFINITIONS

This presentation will contain a moderate number of fairly specialized terms and it is advisable to open with some definitions. Most important is the definition and differentiation of *alexia* and *dyslexia*, terms which are used in several different ways at the present time. While it is not my position to arbitrarily state which contemporary usage is right or wrong, for the remainder of this presentation *alexia* will refer to an acquired incapacity in the comprehension of written or printed words produced by a cerebral lesion, and *dyslexia* will refer to an inherent incapacity to learn to comprehend written or printed words. In other words, I will refer to alexia as an acquired loss of the ability to read and dyslexia as an inborn inability to learn how to read. While these definitions are not universally accepted, there is considerable agreement on this usage at present.

Some authors subdivide alexia into literal and verbal types. By *literal alexia* is meant an inability to identify letters of the alphabet; *verbal alexia* refers to inability to comprehend written words. In the older continental terminology these were called letter-blindness and word-blindness respectively, terms that are still used occasionally.

Agraphia, rather obviously, refers to a difficulty in producing written language. Agraphia is extremely common, but there has been little attempt to study or classify variations in writing disturbances. Some authors use the terms agraphia and dysgraphia to suggest quantitative variations in the degree of writing disability. As there are no meaningful measurements available this appears rather superfluous, so in the present report all writing disturbances will be termed agraphia and will be modified by description as necessary.

Agnosia is a mysterious disturbance that will be mentioned several times. While this is an old and accepted concept, in recent years a number of serious investigators have suggested that there is no true disorder of agnosia; others, the author included, have disagreed with this stand. We will not carry on this controversy here; for present purposes agnosia can be defined most easily as "a percept stripped of its meaning" (51). In other words, a correctly perceived stimulus (most often visual), which cannot be recognized despite fully intact language, intellect, state of consciousness, etc., is the symptom of agnosia.

Some of the other terminology to be used will be general and less controversial. I will frequently use the word *lesion*. By this will be meant damage to the cerebral tissues, producing true structural pathology. We will frequently be referring to aphasia in correlation with alexia. *Aphasia* can be defined as the loss or impairment of language caused by brain damage (10). Some of the terminology will be anatomical, while other terms will be specific to the other neurosciences, to neurology, neurosurgery, or psychiatry. (The anatomical terminology used in this paper is of a fairly elementary nature. If the reader is not familiar with neuroanatomical terminology, reference to one of the standard neuroanatomical textbooks would be advisable.)

HISTORICAL BACKGROUND

While alexia existed and was recorded for many centuries, it is only in recent years that literacy has become widespread and alexia has become a major medical problem. One report of alexia dates back to 30 A.D. and describes a man who lost his ability to read letters after being struck on the head by an axe (11). In 1588 Mercuriale described a patient who suffered a major seizure and afterward the physician noted a "truly astonishing thing"; this man could write but could not read what he had written (11). A few other cases of alexia were described before the time of Broca, but it was only subsequently that a major interest in language problems, including alexia, developed, and in the first years after 1861 only occasional cases of alexia were described.

The real beginning of modern thoughts on alexia came in 1891 and 1892 when the French neurologist, Dejerine, published two beautifully defined case reports of patients with alexia, which included postmortem findings. In the first report Dejerine (15) described a patient who had suffered a stroke and was no longer able to read. Additional examination revealed a mild right-sided weakness, questionable right-sided visual field defect, and mild difficulty in language, including repetition. In addition to a complete alexia, the patient was totally unable to write except to sign his own name. He was evaluated regularly until his death; during this time the aphasia cleared almost completely, while the difficulty with reading and writing remained severe. Post-mortem examination revealed an old, scarred infarct that involved three quarters of the cortex of the angular gyrus and extended deep to the lateral ventricle of the left parietal lobe.

Dejerine's second case (16) included an excellent clinical description of an individual who suddenly lost the ability to read, but had no additional abnormality except for a right homonymous hemianopia. The condition remained stable for a number of years until the patient suffered a second cerebrovascular accident and died ten days later. Post-mortem examination revealed two infarcts, one a large softening that involved much of the angular gyrus and was of very recent origin. The second was an old scarred lesion that involved the medial and inferior aspects of the left occipital lobe, plus infarction of the splenium of the corpus callosum. At the time Dejerine concluded that the original infarct had destroyed the visual pathways of the left occipital area and that the callosal lesion had severed the connection between the right hemisphere's visual area and the left hemisphere. He further conjectured that the dominant angular gyrus acted as a center for the optic images necessary for written language. In Dejerine's view, if this area remained intact but isolated from visual stimulation, the patient would retain the ability to write (along with all other language skills), but would be unable to read.

Subsequent to Dejerine's reports, a number of excellent reports appeared in the literature documenting similar cases. Bastian (7), Wylie (55), and Hinshelwood (30) reported cases of their own and of others. There have been a number of reviews and reports of cases of alexia in the present century, most of which agree with both the clinical and pathological findings outlined in the two papers of Dejerine (8,18,34). These combined studies provide the fundamental basis of alexia that will be discussed in this report.

For the present discussion, I would like to subdivide alexia into three major types. I believe these subtypes have real identity of both a functional and an anatomical nature. I strongly suspect that they also represent very important differences from a physiological point of view. A three-way division of alexia, or the alexias, is not new, in fact none of the subtypes to be mentioned are completely novel. Nonetheless, the tendency to use the term alexia in a blanket (unitary) manner rather than recognizing specific variations is almost universal and leaves much to be desired. It seems probable that there are more factors involved in the process of reading than can be subsumed under the three varieties of alexia to be mentioned here. For the present, however, we will retain the established clinical types from which we can discuss reading loss with some security. For want of accepted terminology we shall classify the three varieties of alexia by the simple breakdown of primary, secondary, and tertiary. Several recognized varieties of alexia will be described under each of these major subtypes. Similarities and differences between the categories will be discussed and will provide a foundation for a clinical anatomical view of reading.

PRIMARY ALEXIA (OCCIPITAL)

Under the title primary alexia we will discuss two separate entities. In reality only one variety of reading disturbance is present, the difference in names referring to other clinical factors. The first is a rare surgical artifact identified by the infrequently used term, hemialexia; the second is more common, the classical entity presently called alexia without agraphia. While the second is the most important, it will be easier to start with a description of hemialexia.

1. Hemialexia

There are a few reports scattered through the literature that suggest that after sectioning of the splenium of the corpus callosum, written language presented to the left visual field is not comprehended, while, in contrast, material presented to the right visual field is immediately "read." The earliest such case report was that of Trescher and Ford (52). They studied a patient who had a colloid cyst of the third ventricle removed through a posterior exposure that necessitated sectioning of the posterior part of the corpus callosum. Postoperatively, words and letters presented to the left visual field could not be comprehended, despite the presence of fully normal visual fields. At that time the authors conjectured that visual material presented to the left visual field reached the right calcarine cortex, but that pathology involving the splenium of the corpus callosum effectively kept this material from being transmitted to the language dominant left hemisphere. Therefore, language material presented to the left visual field could not be interpreted.

In 1948 Maspes reported six cases that had had posterior callosal sectioning (41). When discussing reading he excluded four of the six cases because they had either preoperative or operative damage to the cerebral hemispheres. Two of the patients, however, had no known cerebral hemisphere pathology except for sectioning of the posterior part of the corpus callosum. Both of these patients could comprehend written material presented to the right visual field, but were unable to comprehend similar material presented tachistoscopically to the left visual field. More recently, Sperry, Gazzaniga, and their colleagues (21) have performed similar tests on patients who had undergone complete callosal section. They confirmed the findings of Maspes, but suggested that there was some recognition of words by the right hemisphere. Right hemisphere reading will be discussed in detail later in this paper.

While the studies noted above supported the occurrence of hemialexia, there is a series of reports in the literature with negative findings. Akelaitis (3,4) studied a large number of patients (at least twenty-four) who had part or all of the corpus callosum sectioned and included nine individuals with complete sectioning of the splenium of the corpus callosum. Akelaitis tested six of these patients both pre- and post-operatively for reading ability and could find no significant change. From this he concluded that both hemispheres had equal ability to read. There have been a number of criticisms of the Akelaitis findings (8,23, 41). They particularly note that the patient population studied by Akelaitis was not normal: all of his patients had serious seizure disorder, most of which dated from childhood brain damage and which possibly produced abnormal development of language skills. It has also been suggested that life-long seizure disorder itself may have produced cerebral pathways that are not normally present in other individuals. Thus, the results reported by Akelaitis, which contrast with the results reported by Trescher and Ford and by Maspes, may be explained simply by the fact that patients in the latter studies were normal until the time of surgery, whereas the Akelaitis cases were abnormal. There is an additional difference that is probably of even greater significance. Akelaitis tested reading by using large block letters, 4.5 centimeters in height, which were maintained in position until a response was given. The author states that his best results came when the letter was placed between 2 and 10 degrees lateral to the point of fixation, but he reports no means of detecting lateral eye movements. Neither his technique nor his results are comparable to the results reported by the other authors, particularly the elegant tachistoscopic studies done by the group in California.

In summary there appears to be a condition in which written material presented to the nondominant (almost always left) visual field cannot be understood and that this "hemialexia" follows destruction of the splenium of the corpus callosum.

2. Alexia without Agraphia

This clinical syndrome has been recognized consistently since the report of Dejerine in 1892, but has been called a number of different names. These include alexia without agraphia, pure alexia, pure word blindness, agnosic alexia, occipital alexia, and optic aphasia.

Clinically, alexia without agraphia is a comparatively specific syndrome and is often dramatic. The patient is able to write with ease, but is unable to read what he himself has just written. These two key findings separate alexia without agraphia from all other alexia syndromes. There are additional associated symptoms, but these may vary. The most consistent is a right homonymous hemianopsia and the next most common is color agnosia. Other frequent findings include disturbances of musical notation or number reading, the almost total lack of significant aphasia, and, but only rarely, the appearance of a full-scale visual agnosia. These variations have been summarized in a tabular form by Stachowiak and Poeck (table 1.1) (49).

Alexia

Reading disability is, of course, the most striking characteristic of alexia without agraphia. While considerable variation in the degree of disability exists, the pattern is fairly stable. Many patients can read a few very high-frequency words, such as their own name, their city, U.S.A., etc., but fail on all others. Quite a few patients with primary alexia can read some individual letters. This is done slowly and insecurely, but if several letters are read aloud the patient can then decipher (recognize) the word from the oral spelling and "read" the word. This process is slow and there is a tendency for both misreading of longer words (refrigerator for refrigeration) and omission of words. The ability to recognize words spelled out loud, which is characteristic of alexia without agraphia, leads to an excellent test for this disorder. If the patient cannot read a written or printed word, but easily identifies the same word when spelled aloud, he probably has primary alexia. With improvement (and many of these individuals do improve) this style of "reading" becomes faster, they no longer need to spell aloud, but they still read by identifying individual letters.

Just as patients with primary alexia recognize letters said aloud, they also recognize them tactilely. Thus a block letter can be identified by palpation (by either hand), and letters or numbers written in the palm are easily recognized. Entire words can be spelled and identified in this manner. Similarly, the motor movements necessary to trace a letter with a finger is often sufficient stimulation to allow identification.

Table 1.1. Variations in Clinical Findings Associated with Alexia without Agraphia

Pure alexia	Right-sided hemianopia	Color-naming-deficit	Severe object-naming deficit	Reference(s)
+	–	–	–	Ajax (2) Goldstein, Joynt & Goldblatt (27) Greenblatt (28)
+	+	–	–	Ajax (2)
+	+	+	–	Geschwind & Fusillo (24)
+	+	+	+	Freund & Scheller (20) Lhermitte & Beauvois (35) Poeck (45)

Some investigators even claim that some patients with primary alexia get so adept at identifying kinesthetic stimuli that tracing the form of a letter with the eye will allow identification. In all of these examples, letter identification is normal if appropriate sensory stimuli reach the language area. The patient with primary alexia has not lost the power to read; rather he has suffered a disturbance of transmitting visual stimuli to the language area.

Agraphia

In most cases of alexia without agraphia writing is not entirely normal, but is so much closer to normal than reading that the difference is absolute. Most patients with alexia without agraphia write better to dictation or spontaneously on a given topic than when copying. Attempts to copy written or printed words are performed as though copying an unfamiliar foreign language; each letter is slavishly reproduced, but copying is slow and tedious. The patient with primary alexia will often fail if asked to write a fairly long paragraph. For instance, one patient who was asked to describe the act of shaving could not remember the word aerosol to describe his shaving cream and left a blank so that he could fill in this word later. After completion of the paragraph he was unable to read what he had just written and therefore had no reference to the word needed.

In general, however, written production is sufficiently close to normal that one is unwilling to call this agraphia. There are some exceptions.

Dejerine (17) and Martin (40) both reported that patients with alexia had difficulty in following the lines on paper and in going from one line to the next, suggesting visual difficulties. Martin compared the writing of his alexia patients with normal individuals asked to write with their eyes closed and suggested a similarity. Alexandria Adler (1) reported a single case of alexia without agraphia caused by carbon monoxide poisoning. Her patient wrote adequately soon after the onset of alexia, but when retested five years later, the writing ability had deteriorated greatly. Dr. Adler suggested that this deterioration was based on the patient's inability to practice. Most individuals with alexia without agraphia, however, show no deterioration in writing ability, in fact, they usually show improvement in reading and maintain or improve their writing ability.

Color Identification

A specific defect in the ability to name a color that is presented visually has been noted in many cases of primary alexia. I. Gloning et al. (25) recorded "color-naming disturbance" in 70% of cases of "pure" alexia that they evaluated. Color-naming disturbances of several different varieties are recognized, but a specific type is present in cases of primary alexia. The patients recognize color, i.e., they can separate groups of color chips into appropriate piles by color and can match colors without difficulty. Similarly, they are able to name colors when given verbal stimuli, i.e., if asked the color of a banana they readily respond. What they cannot do is tell the name of a color presented visually, nor point to a specific color when the name is given. This fits the definition of agnosia offered earlier, and the color identification disturbance in cases of alexia without agraphia can be considered a true color agnosia. Some cases of primary alexia, however, have no color identification difficulties. While there has been some conjecture on why color identification is occasionally maintained, no absolute explanation is available (28,49), and most individuals with alexia without agraphia do have a color-naming disturbance.

Other Disturbances

Various reported cases of alexia have had other neuropsychological disabilities. Many have had a mild degree of anomia, some have number-reading difficulties, others true calculation defects. Musical notation reading difficulty is present in some, but not in others. Musical ability, per se, has been intact in several reported cases. Most characteristic is the striking lack of significant aphasia, paralysis, sensory defect, or other elementary neurologic problem, except for the right homonymous hemianopia. Even this is not constantly present (2,28). None of the findings, except alexia, visual field defect, and color agnosia, have been present in any sizable percentage of reported cases. The other findings probably indicate additional damage in that specific patient rather than part of the syndrome of alexia without agraphia.

Pathology

Despite the interest provoked by the dramatic findings of alexia without agraphia, there have been comparatively few clinical studies with post-mortem findings. In 1969 Benson and Geschwind (8), in a review of the world's literature, listed only seventeen cases of primary alexia with autopsy findings. Since that time several additional cases have been published, but the number remains small. The limited number is not crucial, however, as there has been striking agreement concerning the pathological findings. In essence, all cases have had medial occipital pathology, most often infarction, although there have been cases of both brain tumor and A-V malformation that produced primary alexia. In all cases except one, the involved occipital area was in the left hemisphere. Review of the literature suggests (and it must be remembered that the reports span three-quarters of a century, are by different investigators, and vary considerably in terminology, completeness, etc.) that the areas most consistently involved are the two cortical regions rostral to the calcarine cortex, the lingual and fusiform gyri. In addition to involving the cortical areas mentioned, the infarction involves underlying white matter and in most cases acts to separate the left occipital cortex from visual stimuli. This produces the right homonymous hemianopia. A few cases without calcarine cortex involvement have been reported, and in at least one of these (28), the patient did not have visual field abnormality. In addition to this constant occipital lesion, most reports describe infarction that involves the splenium of the corpus callosum. While this is not consistently described, splenial infarction is almost never negatively reported; rather, most reports that fail to describe splenial infarction omit mention at all. In as much as it is quite possible to inspect the splenium grossly and be unaware of infarction, it is probable that the cases in the literature that do not mention splenial infarction actually had this difficulty. There are a few reports in which the splenium definitely was not infarcted; in these cases, however, the pathology produced a disconnection of transsplenial pathways just to the left of the splenium proper.

The above combination of lesions produces an interesting functional situation. The right calcarine cortex and visual association area receive perfectly good visual signals, including written or printed material, but transfer of this material from the nonverbal right hemisphere to the language-competent left hemisphere demands connection through the splenium of the corpus callosum. The patient cannot see or read with his right visual field because of involvement of the primary visual sensory pathways. He can see written material in his left visual field, but cannot transfer these stimuli from the right hemisphere (which apparently cannot read) to the left hemisphere (which can) because of the splenial pathology. The language-competent left hemisphere receives no visual language stimuli and therefore cannot read; in other language functions, including writing, it can function normally.

A number of other etiologies and explanations have been suggested, at least some of which are correct in some cases. These include *asthenopic alexia* (46), an inability to read after regaining sight following a prolonged blindness. Another is *simultanagnosia*, a condition described by a number of authors (32,37,54). When given a picture to analyze the gaze is fixed on a single item to the exclusion of the remainder of the picture, including the relationship of the visualized item to other portions of the picture. These patients have a severe reading disability (called "spelling dyslexia" by Kinsbourne and Warrington), laboriously read single letters, and only occasionally decipher simple words. A somewhat similar explanation is called defective Gestalt formation; the patient can recognize parts of the written material (letters), but is unable to combine them into a meaningful whole (words).

Some authors suggest eye movement disorder as the underlying cause of primary alexia and consider alexia as one symptom of eye movement disorder (38). As an extreme example, Berringer and Stein (12) reported a patient who could read at most one or two letters and then had to close his eyes and nod his head to transfer his gaze to the next letters. By this method he could eventually spell a word out loud and recognize the spelled word. A somewhat similar patient was described by Warrington and Zangwill (53). While abnormal eye movements were easy to demonstrate in these cases, most patients with primary alexia have normal eye movements.

Some investigators consider that visual agnosia is the master disturbance and that primary alexia is merely one symptom of agnosia. Agnosia is difficult to define and when used in its broadest sense could include an inability to read words or letters. It is suggested that the inability to recognize letters or words, while ordinary objects, body parts, etc. can be recognized, merely shows that language recognition is a more subtle and difficult task, and a milder degree of visual agnosia can produce alexia. Agnosia without alexia has been reported, however, suggesting at least some distinction between alexia and agnosia.

Summary.

Primary alexia, then, appears to be a disturbance of reading only, without other significant language disorder. The pathology is located in the medial occipital area of the dominant hemisphere and includes destruction of primary visual pathways of the dominant hemisphere and secondary visual pathways from the nondominant hemisphere. Primary alexia appears to be closely associated with disturbance of visual sensory information, but is not a true language disorder.

SECONDARY ALEXIA (PARIETAL—TEMPORAL)

Even before Dejerine had reported alexia without agraphia, many physicians were aware of alexia with agraphia. By the time Dejerine published his case in 1891 there were many reports of alexia with agraphia in the literature, all with pathology involving the parietal-temporal region of the dominant hemisphere. In fact, as early as 1889 an American neurologist, Starr (50), collected fifty cases of "sensory aphasia," twenty-one had pathology involving the angular gyrus and each of these had reading disturbance. Unfortunately, many of the early examinations did not test writing, but whenever evaluated agraphia was present. This syndrome has also been called "parietal alexia," "cortical alexia," and "aphasic alexia."

Secondary alexia comprises disability of all aspects of written and printed language symbols, both the interpretation and the utilization of these symbols, and may be considered a language defect in contrast to the perceptual defect of primary alexia. While the syndrome, alexia with agraphia, is the classic example of secondary alexia, essentially identical abnormalities of reading and writing occur in several varieties of aphasia. In the classic alexia without agraphia syndrome, the aphasic symptomatology, while almost always present (8), is notably mild in comparison to the severe disturbance of reading and writing. In the aphasic syndromes, on the other hand, the patient has a severe disturbance of auditory language comprehension, with additional problems of reading and writing. A number of investigators separate the alexia associated with receptive aphasia on the basis that these patients have such a severe compromise of language function that inability to read (and write) is secondary. It should be noted, however, that the alexia accompanying certain types of aphasia appears identical to that in the alexia with agraphia syndrome. Secondary alexia, therefore, will be discussed under three separate headings, alexia with agraphia, Wernicke's aphasia, and transcortical sensory aphasia.

1. Alexia with Agraphia

As already noted, this syndrome is common and many descriptions appear in the literature. It may be produced by many disturbances, including vascular accident, A-V malformation, brain tumor, head trauma including gunshot wound, and others. The course of the disorder will depend on the etiology, not the location, of the disease process. The presence or absence of neighborhood signs, however, is dependent upon both the etiology and location of the pathology. Alexia with agraphia may be accompanied by significant neurologic defects, including right-sided sensory loss and, if the lesion is sufficiently extensive, right-sided paresis and/or right-sided visual field defect. Behavioral and aphasic symptoms, including anomia, language comprehension defect, Gerstmann syndrome, constructional disturbance, and even deterioration in intellectual capacity, may be noted as well. None of these are constant, however, and the basic syndrome of alexia with agraphia may occur in almost pure form. The pure form will be described.

Alexia

The loss of the ability to read in alexia with agraphia is almost always severe and includes words, letters, numbers, and musical notes. Cues are of little help, i.e., tracing a letter does not help in its identification. Similarly, when a word is spelled aloud the patient with secondary alexia cannot decipher it, in sharp contrast to alexia without agraphia. The abilities to read aloud and to read for comprehension are involved equally; if a word can be read aloud it will be understood and vice versa.

Agraphia

The writing disturbance in secondary alexia is severe. While some authors have suggested that writing is less disturbed than reading, most believe the disturbances are approximately equivalent. Most patients with secondary alexia write upon request and produce real letters. The letters, however, are liable to be combined into unrecognizable and meaningless words. Copying of written and printed symbols is performed much better, again in contrast to the patient with primary alexia. The patient with secondary alexia can be considered illiterate for written or printed language symbols. This is best exemplified when the alexic patient with a good command of auditory language is asked to recognize a word spelled out loud. When the patient fails, he will state frankly: "I can no longer read." In the patient's mind recognition of an orally spelled word is a reading task which he fails.

There are many demonstrations correlating the alexia with agraphia syndrome with angular gyrus pathology. While similar reading and writing disturbance can occur after involvement of neighboring areas, the syndrome of "pure" alexia with agraphia, with only minimal abnormality of other aspects of language, will almost invariably have an angular gyrus lesion.

2. Wernicke's Aphasia

Wernicke's aphasia is one of the classic varieties of aphasia and a syndrome that is almost universally recognized. The major characteristics include fluent paraphasic verbal output, severe disturbance of comprehension of spoken language, severe disturbances in repetition of spoken language, and defective word finding, reading, and writing. In most cases of Wernicke's aphasia the disturbance in comprehension and production of spoken language is mirrored in written language. In other words, the patient who understands a few spoken words will probably recognize a few written words, and the patient who can produce a few correct words in repetition or naming tasks may also write a few meaningful words. Some, like de Massary (18), consider that the language disturbance in Wernicke's aphasia is so basic that failures of reading and writing are merely part of the overall disturbance and should not be considered with the alexias. Clinically, however, the reading and writing disturbances of Wernicke's aphasia are identical to the alexia with agraphia syndrome, and a relationship must be considered.

The pathology in Wernicke's aphasia almost invariably involves the posterior superior portion of the first temporal gyrus of the dominant hemisphere. This area contains auditory association cortex surrounding the primary auditory cortex (Heschl's gyrus) and in the dominant hemisphere appears to be essential for the decoding (perception) of spoken language. Apparently, pathology localized entirely in the dominant auditory association cortex with no involvement of the angular gyrus will cause alexia. Nielsen (44) documented a number of autopsied cases with temporal lesions but without parietal pathology which, during life, had severe alexia in addition to auditory comprehension disturbance. Thus, it would appear that the auditory association cortex of the dominant hemisphere plays some part in the recognition and interpretation of written language as well as spoken language. In attempting to explain this somewhat unexpected observation it has been suggested that visual language is learned by association with well-established auditory language. This postulation could be confirmed or denied by appropriate pre- and post-mortem studies of "deaf mutes" who had learned written language without first learning auditory language, but such studies are not presently available.

3. Transcortical Sensory Aphasia

The transcortical aphasias are not universally recognized, but are present in many classifications of aphasia. The basic difference between transcortical aphasia and other aphasias is the retention, by the former group, of an essentially normal ability to repeat (10,26). Transcortical sensory aphasia, is identical to Wernicke's aphasia except for one detail: the patient repeats spoken material almost flawlessly. While not common, transcortical sensory aphasia certainly does exist and in pure form is a striking variation. The clinical characteristics include a fluent paraphasic verbal output (often with a good deal of echolalia), severely disturbed auditory comprehension, comparatively intact repetition of spoken language, severe word-finding defect, alexia, and agraphia. The alexia and agraphia are identical to those described above and this patient also appears illiterate. The classic explanation for transcortical aphasia revolves around preservation of the perisylvian language structures, particularly Heschl's gyrus, Wernicke's area, the white matter pathways connecting these to the motor speech area (probably the arcuate fasciculus), and the frontal areas essential for speech production (Broca's area). If these areas are intact, but isolated or separated from other portions of the cortex, a specific type of aphasia featuring preservation of repetition is produced. The location of pathology underlying transcortical sensory aphasia has not been well documented. Some authors suggest that the basic lesion is in the posterior inferior temporal lobe, particularly the second temporal gyrus and Brodmann's area 37. Others suggest the parietal temporal junction area including the angular gyrus. There is too little pathological material available to allow an exact answer. If, as suggested, this syndrome can result from strictly temporal pathology, then we have a third area significant for the production of secondary alexia.

4. Pure Word Deafness

A few words are indicated concerning another dominant hemisphere comprehension problem that is strikingly different. In pure word deafness, the patient has a severe disturbance of comprehension of spoken language and a repetition disturbance identical to that seen in Wernicke's aphasia. The verbal output, however, is either fully normal or contains only an occasional paraphasia. The patient can name readily and, most strikingly, reads and writes normally. While the patient cannot understand spoken language, he easily understands written language, the exact opposite of primary alexia. While pure word deafness is not common it is seen regularly. Several anatomical localizations have been described for the pathology of pure word deafness but the most commonly reported is a single lesion located deep in the dominant temporal lobe, which effectively separates Heschl's gyrus, the primary auditory cortex, from sensory input. What is of greatest importance is that in all reported cases of pure word deafness with pathological correlation both Wernicke's area and the angular gyrus have been intact. This observation offers strong indirect support to the necessity of these areas for the comprehension of written language.

Summary

It can be suggested that a specific disturbance of written language, secondary alexia, occurs after pathology that involves the dominant parietal-temporal junction area. The syndrome is quite specific: the patient loses the ability to read words, letters, numbers, and even musical notation, and, at the same time, loses the ability to combine letters, numbers, etc. into meaningful written language symbols. He truly suffers an acquired illiteracy. The areas where pathology produces secondary alexia include the dominant angular gyrus, the dominant Wernicke's area, the posterior part of the second temporal gyrus, and area 37. We have called this disturbance secondary alexia, but as it affects all language in written form it could well be called aphasic alexia or central alexia.

TERTIARY ALEXIA (FRONTAL)

Following the teaching of Meynert well over a century ago, it has come to be accepted that the posterior portion of the brain primarily performs sensory functions, while the anterior portion deals with motor functions. Since alexia, the loss of the ability to comprehend written material, appars to be a sensory function, it has not been anticipated with anterior hemisphere pathology. Nonetheless, almost since the onset of interest in aphasia there have been sporadic reports of alexia accompanying the anterior aphasias. There are three distinctly different language syndromes that occur with dominant frontal pathology. While the presence of alexia is variable, it does occur with two of the three.

Broca's Aphasia

Patients with Broca's aphasia have little verbal output, what speech is produced demands obvious effort and is poorly articulated. There is a tendency to omit words, phrase length is reduced, and there is a striking disturbance of speech melody. In contrast, comprehension of spoken language is comparatively intact. Both repetition and naming are disturbed, but often are better than spontaneous production of similar words. Severe agraphia is a constant feature. Writing is usually performed with the left hand, because of right-sided paralysis and is sparse, clumsy, and poorly formed, with letter omissions, misspellings, and agrammatic sentence formation. Clincially, Broca's aphasia usually follows pathology involving the posterior inferior portion of the third frontal convolution of the dominant hemisphere.

Transcortical Motor Aphasia

The spontaneous or conversational output in this disorder is similar to that described in Broca's aphasia. Similarly, comprehension of spoken language is good. The striking difference in the two syndromes is the excellence of repetition in transcortical motor aphasia. The demonstration of smooth and fluent repetition of a five- or six-word phrase by an individual who is severely agrammatic and restricted in spontaneous output is both dramatic and diagnostic. As in Broca's aphasia, writing is seriously limited in this syndrome. The pathology underlying transcortical motor aphasia varies but the location is consistent; the lesion is located in the frontal cortex superior and/or anterior to Broca's area, but does not involve Broca's area nor its major afferent or efferent pathways.

Aphemia

The third anterior language syndrome (also called pure word dumbness, cortical anarthria, and subcortical motor aphasia) is analogous to the other "pure" syndromes, alexia without agraphia and pure word deafness, in that only one aspect of language is involved. In aphemia it is speech production that is lost or severely disturbed, while all other language functions, including reading and writing, are intact. The location of the lesion producing aphemia is not well documented. Two case reports with post-mortem correlation give slightly conflicting information. One (7) had a white matter lesion that undercut but did not destroy Broca's area. The second (17) had a lesion that involved Broca's area only, a comparatively small and superficial infarction. In both instances it would appear that the lesion was small, that Broca's area was involved, and that reading and writing were not affected.

Discussion

Alexia accompanying Broca's aphasia has been reported for at least a century. In 1885 Lichtheim (36) offered one explanation for this unexpected combination. He suggested that such cases represented individuals who had originally lost all language function (global aphasia); following recovery from the most reversible disability, word deafness, they were left with alexia and Broca's aphasia. Another nineteenth-century suggestion emphasized that reading was a precariously under-learned attribute for most of the population. To comprehend written material they had to read out loud and even with apparently silent reading were forced to make tongue and lip movements. By interfering with these movements, Broca's aphasia caused a disorganization of reading. Even this plausible explanation was not universally acceptable. In 1894 Freud (19) stated that the combination of Broca's aphasia and alexia was a strong argument against many of the language diagrams being proposed. Using the same basic argument as Freud, many of our contemporaries have suggested a unitary language center in the dominant hemisphere, damage to which underlies all language disturbances. This hypothetical language center has been located posteriorly, in the parietal-temporal junction region. From this view alexia, even that accompanying Broca's aphasia, always indicates posterior damage.

Viewed in another manner, not all investigators agree that alexia occurs with Broca's aphasia. Henschen (29) believed that all such cases recorded in the literature (up to 1923) could be explained either on the basis of Broca's aphasia plus a psychosis or two lesions, one anterior and one posterior. Nielsen (42) and Goldstein (26) both exclude reading comprehension disturbance in their clinical descriptions of Broca's aphasia. Nielsen states: "The patient (with Broca's aphasia) cannot read aloud, but comprehends written language." Goldstein writes, "Reading ability is intact as far as understanding is concerned." In a later paper, however, Nielsen recognized that alexia occasionally occurred in cases of Broca's aphasia with fully normal comprehension of spoken language and called this "one of the unsolved problems of aphasia" (43). From the literature he collected ten cases of Broca's aphasia with lesions strictly confined to the frontal cortex all of whom had alexia. Nielsen concluded that alexia could follow purely frontal lesions, at least in association with Broca's aphasia. Nielsen's paper is disappointing, however, in that he could not always present evidence that reading ability was truly lost. In several cases one must question whether the patient had ever been able to read, and, in several others, the ability to read aloud and the ability to read for comprehension were not distinguished. In addition, several of the patients died within weeks of the onset of aphasia. Whether the alexia was a distinct clinical disturbance or merely the malfunction of a severely ill patient cannot be determined.

In our own clinical experience reading abnormalities occur frequently in patients with anterior aphasia. These patients have good comprehension of spoken language, are fully alert and attentive, but have great difficulty in reading. In fact, when questioned many patients with Broca's aphasia will deny that they can read and obviously refrain from reading. Based on this observation we have reinvestigated the problems of alexia in anterior aphasia. Before discussing our findings, however, a number of fairly obvious sources of a reading problem in anterior aphasia deserve comment.

One possibility is that the patient has always been illiterate. Presently this is rather uncommon, but in reviewing the literature of the past century one must remember that illiteracy has been the rule, not the exception. We had one experience a number of years ago in which a patient with a fairly recent onset of Broca's aphasia showed severe alexia. He could read only a few words, such as cat, dog, etc. Because of the primer-like quality of this reading we became suspicious and with further questioning, particularly of his family, discovered that he had never learned to read, despite considerable special schooling. There was a true developmental dyslexia underlying the recently acquired Broca's aphasia (see later section on pseudoalexia).

A second possibility is that reading ability is judged on the ability to read out loud rather than on the comprehension of written material. Patients with anterior aphasia have great difficulty reading out loud, but comprehension of written material is a totally separate function and we see many aphasic patients who cannot read out loud but readily comprehend written language. Alexia, by the definition given earlier, concerns the ability to comprehend written material not the ability to read out loud.

It is always possible that the diagnosis of Broca's aphasia itself is in error. This occurs easily if the examiner simply divides aphasia into expressive and receptive varieties. Actually, all aphasics have some degree of expressive defect. The expressive difficulties that characterize the anterior aphasias are distinct from the other varieties of aphasia.

Another possible explanation of alexia occurring in a case of Broca's aphasia would be multiple brain lesions. If one lesion involves an anterior area, causing Broca's aphasia, while another involves a more posterior area, producing a secondary alexia, the combination of Broca's aphasia and alexia would easily be explained. In such a situation, careful language and neurological evaluation, searching for significant neighborhood signs such as hemiplegia, hemi-sensory loss, visual field defect, Gerstmann syndrome, etc., can usually demonstrate the multiplicity of lesions.

A final possibility is the one suggested by Nielsen, that a true reading disturbance may coexist with Broca's aphasia without any lesion in the posterior language-dominant hemisphere. I would like to present several clinical observations in support of this postulation.

Our first observation concerns reading problems of patients on our ward (9). We once had three patients with proved posterior lesions and primary alexia and, simultaneously, three patients who were recovering from Broca's aphasia and also were alexic. While all six patients had serious reading difficulties, their problems were quite different and their approach to reading was opposite. The patients with the posterior lesion all attempted to read each letter aloud, then put the letters together to recognize the spelled word. In contrast, the patients recovering from Broca's aphasia often could interpret words and, even more particularly, sentences, as a unit while they failed to read most single words aloud and were characteristically unable to read a sentence aloud or name a letter. In older terminology, the first group had word blindness but not letter blindness, while the second had letter blindness but not word blindness. One could consider that the reading problem in the anterior aphasia patients was limited to verbalizing (naming) what they read. That this was not true will be seen.

Our second observation comes from a study performed many years ago but never published. Ten patients with the clinical diagnosis of Broca's aphasia were given a short test (six true/false questions and six multiple choice fill-in statements). Of the ten patients, seven attained perfect scores on the twelve questions, which were presented in both written and oral form. The time necessary to comprehend the written material, however, was extremely long, up to thirty minutes for the twelve questions. These patients were not completely alexic, but reading was so inefficient for them that they never attempted it. Even when reading materials (newspapers, magazines) that they had formerly used regularly were made available, they would never attempt to read them. If one accepts the definition of alexia given earlier, an impairment of the ability to comprehend written or printed language symbols, then this anterior aphasic group would qualify. Functionally they were just as impaired in reading as patients with the other varieties of alexia. In my opinion, this represents a third, very real variety of alexia and deserves recognition in any analysis of reading problems.

When attempting to find the cause of reading difficulties in these patients several problems became apparent. First, they had difficulty in moving their eyes from line to line and from word to word; many of them used their finger as a guide. It seemed possible that this was caused by a visual-motor defect, probably related to frontal eye field damage. In addition, it has been demonstrated that many patients with frontal lesions (including those with Broca's aphasia) have great difficulty in maintaining information in sequence (5). For example, when multiple objects are presented in an array and the patient with an anterior aphasia is asked to point to objects individually he performs readily. When asked to point to several objects in the exact sequence presented by the examiner, however, he often fails or performs well below the level attained by normal subjects. Thus these patients comprehend individual portions of a spoken or written sentence, but apparently cannot maintain the sequence of information needed to comprehend the entire sentence. A combination of a visual-motor defect and defective ability to handle sequential material could make reading extremely difficult.

Summary

Alexia occurs with two of the varieties of aphasia produced by anterior lesions, Broca's aphasia and transcortical motor aphasia. While these patients often comprehend some written words, and if these are key words they can interpret the sentence, failure is frequent and reading is such a difficult chore that it is avoided. Both visual motor disorder and defective ability to handle sequential material has been demonstrated in some patients with anterior aphasia. Either of these disorders would appear to make reading difficult. Thus, a third form of alexia can be recognized that is clinically quite different. The exact location of the pathology producing this variety of alexia remains uncertain, but it can be limited to the frontal lobe of the dominant hemisphere.

PSEUDOALEXIA

After postulating three types of reading disturbance that fit the definition of alexia, we should look at disturbances of reading that do not fit the definition. We will call these pseudoalexia. In evaluating reading ability or when studying the literature on reading disturbances one must be cautious not to mistake one or more of these entities for true alexia.

1.Reading aloud

It has been already noted that differentiation of the ability to read out loud and the ability to comprehend written material is essential. Many aphasic patients cannot read out loud, but if appropriately tested, will demonstrate considerable reading comprehension. This is particularly true in conduction aphasia, but also occurs in some individuals with anterior aphasia. The novice examiner may incorrectly base the diagnosis of alexia on the ability to read out loud.

2. Unilateral Paralexia

After an acute homonymous visual field defect, some individuals are inattentive to their defective field; when reading words or sentences they visualize only one-half of the word or phrase. Thus, a patient with a right visual field defect may read the word "northwestern" as "north" while a patient with a left visual field defect may read the same word as "western." At times the patient may substitute (confabulate) portions of the word that fall in the damaged fields, i.e., "medical" may be read as "medicine." Obviously, such patients have considerable difficulty in reading and comprehending a full sentence. Unilateral paralexia is easily mistaken for alexia.

It can be demonstrated that unilateral paralexia is not a true alexia however. Kinsbourne and Warrington (32), in a study of unilateral paralexia, noted that words that were misread when presented in the normal, horizontal manner were immediately recognized and comprehended when printed in a vertical orientation. A current study by Rubens and Butler (47) of individuals with unilateral paralexia is of particular interest. After demonstrating that certain patients with homonymous visual field defects could read only part of a given word, the eardrum was stimulated by ice water forcing the eyes toward the hemianopic side. The patient could then read the entire word flawlessly. Both of these investigations demonstrate that unilateral paralexia is actually a visual gaze disturbance, not a true alexia.

3. Developmental Dyslexia

Some individuals never learn to read, but are sensitive and do not admit their reading problems. Following acute neurological disturbance such a patient will have an inability to read; without specific history from the patient or the family this may be diagnosed as alexia caused by the new neurological disease. Only careful history taking can save the examiner from an incorrect diagnosis.

4. Mental Retardation

Similarly, many individuals with mental retardation cannot comprehend written material, and evaluation after an acute neurologic insult may suggest alexia. History of previous reading capability is necessary to exclude this pseudoalexia.

5. *Psychogenic Disorders*

On rare occasions a disturbance of reading ability may be seen in "psychogenic disorders." Acutely anxious, seriously depressed, or deteriorated schizophrenic patients may refuse to read, suggesting alexia. The alexia usually does not stand out when compared to other psychiatric symptoms, however. Only rarely does hysteria present as alexia, and when viewed in context such patients should not be diagnostic problems.

Thus, in addition to the three varieties of alexia there are a number of false conditions, difficulties with reading that are not true alexias. One additional idiosyncrasy of reading should be mentioned, that of paralexia. In this condition the symptoms appear to be related to right hemisphere reading and will be discussed in a later section.

ALEXIA IN ORIENTAL LANGUAGES

Most reported studies of alexia have concerned Indo-European languages. There is good reason to suspect that acquired disturbances of written language may be different in Oriental languages, at least in those Oriental languages in which ideographic characters are utilized. The medical literature contains comparatively few reports of alexia in Orientals, but these few are worth studying. In particular, reports from Japan are of interest because most Japanese learn two forms of written language, *Kana* with phonetic, syllabic characters, and *Kanji*, nonphonetic, logographic or ideographic characters, similar but not identical to Chinese characters. The possibility of a dichotomous loss of reading ability is apparent. *Kana*, with its auditory basis may involve a different neuroanatomical substratum than the strongly visual *Kanji*. Recorded case reports support this dichotomy, but there are too few cases to allow secure localizations.

The earliest reports by Imura (31) and Asayama (6) both discuss reading disturbances in Japanese in the manner just suggested. Asayama described an individual with a lesion in the dominant hemisphere causing nearly total alexia and agraphia in *Kana*, but only a negligible disturbance of *Kanji*. Several authors have suggested that this is the prevalent clinical picture of alexia in Japan, but there are few case reports (48,56). Recently, Sasanumo (48) reported one case of probable alexia without agraphia, caused by infarction of the left posterior cerebral artery. Disturbances of reading in both *Kana* and *Kanji* scripts were observed but the disturbances were different. When attempting to read the *Kana* script the patient read each syllabic character separately, often using his fingers to trace the outline of the character in the air until he recognized it.

He then attempted to combine the syllables aloud to sound out the word. At that point he could grasp the meaning. This process seems identical to the recognition of spelled words described in primary alexia. If Sasanumo's patient was unable to sound out the word correctly, he could not understand the word. This reading was tediously slow but accurate. In the reading of *Kanji*, on the other hand, many of the characters were recognized and named immediately. When not immediately recognized, however, there was great difficulty. He would try to trace the figure and sound out the word, a process that usually failed or produced a paraphasic response. Thus, while he was extremely slow in reading *Kana*, finding it necessary to sound out each individual character and join them for recognition, he was accurate. In reading *Kanji* script, on the other hand, some characters were recognized instantaneously, but when this failed he was forced to guess and usually failed completely or produced confabulatory errors.

In a similar vein, there is a patient reported by a neurosurgeon from Shanghai (39). The patient was an educated Chinese merchant, fluent in both Chinese and English, who had a left parietal-occipital tumor removed. He made a good recovery from surgery, but was found to have an unusual and unexpected disturbance of written language. While he remained fluent in reading and writing English, his second language, he was unable to read and write Chinese, his native tongue. The author conjectured that the posterior location of the lesion produced a more severe interference with visually oriented Chinese characters than with the more auditorially associated English letters.

Review of this limited literature suggests a difference based on the neuroanatomical areas needed to read the visually associated pictographic characters of Chinese and the *Kanji* script of Japan and for the auditorially associated phonetic alphabet of the Indo-European languages and the *Kana* script of Japan. This observation appears logical, but at present the amount of supporting proof is inadequate and additional observations are needed.

READING WITH THE RIGHT HEMISPHERE

In the early discussion of hemi-alexia attention was drawn to the works of Akelaitis who suggested, based on study of patients following section of the corpus callosum, that reading was performed equally by either hemisphere. Many clinical observations disagree with this suggestion. The most telling example is the syndrome of alexia without agraphia in which right hemisphere function is apparently normal but reading competency is severely disabled. On the basis of such clinical findings, most authorities believe that the right hemisphere does not handle written language. While there are some patients with bilateral language function and a few exceptional individuals with totally reversed hemispheric dominance for language, for most individuals comprehension of written material is apparently the exclusive province of the left hemisphere.

Some very sophisticated studies performed in recent years, however, question the absolute dominance of the left hemisphere for reading. A group in Los Angeles (13,21,22) has studied several patients after total section of the corpus callosum and by using sophisticated tachistoscopic presentations has demonstrated that the right hemisphere can respond, at least in a limited fashion, to written material. In their classic demonstration, the patient sits before a tachistoscope with his gaze fixed on a central point. When a word is flashed in the left visual field the patient verbally denies that anything appeared. If the left hand is left free, however, it often reaches out and picks up the object named in the tachistoscopic flash. Appreciation of object names and an ability to match the printed name with the actual object by the right hemisphere has been clearly demonstrated. Obviously, this type of reading fails for sentence length material, abstract words, etc. Nonetheless, in this selected group of patients, some ability of the right hemisphere to decipher written symbols cannot be denied. Interpretation of these results, however, must be viewed with our usual degree of suspicion. Each patient that demonstrated right hemisphere reading had suffered severe brain damage early in life. In such circumstances we must question the normal lateralization of language dominance. Only one patient had callosal section for seizure disorder with onset after he became an adult; this patient did not show right hemisphere reading ability. Thus, the possibility that the patients reported by the Los Angeles group had an idiosyncratic reading capability based on long-standing brain injury must be considered.

The development of limited right hemisphere reading capability long after left hemisphere damage is further supported by study of patients with the onset of alexia early in life. Some such individuals develop an abnormal reading style that has been called *paralexia*, an ability to recognize a number of words as visual wholes (similar to object recognition). As an example, a patient aged thirty-four years who had been totally alexic after a major left parietal infarct at age twenty-four could "read" words such as milk and bread. The patient believed she recognized the words as a visual pattern. Only the printed form was recognized; the same word in script was incomprehensible. She made many incorrect (paralexic) interpretations of words. For instance, she read the printed word "kitten" as "a small cat." When the word "living room" was written the patient said "Oh, I know what this is, that is the place that my husband and I go after supper and drink our coffee and watch television." The printed word "automobile" was read as "car," "infant" as "baby," etc.

In paralexic reading it can be conjectured that the letters making up the words lead to a visual image of the object. The visual image is translated into a name that may or may not be the same as what was written. Even if not correct, however, it is a reasonable substitution or description of the written word. Paralexia of this type is not common and almost invariably occurs in individuals who sustained dominant parietal lobe injury at an early age.

In summary, it would appear that the right hemisphere can function, at least to some degree, in the comprehension of written symbols. Most evidence suggests that this is done by associating the written symbols with a visual image and then naming the visualized object. The efficiency and accuracy of right hemisphere reading, therefore, is limited.

DISCUSSION

Based on the material just presented, some conclusions are rather obvious and a number of implications can be made. However, most of the really significant questions about the acquisition and operation of reading skills remain unanswered. In discussion I would like to emphasize the points that are fairly definite and leave conjecture concerning the many unanswered questions to future investigators.

The review of pathological correlations suggests that the left hemisphere is strongly dominant for reading in almost all right-handed individuals. There is no indication that this dominance is either stronger or weaker than the similar left hemisphere dominance for spoken language, but there is little in the world literature suggesting "mixed dominance" for reading. In fact, review of the literature rather strongly suggests that reading with the right hemisphere is distinctly unusual. There probably are individuals with mixed dominance or true reversal of dominance for reading, but for most adults it appears that the left hemisphere is necessary for the comprehension of written material. The apparent exceptions to this rule, reading by the commissurotomized individual and the paralexic reading seen on rare occasions, would actually indicate the strength of the left hemisphere dominance rather than the presence of significant exceptions.

A second point of anatomical significance can be gathered from the review of the literature concerning alexia in Oriental languages. While the amount of published data is still limited, there is considerable agreement concerning differences in handling the pictographic characters that appear to be visually oriented and the more auditorially oriented phonetic characters. In essence, a more posterior localization of pathology (parietal-occipital) produces alexia for pictographic characters and a more anterior, temporal-parietal localization underlies alexia for phonetic script. This is compatible with anticipated localization of visual and auditory functions based on prior experience.

As a third point, this presentation has attempted to demonstrate the presence of three clinically different varieties of alexia secondary to three different anatomical localizations of pathology. For simplicity, these have been called primary, secondary, and tertiary, but a number of other names have been or could be used for these syndromes. Table 1.2 lists some of the many terms in use.

Table 1.2. Synonyms for the Three Varieties of Alexia

Primary	Secondary	Tertiary
Occipital alexia	Parietal-temporal alexia	Frontal alexia
Sensory alexia	Associative alexia	Motor alexia
Posterior alexia	Central alexia	Anterior alexia
Pure word blindness	Word & letter blindness	Letter blindness
Verbal alexia	Verbal & literal alexia	Literal alexia
Agnosic alexia	Aphasic alexia	
Alexia without agraphia	Alexia with agraphia	
Optic aphasia	Cortical alexia	
Pure alexia	Angular gyrus syndrome	

Primary alexia appears to be associated directly with a visual-sensory disturbance. The patient can read in any manner except through visual input, thus producing a sensory alexia. Tertiary alexia is associated with disturbances of motor speech and eye movements and can be considered a motor alexia. Secondary alexia appears to fall between these two extremes; it is often associated with disturbed language comprehension, with serious word-finding defects, and with difficulty in auditory association. It would appear that secondary alexia is a disturbance of integration in which the patient is unable to associate visual input (the written word) with auditory or other sensory knowledge or to transform these associations into appropriate units for reading out loud or semantic comprehension. The three varieties of alexia outlined above produce different clinical findings, both in the alexia itself and in the associated clinical findings. Table 1.3 outlines some of the important clinical differentiating points.

There is an anatomical differentiation that is just as definite; primary alexia occurs exclusively with medial occipital pathology, secondary alexia follows parietal-temporal pathology, and tertiary alexia occurs with frontal pathology. All of the lesions involve the dominant hemisphere.

The findings mentioned above can be considered to represent an outline of the pathology that underlies reading disturbances, in other words, a pathology of reading. Future studies of reading capability, including reading acquisition, reading loss, etc., should attempt correlation with this pathology. Without question, however, there are additional factors underlying the ability to acquire reading. Such factors as auditory memory, visual memory, attention, visual discrimination, cognitive ability, as well as social and educational factors deserve consideration. It can be conjectured, however, that the anatomical areas noted above are important for the developing child and that structural abnormalities in

Table 1.3. Clinical Findings Associated with the Three Varieties of Alexia

	Primary	*Secondary*	*Tertiary*
1) Alexia	+	+	+
literal	–	+	+
verbal	+	+	–
2) Agraphia	–	+	+
3) Letter-naming	+	–	–
4) Comprehension of spelled words	+	–	–
5) Spelling aloud	+	–	–
6) Aphasia, fluent	–	+	–
Non-fluent	–	–	+
7) Right visual field defect	+	±	–
8) Right hemiparesis	–	±	+
9) Right hemisensory loss	–	+	±
10) Gerstmann syndrome	–	+	–

these areas may interfere with the acquisition of reading. Reading is not a unitary process, and the variations of reading disturbances described above should be considered in any serious attempt to investigate reading disability.

REFERENCES

1. Adler, A. 1950. Course and outcome of visual agnosia. *J. Nerv. Ment. Dis.* 3: 41.
2. Ajax, E. T. 1967. Dyslexia without agraphia. *Arch. Neurol.* 17: 645.
3. Akelaitis, A. J. 1941. Studies of the Corpus Callosum II. *Arch. Neuro. Psychiat.* 45: 788.
4. ———. 1943. Studies of the corpus callosum VII. *J. Neuropath. Exptl. Neurol.* 2: 226.
5. Albert, M. L. 1972. Auditory sequencing and left cerebral dominances for language. *Neuropsychologia* 10: 245.
6. Asayama, T. 1914. Über die Aphasie bei Japanern. *Deutsches Arch. f. Klin. Med.* 113: 523.
7. Bastian, H. C. 1898. *Aphasia and other speech defects.* London: H. K. Lewis.

8. Benson, D. F., and Geschwind, N. 1969. "The alexias," in Vinken, P. J., and Bruyn, G. W. (eds.), *Handbook of neurology*. Amsterdam: North Holland Publishing Co.
9. Benson, D. F., Brown, J., Tomlinson, E. B. 1971. Varieties of alexia. *Neurology* 21: 951.
10. Benson, D. F., and Geschwind, N. 1971. "Aphasia and related cortical disturbances," in Baker, A. B., and Baker. L. H. (eds.), *Clinical neurology*. New York: Harper & Row.
11. Benton, A. L. 1964. Contributions to aphasia before Broca. *Cortex* I: 314.
12. Berringer, K., and Stein, J. 1930. Analyse eines Falles von Reiner Alexie. *Ztschr. f.d. ges. Neurol. u. Psychiat.* 123: 472.
13. Bogen, J. 1969. The other side of the brain II: An appositional mind. *Bull. Los Angeles Neurol. Soc.* 34: 135.
14. Davidenkov, S. N. 1956. Visual agnosias, Lectures 8 & 9—impairment of higher nervous activity. Leningrad: State Publishing House of Medical Literature.
15. Dejerine, J. 1891. Sur un cas de cécité verbale avec agraphie, suivi d'autopsie. *Mem. Soc. Biol.* 3: 197.
16. _____. 1892. Contribution a l'etude anatomo-pathologique et clinique des differentes varietes de cécité verbale. *Mem. Soc. Biol.* 4: 61.
17. _____. 1914. *Hemiologie des affections du systema nerveaux*. Paris: Masson.
18. de Massary, J. 1932. L'alexie. *Encephale* 27: 134.
19. Freud, S. 1953. *On aphasia* (trans. E. Stengl). New York: Int. Univ. Press.
20. Freund, C. S. 1888. Uber optische Aphasie und Seelendlindheit. *Aich Psychiat. Nervenker* 20: 276–97.
21. Gazzaniga, M. S., and Sperry, R. W. 1967. Language after section of the cerebral commissures. *Brain* 90: 131.
22. Gazzaniga, M. S., Bogen, J. E., and Sperry, R. W. 1965. Observations on visual perception after disconnexion of the cerebral hemispheres. *Brain* 88: 221.
23. Geschwind, N. 1965. Disconnexion syndromes in animals and man. *Brain* 88: 237.
24. Geschwind, N., and Fusillo, M. 1966. Color naming defects in association with alexia. *Arch. Neurol.* 15: 137.
25. Gloning, I., Gloning, K., and Hoff, H. 1968. Neuropsychological symptoms and syndromes in lesions of the occipital lobe and the adjacent areas. Paris: Gontheir Villar.
26. Goldstein, K. 1948. *Language and language disturbance*. New York: Grune & Stratton.
27. Goldstein, M., Joynt, R., and Goldblatt, D. 1971. Word blindness. *Neurology* 21: 873.
28. Greenblatt, S. H. 1973. Alexia without agraphia or hemianopsia. *Brain* 96: 307.
29. Henschen, S. E. 1920–22. *Pathologie Des Gehirns*. Frontalaphasie und Wortblindheit, vol. 7. Stockholm: Nordiska Bokhanddeln.
30. Hinshelwood, J. 1900. *Letter-word-mind-blindness*. London: H. K. Lewis.
31. Imura, T. 1943. Aphasia, its characteristics in the Japanese language. *Psychiat. Neurol. Jap.* 47: 196.
32. Kinsbourne, M., and Warrington, E. K. 1962. A variety of reading disability associated with right hemisphere lesions. *J. Neurol. Neurosurg. Psychiat.* 25: 339.

33. _____. 1965. A case showing selectively impaired oral speech. *J. Neurol. Neurosurg. Psychiat.* 28: 563.
34. Leischner, A. 1957. *Die Storungen der Schriftsprache.* Stuttgart: Georg Thieme Verlag.
35. Lhermitte, F., Beauvois, M. F. 1973. A visual-speech disconnexion syndrone. *Brain* 96: 695.
36. Lichtheim, L. 1885. On aphasia. *Brain* 7: 434.
37. Luria, A. R. 1959. Disorders of simultaneous perception in a case of bilateral occipito-parietal brain injury. *Brain* 82: 437.
38. _____. 1966. *Higher cortical functions in man.* New York: Basic Books.
39. Lyman, R. S., Kwan, S. T., and Chao, W. H. 1938. Left occipito-parietal brain tumor with observations on alexia and agraphia in Chinese and English. *Chinese Med. J.* 54: 491.
40. Martin, J. P. 1954. Pure word blindness considered as a disturbance of visual space perception. *Proc. Roy. Soc. Med.* 47: 293.
41. Maspes, P. E. 1948. Le syndrome experimental chez l'homme de la section du splenium du corps calleux alexie visuelle pure hemianopsique. *Rev. Neurologie* 80: 100.
42. Nielsen, J. M. 1936. *Agnosia, apraxia, and aphasia: Their value in cerebral localization.* New York: Hafner Publishing Co. (2nd ed.).
43. _____. 1938. The unsolved problems in aphasia, part I. *Bull. L.A. Neurol. Soc.* 4: 114.
44. _____. 1939. The unsolved problems in aphasia, part II. *Bull. L.A. Neurol. Soc.* 4: 168.
46. Potzl, O. 1919. Über die ruckbildung einer reinen wortblindheit. *Ztschr. ges. Neurol. u. Psychiat.* 52: 241.
47. Rubens, A. B., and Butler, R. B. 1974. Conjugate gaze defect (in preparation).
48. Sasanuma, S., and Fujimura, O. 1971. Selective impairment and non-phonetic transcription of words in Japanese aphasic patients. *Cortex* 7: 1.
49. Stachowiak, F. J., and Poeck, K. Functional disconnection in pure alexia and color naming deficit demonstrated by deblocking methods. *Brain and Language,* in press.
50. Starr, A. 1889. The pathology of sensory aphasia, with analysis of fifty cases in which Broca's centre was not diseased. *Brain* 12: 82.
51. Teuber, H. L. 1968. "Alteration of perception and memory in man." in Weizkrantz, L. (ed.), *Analysis of behavioral change.* New York: Harper & Row.
52. Trescher, J. H., and Ford, F. R. 1937. Colloid cyst of the third ventricle. *Arch. Neurol. Psych.* 37: 959.
53. Warrington, E., Zangwill, O. L. 1957. A study of dyslexia. *J. Neurol. Neurosurg. Psychiat.* 20: 208.
54. Wolpert, I. 1924. Die simultanagnosie-störung der gesamtauffassung. *Ztschr. f.d. ges. Neurol. u. Psychiat.* 93: 397.
55. Wylie, J. 1894. *The disorders of speech.* Edinburgh: Oliver and Boyd.
56. Yamadori, A. 1975. Ideographic reading in alexia. *Brain* 98: 231.

2

Doris R. Entwisle

Young Children's Expectations for Reading

Looking just at the titles of the papers presented in this symposium forcefully reminds one that reading is a multifaceted activity. Reading draws on skills in visual processing. It draws on knowledge of structure and syntax. It draws on general information about the world. It draws, furthermore, in different amounts on different skills as the reader matures. My thesis is that *all* facets of the multifaceted activity we call "reading" are influenced by social variables—such things as views of one's social group and one's place in it, things in the environment to which one pays attention, the social reinforcements one gets—for the visual cues the child attends to, the variant of syntax he knows, and his store of general information all depend on what social group he belongs to. Perhaps most important, reinforcements for learning to read, which are mainly *social* in nature, differ strikingly from one group to the next. To explain the large differences in reading achievement that occur from one subculture to another in the United States, or to explain the sex differences that favor boys in one country, girls in another, one must look to socio-

This research program was supported by Office of Education grant OEG-3-71-0122 and National Institute of Education grant NIE-G-74-0029. We gratefully acknowledge this financial support.

Most of this work was done in collaboration with Leslie Hayduk. He has had a major role in preparation of the results presented here. Earlier Murray Webster contributed many useful suggestions and I am grateful for his help. Linda Olson has coordinated the day-to-day operations of the research and helped in every phase of it, including preparation of this chapter. I also wish to thank Eileen Rudert and Murial Berkeley for their help. I would also like to acknowledge the valuable assistance of Dr. John Crew of the Baltimore City Public Schools, Dr. George Gabriel of the Baltimore County Public Schools, the principals, staff, students, and parents. The participants must remain anonymous, but the research would have been impossible without their cooperation.

logical variables. Formal learning theory and reading research both ignore sociological variables.

For many years I have been interested in children's linguistic development and how this relates to reading competence. But, to my mind, studies of linguistic development and educability both here and abroad suggest that differences in reading achievement may depend much more heavily on the social differences that separate groups of children rather than the linguistic factors separating them. Experiments in Montreal, for example, by Wallace Lambert and his associates (see, e.g., Lambert & Tucker 1972) demonstrate that even maximum cleavage between the language a child speaks and the language he hears in school does not impair reading achievement. In their studies Anglophone children in Montreal heard nothing but French from the time they started school and learned to read with little difficulty. These data and similar data from other bilingual programs suggest that social factors may overshadow linguistic factors in explaining differences in reading performance. Differences in reading achievement, like the differences seen in the United States between children from various socioeconomic strata, depend, in my opinion, much more on the social matrix in which the child is embedded than on the level of the child's syntactic development or the phonological system he uses.

Hundreds of studies show that social class is relevant to linguistic performance or to reading performance. Data are scarce, though, to specify *exactly* what happens day by day to produce social class differences. Bernstein and his colleagues in Great Britain suggest that social roles within the family shape the kind of language used, in particular, how context-free or context-dependent the child's language is. Bernstein (1970) speculates that difficulty in school and, by presumption, difficulty in learning to read springs from "code" differences and the sociolinguistic customs that separate middle-class teachers and working-class children.

I have pointed out elsewhere (Entwisle 1975) that both how a child structures problems and how he goes about solving problems may depend to a surprising degree on the child's social class. Children's attitudes toward work are also very different across social classes. Such cognitive style variables could be very influential in how the child perceives the task of reading, how he perceives feedback as he tries to read, and whether or not his early attempts at reading are judged successful in his own eyes. These notions are all of a hand-waving variety, however, for to my knowledge no extensive data base supports them as they apply to reading *per se*.

Children's expectations may provide a key bridge between cognitive style and social class differences. What a child *expects* and what others expect of him are socially defined parameters. If a child expects to learn to read on the first day of school, he is bound to be disappointed. If a mother expects that her child will function within a school role that allows the child little discretion, then the child is likely to expect the same and act accordingly. If a teacher expects a child to do well, or poorly, a whole shower of studies show the influence of such expectations. Lately, careful studies have appeared, for example, showing that teachers' experiences with older siblings strongly influence their reactions to younger siblings (Seaver 1973). The younger sib of a high achiever is held to different standards from the younger sib of a poor achiever. Teachers' expectations can bias perceptions in startling ways, for Bikson (1974) observed that teachers perceived *no* differences between the verbal fluency of black or Chicano third-graders and white third-graders, when the verbal productions of the minority group children were almost twice as long as those of the white children. Another study shows that gifted white and black children receive very different treatment at the hands of student teachers (Rubovits & Maehr 1973), presumably because different expectations are held for blacks and whites.

The work I have just touched upon and other work in the same vein caused me to turn my attention five or six years ago toward social interaction of children in small groups to see what affected performance, or affected their willingness to perform. A set of experimental studies (Entwisle & Webster 1972, 1973, 1974*a*, 1974*b*) used a story-telling task, and children's expectations for success at that task, to study how adults might raise children's expectations. What I want to present here, however, is a preliminary report on some other research that centers on *observational* studies of children's expectations *over time* in natural settings. This research asks first, how do children develop expectations for their performance and how do these expectations influence that performance, and second, how do other persons' expectations—parents, peers, teachers —impinge on the child's expectations for himself?

The observational data focus on children in first and second grade in a white middle-class school and in an integrated lower-class school. We have followed individual children from the time they start first grade to see how their expectations for their own performance in reading (and arithmetic and conduct) develop. Their expectations for themselves, and their parents' and classmates' expectations for them, are repeatedly measured. The children's expectations in the three subject areas have been tabulated twice each year (before the first report card in the fall term and just before the end of the spring term). In addition, other data— IQ, school marks in reading, arithmetic, and conduct, self-esteem scores, and the like—have been studied over the same time to see how children's expectations relate to them (e.g., in the case of IQ) or how children's expectations respond to them (e.g., in the case of marks). Some of the data and results presented below are discussed more fully in Entwisle and Hayduk (1974).

PSYCHOLOGICAL AND SOCIOLOGICAL PARADIGMS

This research tries to trace out how sequences of events or patterns of social interaction lead children to take particular views of themselves as performers in school. The unit of analysis is the *school-child nested in a group* of significant others, his parents, his peers, his teacher. This unit bridges both the psychological and sociological units of analysis and focuses on the articulation of the child with his group of significant others. The aim is to trace how social factors and processes are translated into expectations of children and how these expectations, in turn, affect children's performance. The design and analysis draw upon both the psychological and sociological tradition of research.

Like longitudinal research in psychology, children are measured at several time points. The child's expectations for himself are assessed repeatedly from a time before he receives his first report card to the end of the second grade in some cases. Individual curves can be derived that show how a child's hopes for his own achievement change over time, indicating whether, for example, a given child's expectations remain stable or move. With expectations rising *on the average* over the first-grade year (as they do, for instance, in the white middle-class school) there is opportunity to see whether all children's expectations rise a little, or whether some rise a great deal, while others decline slightly. It could turn out that a child's expectations decrease if his earliest expectations are not confirmed, or equally well that his expectations remain fixed and his performance improves.

The research also draws from the sociological tradition. Like sociological studies, this work studies contextual variables and tries to impose a causal paradigm. Children's expectations at the end of first grade, for example, are studied in the context of (1) expectations of the child earlier that year; (2) parents' expectations; and (3) previous marks received. The number of cases involved (so far 150 at the maximum) and the nature of the measurement (usually ranks) does not permit a full correlational path-analysis at this stage in the research. However, repeated cross-tabulations are carried out, where *change* in one variable is tabulated against change in another variable. Such an analysis can examine whether children with low initial expectations revise their expectations upward after receiving high marks, or whether marks and expectations change simultaneously so as to increase the agreement between them from one time point to the next. Or, to take another example, if parents, on the average, expect boys to do more poorly than girls in reading, what is the course of particular boys' expectations whose parents hold very low expectations and how are the expectations of both parents and boys affected by marks the boy receives? Or, to take still another example, if black children have higher expectations at the start of school than white children, is this linked to higher expectations of black parents, black teachers, or peers for these children, and does this elevated state persist?

The melding of the psychological and sociological approaches found in this research is novel and allows study of a *dynamic causal* model (see fig. 2.1). The longitudinal method is often extolled, because it allows one to observe change in behavior as the individual grows. Obviously, however, time cannot be viewed as the independent variable in the sense of causation. Rather this method allows study of sequential intraindividual variation. If hopes of children in one cohort assessed at the end of first grade, are weighed against hopes of other children in second grade one might conclude, other things being equal, that the average level of hope had risen or fallen. One might also calculate the correlation between hopes and marks *within* the first-grade sample or within the second-grade sample. One could not, however, conclude that high hopes in the second grade were preceded (or caused) by high marks in the first. Thus the advantage of the longitudinal method lies in teasing out causal patterns *not in detecting successive differences with greater power*, an aim often cited by developmental psychologists and by sociologists who carry out panel studies.

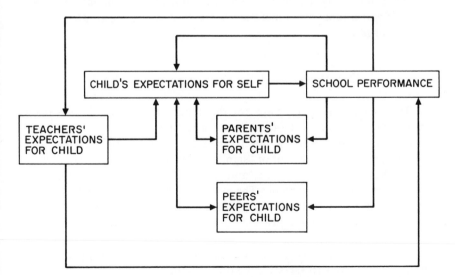

Fig. 2.1. The Dynamic Model

EARLY STAGES IN THE LIFE CYCLE

The present research measures variables in young school children that may be potent determinants of later achievement and of ultimate status attainment. To our knowledge, these variables have not previously been studied in a sociological-type causal framework. Several studies suggest that by the end of third grade the prediction of eventual attainment may be almost certain. Both national (Bloom 1964; Kraus 1973) and cross-national studies (Husèn 1969) show very little change in children's achievement levels in school after that time. These findings, it should be noted, are in accord with much folk wisdom as well. If this kind of early asymptote then exists, two conclusions may be drawn. (1) Status attainment may be predictable from points very early in the life cycle. Despite data showing that peers and the social context in high school may account for considerable variance in later attainment, these peers may be surrogates, in a sense, carriers of influence for peers who intervened much earlier. If a person's level of educational attainment is set by the end of third grade, then perhaps his peers before that time have shaped his tendencies to achieve. His peers later, in high school, are "influential" because they match his earlier peers in their characteristics. It is only because he remains in a fairly constant environment that both sets of peers appear equal. (2) Policy-oriented or action research should perhaps focus on school children at a much earlier point in the life cycle, before the point when eventual attainment becomes predictable. There may be little use in altering school or school environments after the early primary years if educational attainment levels are as stable as the studies quoted above suggest.

THE IMPORTANCE OF SOCIAL CONTEXT

The social context germane for this longitudinal study derives from two separate theoretical orientations. The first, the nest of significant others, can be linked to the developmental "looking-glass" of Mead and Cooley and to Sullivan's set of "significant others." The set of significant others has been an important and continuing concern in sociological studies of status attainment. The only difference in its use here is its application to students who are much younger than those previously studied, those who have just emerged from the protective circle of the family.

The second theoretical strand, more macrosociological in its roots, links this research to the stratification system of the society as a whole. The cross-sectional study of social class differences is firmly established as a research paradigm in both education and sociology, for example, studies of school achievement over various levels of social class. The repeated demonstration of social class differences has reached a point of diminishing returns, however, as already mentioned. Middle-class children are, on the average, better readers at every grade than lower-class children. This fact is well established. What is not known is the causal priority to be assigned to social factors leading to the association between social class and performance.

Rosenberg and Simmons's (1971) work is especially informative with respect to the impact of social context. In a large cross-sectional study of children at third grade and higher, they note that minority group children in certain contexts have higher self-esteem. The overall picture for minority group children is for higher self-esteem because most of them are in consonant social contexts that protect self-esteem. The black child in an all-black neighborhood and all-black school compares himself with those around him. He does not use children or families with which he has no contact as reference groups. For this reason, if his parents are separated or divorced or if his actual father is unknown, his family status is not a source of embarrassment or sorrow, because many of his confreres have the same problem. A black child from a broken family who attends an integrated school, however, rates himself in comparison with his classmates whose families are intact. In this atmosphere a broken family produces social stigmata.

The impact of other facets of school life that might also be thought to lower self-esteem is cushioned by self-reference to protective groups. The low-IQ black child, for example, reports that his parents believe that being smart is not very important for getting higher grades. Or, for another example, the black child with very dark skin rates color as less important in assessing physical attractiveness than the child with light skin color.

The important outcome of Rosenberg and Simmons's work for the present research is that self-esteem, which can be termed a "global set of self-expectations," is highly dependent on context. Rosenberg and Simmons could not investigate causal priorities directly because their data are cross-sectional, but their data (retrospective reports of racial taunts) implicate the kinds of interpersonal events that could lead to lower self-esteem in minority group children. Certainly, racial taunts are more likely in a mixed than in a segregated context.

Social context and its impact on expectations has also been pointed up in small-scale experimental work. The study of interventions to raise expectations of black children in small mixed racial groups (see work by Cohen and her associates) when balanced against some small experimental studies of our own (Entwisle & Webster 1974*a*, 1974*b*) point even more strongly to contextual effects and their importance. In brief, in mixed racial work-groups of children brought together for experiments, Cohen found that black children held low expectations for their own success and that these feelings were shared by white work-mates. Blacks who up to the time of the experiment were resident in all-black contexts did poorly in the mixed-race experimental context, even when much preparation before the experiments guaranteed the superior competence of the blacks. In our experiments where blacks also worked in mixed racial groups, neither white children nor black children held low expectations for blacks. These black children had attended an integrated school from kindergarten on. The social contexts from which these two sets of experimental subjects were drawn apparently made them behave very differently.

Guided by the importance of social context in both the large-scale Baltimore study of Rosenberg and Simmons and the small-scale experimental work, the present research focuses on children within two contexts—one all-white and one mixed racially, 60% black. (Later work will examine all-black contexts.) The present research can examine more events, and more specific events, than that of Rosenberg and Simmons and also, of course, looks at effects over time. If a child is asked to recall racial taunts, as in the Rosenberg and Simmons study, such a report has weaknesses too well-known to be enumerated here. Without being at all critical of the Rosenberg and Simmons work, one can note that self-esteem covers many aspects of the self. To understand its ups and downs or the underlying factors that comprise it, considerable precision is required. The causes of self-esteem are no doubt manifold and subtle, and a single overall measure is probably inadequate for explaining its causes. The present research attempts to look at the course of development of the academic self-image in particular areas, how performance feedback shapes that self-image, and how feedback from particular persons operates on the self-image. The social context (in the persons of particular actors) shapes the image, subject to overall constraints in the social milieu. Specifically, peer feedback in an integrated environment may have effects different from such feedback in a segregated environment. From a methodological standpoint it would be fruitless to try to gauge the self-image with either the localized or general context erased. Up to this time, studies have not combined both social context and a detailed dynamic feedback mechanism in a research paradigm.

DESIGN

Three cohorts of children have been followed from the time they began first grade. Two cohorts are in a white middle-class suburban school. One (S–1) began first grade in 1971, the other (S–2) began first grade in 1972.

A third cohort (L–1) in a mixed race (60% black), urban lower-class school began first grade in 1972. Insofar as possible, similar data and information were obtained for all three cohorts.

The time chart in figure 2.2 shows the sequence and timing of several of the repeated measures over a two-year time span. Only cohort S–1 has been followed for the entire two-year period. Cohorts S–2 and L–1 have been followed on the same plan as S–1, but for only one year. The measures identified on the time chart will now be described.

The Children's Expectation Measure

To provide a measure of the child's expectations for his own school performance, children were asked to "guess what your next report card will look like. Guess what you will get in reading . . . in arithmetic . . . and in conduct." How elaborate the interviewing procedure was that accompanied this "guessing" depended on whether the child was new to the study or had been interviewed previously.

For the initial measuring of expectations, a large plastic brightly colored sheet (approximately 2′ × 3′) was prepared, with titles of school subjects (arithmetic, reading, conduct) and squares for entering marks in it like a report card. This sheet was spread out on a table or sometimes on the floor. Next to the sheet were a number of piles of cardboard squares with large numerals (1, 2, 3, 4) inked on them.

Children, interviewed individually outside their classroom or in a separate room nearby, were told that "we are going to play a game—guessing what you will get on your report card." Before "playing the game," the child was asked if he knew what a report card was, what the numerals meant, and what "reading," "arithmetic," and "conduct" meant. Enough discussion then ensued so the interviewer felt reasonably confident that the child understood what school report cards signified and how marks were coded. The child was then asked to pick a number from the pile of numerals and put it in a square next to "reading" to "guess what you will get in reading." He was similarly asked to pick numerals to represent his guesses for arithmetic and conduct.* Initial interviews for measuring expectations in reading, arithmetic, and conduct were held slightly before the child received his first report card in first grade. Report cards are issued three times in grade one, midyear, year end, and half way between midyear and year end. Only midyear and year-end report card information is used. In second grade, report cards are issued four times—roughly corresponding to the end of each of four quarters of the school year.

---

*At a later time a separate interview was conducted with each child by a different interviewer. These interviews verified the child's understanding of marks and marking systems without reference to the guessing task. The independent verification is discussed in connection with results.

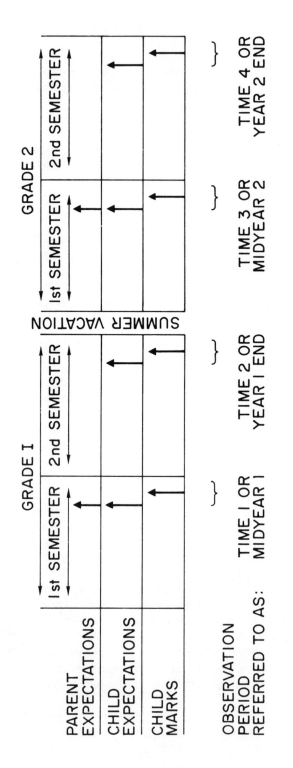

Fig. 2.2. Observation Periods

As the child made his guesses the interviewer unobtrusively recorded check marks on a small $3'' \times 5''$ card. The cards were kept out of sight, and it is doubtful if any of the children were aware that their guesses were being recorded.

This same guessing procedure was carried out twice yearly during each school year. In first grade it occurred once before the child received his first report card (November for L–1, December–January for S–1, and S–2), and again before the end of the school year in late May or early June. In second grade it was carried out just before the end of the first semester and again near the end of the school year.

The expectation measure appears to have a fair degree of validity and reliability indicated by reinterviews, meaningful relationships that emerge between it and other variables, and a substantial degree of test-retest agreement when guesses for the same child are matched between one session and the next. A special reliability check run on a small sample of first-graders with a short time span (one week between test and retest) indicates a high degree of concordance between expectations elicited on the two occasions (.76).

The details of how other variables were measured may be found in Entwisle and Hayduk (1974).

Teachers' Marks

The reader should note carefully that the teacher's basis for assigning marks, according to the report card definition, is quite different in the two schools. In the middle-class school the teacher attempts to mark the child in relation to his own ability. In the lower-class school the teacher attempts to mark the child in relation to others of his grade level.

Parents' Expectations and Questionnaire

Parents in the middle-class school were interviewed in many instances, the occasion being their appearance to visit their child's classroom during American Education Week (late October). Those not available were sent questionnaires by mail.

Parents in the lower-class school were also interviewed at school if they came for activities in connection with American Education Week. A much lower percentage attended, however, and the difficulties in securing the needed information from interviews in school led us not to mail questionnaires to these parents, but rather to send out interviewers to the homes to secure the information. Children carried home a note a day or two in advance of the interviewer's call, notifying the parent that an interviewer would be coming, and explaining that this was a routine research request, not an indication that their child was in difficulty at school. Black adult female interviewers were dispatched to homes of black children, and white adult female interviewers saw parents of white children. Refusal rates and other data are given with the results.

The data procured from parents was, insofar as possible, identical for the two schools. The parents were asked to "guess" what their child "would get on his next report card," and the interviewers recorded guesses on sheets of paper with replicas of part of the report card appearing upon them.

ANALYSIS

All data were coded and punched on cards. Data reduction was accomplished mainly through use of standard DATATEXT programs. Further analyses and tests were calculated as needed.

RESULTS

The Middle-Class School

Means and standard deviations for the variables used in subsequent analyses and cross-tabulations are given in table 2.1. The mean IQ for 183 children (those in the sample, 82% for whom IQ data were available from school records) is 113.5, with a standard diviation of 11.

A number of conclusions, borne out in both cohorts separately, are even clearer in the data for combined cohorts.

1) Expectations were obtainable from 86% of parents. All were contacted at least twice. Parents have lower expectations than children for reading and arithmetic, but only the difference for reading approaches significance ($t = 1.95$ for the combined cohorts). Parents' expectations levels are uniform across subject areas when the two cohorts are combined.

2) Children in Cohorts 1 and 2 show significant differences in their expectations, those in the second cohort being lower. For reading the difference (0.16) is small in absolute terms and not significant ($t = 1.17$).

3) At the middle of grade one children have highest expectations in reading; next highest in arithmetic, and least in conduct. These differences between subject areas are consistent in both cohorts, but only the reading-conduct difference reaches significance ($p < .05$) in the combined cohorts. Differences between areas are small in Cohort 1.

4) Children's expectations in reading increase significantly over the first-grade year ($t = 2.60, p < .05; t = 3.60, p < .01$, respectively for the combined cohorts).

Table 2.1. Means, standard deviations for separate cohorts and sum of cohorts during first-grade year, middle-class school

	Cohort 1			Cohort 2			Combined cohorts		
	N	Mean	S.D.	N	Mean	S.D.	N	Mean	S.D.
Parents' expectations—T1									
Reading	84	1.96	0.57	76	1.80	0.67	160	1.89	0.62
Arithmetic	84	1.83	0.60	76	2.04	0.74	160	1.93	0.67
Conduct	79	1.89	0.55	75	1.97	0.70	154	1.93	0.63
Child's expectation—T1									
Reading	90	1.63	0.90	96	1.79	0.96	186	1.72	0.94
Arithmetic	90	1.66	0.90	96	1.94	0.79	186	1.80	0.86
Conduct	90	1.68	0.90	96	2.13	1.05	186	1.91	1.00
Child's expectation—T2									
Reading	90	1.42	0.60	94	1.65	0.60	184	1.54	0.61
Arithmetic	90	1.64	0.81	94	1.75	0.75	184	1.70	0.78
Conduct	90	1.49	0.72	94	1.71	0.73	184	1.60	0.73
Child's marks—T1									
Reading	85	1.77	0.65	93	1.77	0.63	178	1.77	0.64
Arithmetic	85	1.82	0.49	93	2.01	0.62	178	1.92	0.57
Conduct	85	1.75	0.75	93	1.96	0.67	178	1.86	0.72
Child's marks—T2									
Reading	86	1.69	0.76	94	1.77	0.59	180	1.73	0.68
Arithmetic	86	1.66	0.59	94	1.77	0.66	180	1.71	0.63
Conduct	86	1.88	0.83	94	1.76	0.67	180	1.82	0.75

Summary of changes over year

	Cohort 1			Cohort 2			Combined cohorts		
	N	Mean	S.D.	N	Mean	S.D.	N	Mean	S.D.
Mark Discrepance (T1 Mark minus T2 Mark)									
Reading	78	0.10	0.70	93	0.01	0.62	171	0.05	0.65
Arithmetic	78	0.19	0.56	93	0.25	0.64	171	0.22	0.60
Conduct	78	-0.04	0.63	93	0.20	0.60	171	0.09	0.63
Expectation discrepance (T1 expectation minus T2 expectation)									
Reading	85	0.24	0.88	89	0.18	1.14	174	0.21	1.02
Arithmetic	85	0.00	1.14	89	0.23	0.84	174	0.12	1.00
Conduct	85	0.21	1.03	89	0.47	1.19	174	0.35	1.12
Mark-expectation discrepance T1 (T1 mark minus T1 expectations)									
Reading	82	0.18	1.07	90	-0.03	1.08	172	0.07	1.07
Arithmetic	82	0.18	0.97	90	0.04	0.91	172	0.11	0.94
Conduct	82	0.10	1.06	90	-0.18	1.20	172	-0.05	1.14
Mark-expectation discrepance T2 (T2 mark minus T2 expectation)									
Reading	84	0.27	0.87	91	0.11	0.71	175	0.19	0.79
Arithmetic	84	0.02	0.88	91	0.02	0.86	175	0.02	0.86
Conduct	84	0.37	0.92	91	0.03	0.90	175	0.19	0.92

5) Reading marks remain relatively stable over the year in both cohorts.

Before the First Report Card What Do Children Expect?

First, a word is needed about how marks are assigned. At the first marking period (around the end of November) first-graders do not receive report cards. At the end of the first semester (around February 1) they receive a report. The card says: "This report is designed to measure the progress of your child in terms of his own maturity and ability. Comparison with other children or groups of children is avoided." Thus children are being judged in terms of what they are theoretically capable of doing—their performance, in other words, is assessed with IQ partialled out.

Discrepancies between Initial Expectations
and the First Report Card

As was true for each cohort taken separately, there is *not* a significant degree of matching in the combined cohorts between children's expectations and the marks they actually receive on their first report card in reading. (As can be seen in table 2.1, the variability in expectations exceeds that in marks.) A high percentage of children expect A's (55% expect A's in reading) and also a sizable percentage (6%) expect failure. Actually, no one fails. As can be seen in table 2.2, the outstanding characteristic is the large number of children expecting 1's who get 2's, far outbalancing the number who get 1's but expect 2's. This kind of overoptimism is the principal source of disagreement between expectations and first marks.

Discrepancies between Expectations
and Report Cards at End of First Grade

By the end of the first grade, children show some improvement in their ability to forecast marks accurately. For reading 53% of children ($z = 2.82$, $p < .01$) are correct. (At midyear 32% of the children had accurately forecast their mark.)

The discrepance between year-end marks and expectations will be treated in more detail later in relation to other variables.

How Do Children's Expectations Change
over the First-Grade Year?

It has already been pointed out that the average level of children's expectations increases over the first-grade year. How does this change

Table 2.2. Reading mark versus expectation, time 1, middle-class school

		Reading mark, time 1				
		1	*2*	*3*	*Total*	*Percent*
	1	30	55	10	95	55.2
	2	23	21	2	46	26.7
Reading	3	3	13	4	20	11.6
expectations,						
time 1	4	3	6	2	11	6.4
	Total	59	95	18	172	
	Percent	34.3	55.2	10.5		100.0

appear at an individual level? Much of what follows addresses this question by looking at changes in expectations in relation to marks received, to the expectation-mark discrepancy at midyear, to parent expectations, and the like. The simplest question is to ask how much matching at an individual level there is at midyear and at the end of the year, and this question will be answered first.

About 48% of children hold the same expectations for reading at the end of the year as in the middle of the year, as table 2.3 shows. While 40% would be expected to show the same expectation by chance, the amount of persistence observed is too large to attribute to chance ($z = 2.18, p < .05$). More important, those whose expectations change tend to move up—60% move up while 40% move down—although the trend does not quite attain significance ($\chi_1^2 = 3.18$).

To sum up: Children's expectations in reading (and arithmetic) are quite stable over the year and tend to change little. When there is a change, it tends to be in an upward direction, but it is not significant.

What Is Impact of First Mark on Expectations Later?

If a child got an A in reading on his first report card, in 72% of the cases he expects an A at the end of the year. If he got a B, in 54% of the cases he looks for a B again, but in almost the entire remainder of the cases, he looks for an A (41%). If he got a C, in only 10% of the cases does he look for a C again; in 45% of the cases he looks for a B and in 45% of the cases he looks for an A!

There is some improvement in forecast accuracy over the year. Can it be accounted for in terms of improved accuracy of only those who receive the higher marks? That is, marks between midyear and year end are

Table 2.3. Reading expectation, time 2, versus expectation, time 1, middle-class school

		1	*2*	*3*	*4*	*Total*	*Percent*
		Reading expectation, time 2					
	1	57	33	4		94	54.0
	2	23	23			46	26.4
Reading expectation, time 1	3	4	15	2		21	12.1
	4	8	3	1	1	13	7.5
	Total	92	74	7	1	174	
	Percent	52.9	42.5	4.0	0.6		100.0

relatively stable (68% of the children receive identical reading marks both times; 99% receive reading marks less than 2 points away from their midyear mark), so it would seem that following anything other than a rule, such as "if you got a C this time (midyear) expect a C next time (year end)," would lead to inaccuracy. Since accuracy improves, it might seem that children with C's who expect A's and B's are not the ones providing for any improvement.

If we look at table 2.4, however, we see that accuracy can be improved by children who get C's. We see that 70% of the children who received a C at midyear in reading get a B at year end. Their marks actually improved, which means expecting an improvement should increase accuracy for them. It would be incorrect to conclude that only the children with A's and B's are producing the improvement in mark-expectation matching, despite the seeming contradiction that children with initially low marks maintain relatively high expectations.

One should note that the children who receive C's at midyear are atypical in that the mark they should expect at year end is *not* the mark they received at midyear, as is the case with children who received A's and B's. The relatively small number of children that receive C's means this distinction can go unnoticed if one simply uses "percent receiving identical marks" in the whole table, as above.

Of the children who received C's at year end, 78% had received a B at midyear. The probability of getting a C after having a B at midyear is smaller than the probability of getting a C after a C at midyear (.15 as compared to .20), but the larger number of cases to which the former

Table 2.4. Reading mark, time 2, versus mark, time 1, middle-class school

		1	*2*	*3*	*4*	*Total*	*Percent*
				Reading mark, time 2			
	1	42	16			58	33.9
Reading mark, time 1	2	24	55	14		93	54.4
	3	1	14	4	1	20	11.7
	Total	67	85	18	1	171	
	Percent	39.2	49.7	10.5	0.6		100.0

applies results in a larger proportion of the year-end C's having a midyear B (14 cases), rather than a midyear C (4 cases). In reading, only 22% of the children who received a C at midyear received a C at year end. More is said about this differential accuracy in the next section.

How Does Children's Expectation-Mark Agreement Vary with the First Mark Received?

In order to discuss table 2.5, of which other examples will appear in this report, we must first acquaint the reader with the possible patterns of outcomes, and the substantive significance of these patterns. First, if a student receives a mark of 1, his expectation can only be equal to or lower than the mark. Only values 0, $+1$, $+2$, and $+3$ on the mark-versus-expectation variable are possible for such a person. Similarly, with a mark of 4, expectations can only be equal to or higher than the mark; only -3, -2, -1 and 0 are possible values of the mark-versus-expectation variable. For a mark of 2, only -1, 0, $+1$ and $+2$ are possible, and for a mark of 3, only -2, -1, 0, and $+1$ are possible values.

Second, one must identify the pattern of outcomes expected if children were (a) able to judge accurately or test the reality of their performance and adjust their expectations accordingly, or (b) acting independently —without any feedback or knowledge—of school performance.

If children formulate their expectations independently of actual performance (marks), the distribution of expectations would be the same for all mark categories. It would, furthermore, be the same as the overall expectation distribution. For example, with an overall expectation distribution of $1 = 55\%$, $2 = 27\%$, $3 = 12\%$, and $4 = 6\%$ we would expect the following pattern.

Mark-expectation prediction
independent of performance
(percentages along rows)

	-3	*-2*	*-1*	*0*	*+1*	*+2*	*+3*	
1				55	27	12	6	100
2			55	27	12	6		100
3		55	27	12	6			100
4	55	27	12	6				100

If, on the other hand, children were adjusting their expectations according to their accurate perceptions of their actual performance, the bulk of the cases would fall in the column headed "0" (i.e., no mark-expectation difference) for each of the mark categories, and most of the remaining cases would cluster in the –1 and ∓1 columns (i.e., small mark-expectation discrepancies for all mark categories). The actual amount of clustering cannot be predicted, of course, from the assumptions given above, so the percentages presented in the following table are hypothetical and made roughly consistent with the previous example for ease of comparison.

Mark-expectation prediction,
assuming performance monitoring
(hypothetical percentages along row)

	-3	*-2*	*-1*	*0*	*+1*	*+2*	*+3*	
1				55	27	12	6	100
2			19	55	20	6		100
3		6	20	55	19			100
4	6	12	27	55				100

Under the "chance" or "marginal probability" assumption, the bulk of the cases fall on the diagonal that rises from the lower left corner of the table, and a declining set of percentages equivalent to the marginal percentages is expected in the column headed "0" discrepance. Under the "reality testing" assumption the bulk of the cases fall in the column headed "0" discrepance. Note that the two assumptions give similar shaped distributions in the row headed "Mark = 1." In any given case, however, it *may* be possible to decide between the reasonableness of the two assumptions by looking at the magnitude of the percent in row = 1, column = 0 cell. If, for example, 95% of cases appear in this cell, the data are not inconsistent with "reality testing" assumption that only claimed the bulk of the cases would be found in this cell. Such a finding would be inconsistent with the "marginal probability" assumption that specified the

Table 2.5. Expectation-mark agreement versus reading mark, time 1, middle-class school

		\-3	\-2	\-1	0	+1	+2	+3	Total	Percent
				*Expectation-mark, reading, time 1*						
Reading mark, time 1	1				51% 30	39% 23	5% 3	5% 3	59	100%
	2			58% 55	22% 21	14% 13	6% 6		95	100%
	3		56% 10	11% 2	22% 4	11% 2			18	100%
	4									
	Total		10	57	55	38	9	3	172	

magnitude of this percent as approximating the overall percent of expected marks (i.e., in our example 55%).

With these two assumptions and their resultant models in mind, let us examine table 2.5, which presents the data for reading marks and expectations at midyear. The distribution of reading expectations at midyear was 1's = 55%, 2's = 27%, 3's = 12%, and 4's = 6%. The reader will recognize these as the percents used in the "hypothetical" example above, which can be used for a direct comparison. The data clearly tend to follow the "marginal probability" model. The bulk of the cases, for the 3 marks the teachers assign, fall on a diagonal, decreasing to the left of the mark = 1, mark-expectation = 0 cell. Furthermore, all these cells (51%, 58%, and 56%) approximate the 55% expected on the basis of our overall percent of 1's expected. The data do not perfectly fit the "marginal probability" model, but approximate it more closely than the "reality testing" model (remembering the mark = 1 distribution is consistent with both).

It appears, then, that reading performance (as judged by teachers) is not information that children incorporate into their midyear reading expectation. This appears to be specifically so for those children who receive 2's and 3's, and possibly so for those who receive 1's (although here it is hard for the model to be wrong in the case of 1's).

By noting that those children with low marks have larger proportions of extreme and moderate discrepancies between their expectations and their marks, one might take table 2.5 to show that children with the poorest marks are also the children who are poorest at forecasting their marks. The discussion of the "marginal probability" model that fits the data, however, suggests that *all the children may be using an equivalent forecasting scheme that is independent of performance.* Children who do better may be better at forecasting than children who do poorly, but at this stage of the analysis it seems prudent to explain the finding on the basis of the simplest model that fits the data.

In summary, most of the data support the statement that *children of all ability levels may formulate their expectations for reading marks the same way before the first report card is received, in a way independent of performance as viewed by teachers.*

How Does Children's Expectation-Mark Agreement Vary with the Mark Received at the End of First Grade?

By the end of first grade there is a noticeable movement toward a pattern of expectation-mark discrepancies consistent with the reality-testing model for reading *for the students who get high marks.* There is both the predicted piling up in the row = 1, column = 0 cell, and a marked shift in the row = 2 distribution. For the row = 3 children, results are mixed. It appears that optimism has moderated, but guesses about performance are still biased strongly in a positive direction (see table 2.6). (Despite the fact that conduct should be more capable of monitoring by the child than reading, it only shows a slight tendency toward reality-testing.)

In sum: There seems initially, before the first report, a considerable *push for expectations to be high and for expectations to be similar regardless of the child's actual level of performance at midyear.* By the end of the second semester, a noticeable, though not extreme, shift toward reality-testing has occurred for reading. *At year end, expectations remain largely independent of actual performance in arithmetic and conduct, while a slight dependence is exhibited in reading.*

All children seem very optimistic before they get a first report card and optimistic in much the same way. Children whose marks are already at or near the ceiling cannot be more optimistic than their performance, and this leads to a confounding of effects that must be acknowledged in interpreting the findings.

How Does Children's Expectation-Mark Agreement Vary with Expectation Level?

As already noted there is a marked optimism seen in children's initial expectations in reading, for 55% look for A's on the first report card (34% receive one) and 82% look for an A or a B. This overall optimism, however, disguises some interesting pessimism when expectation-mark agreement is broken down by expectation level (see table 2.7). (The reader should note that by examining diagonals in this table, one can locate

Table 2.6. Expectation-mark agreement versus reading mark, time 2, middle-class school

		Expectation-mark, reading, time 2								
		−3	−2	−1	0	+1	+2	+3	Total	Percent
	1				68%	29%	1%	1%		100%
					47	20	1	1	69	
	2			43%	51%	6%				100%
				37	44	5			86	
Reading mark, time 2	3		32%	63%	5%					100%
			6	12	1				19	
	4	100%								100%
		1								
Total			7	49	92	25	1	1	175	

persons who received a particular mark. Thus reading down the right-most marginal, 30, 23, 3, 3, one has a summary of those children, 59, who received an "A" in reading on the first report card.)

The majority of children actually receiving an A expected one (30/59 or 51%), but many more children expecting A's did *not* receive one (65/95 or 68%). The majority of extraordinarily high hopes were therefore not confirmed. On the other hand, half the children expecting B's (23/46 or 50%) actually received an "A," so children expecting B's are generally under- rather than overoptimistic. The underoptimism is even more noticeable among those children who expect C's or D's—only 13% of the total (4/31) actually receive a C and none receives a D. Altogether 32% of children forecast their mark exactly, and most of these get an A. The general trend seems therefore to be one of inaccuracy—the overall mean suggests an inaccuracy based on overoptimism but further analysis suggests both over- and underoptimism.

The presence of both over- and underoptimism, while worth noting because of its substantive impact, is not entirely unexpected. If one disregards exact matching of marks and expectations, it is easy to see that children expecting a 4 can only underestimate. Likewise, a child expecting a 1 can only overestimate (or "exactly" forecast his mark). Those expecting 2's and 3's can either over- or underestimate, but these categories can lead to extreme discrepancies occurring in only a single direction. Therefore, given some children expecting 3's and 4's, the presence of some underestimation is guaranteed.

One can ask whether children with naturally high expectations are superior (or inferior) at providing accurate forecasts. If children of all

Table 2.7. Expectation-mark agreement versus reading expectation, time 1, middle-class school

		-3	*-2*	*-1*	*0*	*+1*	*+2*	*+3*	*Total*	*Percent*
			Expectations-mark, reading, time 1							
	1	11% 10	58% 55	32% 30					95	100%
Reading expectation, time 1	2		4% 2	46% 21	50% 23				46	100%
	3			20% 4	65% 13	15% 3			20	100%
	4				18% 2	55% 6	27% 3		11	100%
	Total	10	57	55	38	9	3	172		

expectation levels showed no accuracy at all in forecasting their marks, each expectation level would be assigned a mark distribution corresponding to the overall mark distribution (i.e., 1's = 34%, 2's = 55%, and 3's = 11%). This leads to the table of expected values shown below.

Expected values for complete lack of
forecast accuracy

		-3	*-2*	*-1*	*0*	*+1*	*+2*	*+3*	
			Expectation-mark, reading, T1						
	1		11	55	34				100%
Child's reading	2			11	55	34			100%
expectation, T1	3				11	55	34		100%
	4					11	55	34	100%

(The reader should note the parallel between this analysis and that done previously for children who received various marks.) A comparison of this table with table 2.7 indicates a reasonable similarity, indicating lack of a superior forecast ability on the part of children at any of the expectation levels. Indeed, the most noticeable discrepancy in terms of difference between percentages and the case base for the percentages occurs for the children who expect a 2 and actually get a 1. This cell is overrepresented indicating these children are doing worse at forecasting than if their forecast bore no relation to their mark! As a general statement, however, forecast ability does not seem to vary much with expectation level, and the accuracy of forecasting seems to be at about chance levels. While the above discussion is couched in terms of "forecasting ability," the reader should note it could just as reasonably have been discussed in terms of the causal efficacy of expectations. If expectations highly influenced marks, or even if different expectation levels had different effects on marks, some deviation from the "chance" model would have been expected. That is, the mark distributions within each expectation level should have deviated from the marginal distribution. In particular, the column headed "zero discrepance" and those with small discrepancies (+1 or –1) should have been overrepresented if expectations were displaying substantial causal efficacy.

In summary, both over- and underoptimism is present—the overoptimism naturally occurs for children with high expectations and underoptimism occurs for those with low expectations. Children of all expectation levels show only a chance level of forecasting their marks or, equivalently, in all three areas the children's differential expectations are not differentially influencing mark distributions at midyear (i.e., the midyear mark distribution is the same no matter what level of children's expectations is considered). This lack of a midyear effect contrasts with that noted in the next section concerning both midyear and year-end observations.

Reading: Feedback Effect on Marks

About 23% of the marks in reading went up between the middle and end of the first grade, 58% remained stable, and 19% declined (based on a sample of 165 children). With one exception all movement was confined to a single step (i.e., from B to A, C to B, etc.).

If a child's year-end mark improved over his midyear mark ($N = 38$), in 63% of the cases his mark at the middle of the year had been less than he expected. If a child's marks deteriorated ($N = 31$) in 39% of cases his mark was better than he had expected. The 3×3 table, table 2.8, is a collapsed version of a 7×7 table that relates all possible types of mark changes to all possible types of mark-expectation relationships at midyear. A χ^2 test on the four corners of the table shows the effect of expectations upon later improvement (or deterioration) in marks to be highly significant ($\chi_1^2 = 9.18$, $p < .01$), given an initial discrepancy between mark and expectation. There is a significant tendency for marks and expectations to move toward consistency. But a more interesting comparison is one that can be applied to the entire table and one which has a causal frame of reference. In terms of causation, expectations being higher than the mark should lead marks to rise; expectations being the same as the mark should lead to no change in mark; expectations being lower than the mark should lead the mark to fall. In a perfect causal system in which expectations were the only causes, all cases would fall on

Table 2.8. Observed change in reading mark, time 1 to time 2 versus time 1 expectation-mark agreement, middle-class school

		Change in reading mark, T1 to T2			
		Up	Same	Down	
Child previously (T1) did *B,S,W* than	Better	4	32	12	48
he expected	Same	10	32	9	51
	Worse	24	32	10	66
		38	96	31	165

the "minor diagonal" of the table if consistent with the pattern just outlined.

With the margins as given, the expected values are those given in table 2.9. The cells on the minor diagonal (enclosed) sum to 53.89, and their sum departs from the observed data in the direction predicted by the causal hypothesis—9 more children (24–15) have marks that rise, 3 more children have marks that fall, and 2 more have marks that stay the same. The easiest way to assess the "minor diagonal" effect is by the same statistic used earlier to assess the major diagonal (match) effect. Such a test here reveals a significant effect ($z = 2.43, p < .01$). The magnitude of this effect is hard to assess, but in that column representing those whose marks improve one can see that *most (63%) are recruited from students who did not do as well as they expected earlier.*

Reading: Feedback Effect on Expectations

Marks are affected by an earlier mark-expectation discrepance but the inertia of marks seems relatively large—there is a strong tendency for marks to stay the same no matter what the discrepance. Expectations, though, are more responsive in an optimistic direction, for of those (47) whose mark was higher than expected, 38 (81%) raise their hopes. Expectations at the end of the year are more responsive to earlier marks than are the marks at year end. This is hardly surprising, since a child's expectations are something he himself controls, whereas his mark depends on someone else's behavior.

If a child receives a mark higher than he expected in reading at the end of the first semester (as 28% of 166 children do), then his response is very likely (chances are better than 4:1) to increase his expectations at the end of the second semester. If he gets exactly what he expected at the end of the first semester (as 33% do) then he will be likely to keep that expectation (chances are 3 out of 5); but if he does change, he is about

Table 2.9. Predicted change in reading mark, time 1 to time 2 versus time 1 expectation-mark agreement, middle-class school

		Up	Same	Down	
		Predicted reading mark change, T1 to T2			
Child previously did *B,S,W* than he expected	Better	11.05	27.93	9.02	48
	Same	11.75	29.67	9.58	51
	Worse	15.20	38.40	12.40	66
		38	96	31	165

twice as likely to increase his hopes as to decrease them. If he gets a lower mark than he hoped for (as 39% do), then he will not increase his expectations at the end of the second semester, but he is somewhat more likely to hold to his original expectation than to lower his sights (chances are 6 out of 11).

This analysis, based upon combined cohorts, presents a more complete picture of the response of expectations to previous marks than is available in either cohort and documents with more certainty the trends seen there.

The matter can be explored most easily by condensing a 7×7 table of discrepancies vs. changes in expectations to a 3×3 table, table 2.10. First, the degree of matching above chance is highly significant ($z = 8.05$, $p < .01$) and amounts to 61%. Thus, if a child received a higher mark than he expected, his hopes tend to rise. If he got what he expected, his hopes tend to remain stable. If he got less than he expected, his hopes tend to decrease. But, and this is perhaps the most important part of the table, if he got less than he hoped, his hopes are more likely to remain fixed than to drop (36 vs. 29 children). That is, there is some tendency for these children's expectations to decline, but the chance of decline is still less than even. If he got more than he hoped, on the other hand, his hopes respond vigorously (38 vs. 9 children) and the odds for an increase are over 4:1. If he got exactly what he expected, his hopes may change in either direction, with perhaps some bias in the positive direction. This receptivity to good news and relative resistance to bad news can be termed a "buoyancy effect."

Summary of Feedback Effects on Marks

In all cases the majority of children received the same mark at the end of first grade as at midyear of first grade. That is, for reading, arithmetic, and conduct generally and for all the breakdowns of each of these into distributions of students who did better, the same, or worse than they

Table 2.10. Change in reading expectation, time 1 to time 2 versus time 1 expectation-mark agreement, middle-class school

		Change in reading expectations, T1 to T2			
		Up	Same	Down	
Child previously did *B,S,W* than he expected	Better	38	9	0	47
	Same	12	35	7	54
	Worse	0	36	29	65
		50	80	36	166

expected, the *majority in any breakdown can expect to get the same mark at year end as at midyear.*

There is also, however, a consistent (and significant in the case of reading and conduct) pattern for cases on the minor diagonal to appear with greater than chance expectations. More specifically, there is a consistent observation of the following types of cases occurring more often than would be expected by chance:

(a) A child's *marks going up at year end and after the child did worse than he expected at midyear.*

(b) A child's *mark remaining the same* at year end, *after* the child got the *same mark he expected at midyear.*

(c) A child's *mark going down* at year end, *after* the child did *better than he expected at midyear.*

These observations are consistent with the notion that student expectations causally affect the marks students receive, even if the degree of association is rather small. As noted earlier, the restriction in range on the marking scale and the similar margins at mid- and end-of-year mitigate against effects being displayed. (The power of tests is low.)

Summary of Feedback Effects on Expectations

In all three areas (reading, arithmetic, and conduct) there is a significant tendency for children's expectations to move toward being consistent with the mark they received at midyear. If the midyear mark was above the children's expectations, their expectations moved up substantially; if the midyear mark equalled the children's expectations, their expectations showed less change than would be expected by chance; and if the midyear mark was below the children's expectations, their expectations showed a greater than chance tendency to decline, but in all three cases (reading, arithmetic, and conduct) this decline was not as pronounced as the previous two effects (the majority of children maintained their expectation at the same level it had been at midyear).

When information on marks is combined with that on expectations, it appears that when a child gets less than he hoped he does not lower his sights—his expectations remain the same, and there is a tendency to bring marks in line. If he gets more than he hoped, his expectations immediately rise and his marks stays the same. There is altogether what might be called a buoyancy effect—a tendency for marks or expectations to rise to narrow the discrepancy between them. If the child does better than he expected, his hopes rise; if he did worse than he expected, his marks rise. If he gets good news, he is receptive, whereas, he seems relatively impervious to bad news. (The strongest trends observed in the data are stated without qualification in the above summary—i.e., without regard for weak reverse trends—for simplicity of presentation.)

The Effects of Parents' Expectations on Children's Marks over the First-Grade Year

Changes in reading marks over the first-grade year as a function of parents' expectations vs. first marks are summarized in table 2.11. The sum of the elements on the minor diagonal gives a measure of the extent to which children's marks move in a direction consistent with parents' expectations. The movement is highly significant ($z = 2.52$, $p < .01$). Looking at the four corners of the table one sees that the movement consistent with parents' expectations is impressive in both directions, while that inconsistency is almost invisible (1 in each cell). Thus, though parents' accuracy in forecasting marks drops from first to second semester, movement in children's marks is consistent with parents' expectations.

It is of some interest to compare table 2.11 with the similar table for children (table 2.8). The four corner cells there account for 50 cases, of which approximately two-thirds (36) move to increase agreement. In table 2.11 the four corner cells account for 27 changes, and of these 93% move consistently. What is perhaps most interesting is the size of the cell representing children whose marks move down to increase agreement, that is, those who earlier did better than their parents expected.

In sum, children's year-end marks in all three areas show significant trends toward agreeing with parents' midyear expectations. The over-representation on the minor diagonal is consistent with a causal hypothesis viewing parents' expectations as the independent variable.

The Lower-Class Integrated School

For the lower-class school where one cohort is available for one year (the first grade beginning school in September 1972), I will not attempt as comprehensive a report as that just given for the middle-class school. Rather, after giving an overview of tabular data similar to that given in

Table 2.11. Change in reading mark time 1 to time 2 versus time 1 parents' expectation-mark agreement, middle-class school

		Change in reading mark, T1 to T2			
		Up	Same	Down	
Child previously did B,S,W than parent expected in reading	Better	1	28	12	41
	Same	18	50	13	81
	Worse	13	11	1	25
		32	89	26	147

table 2.1, I will attempt to concentrate on the differences between social classes or racial groups.

Means and standard deviations for variables used in subsequent analyses and cross-tabulations are given in table 2.12. The mean IQ (Primary Mental Abilities) for 130 children for whom IQ data were available from school records (88%) is 104.65, with a standard deviation of 13.7. The data are given for the entire cohort and also separately for white students and black students. The overview will be given first for the entire cohort and then separately for its white and black portions.

Entire Cohort

1) In the lower-class integrated school, parents' expectations in all three areas are much lower than children's expectations (significant beyond the .01 level for reading, arithmetic, and conduct). The mean expectations of parents and children, respectively are 2.33 vs. 1.28 in reading, 2.23 vs. 1.74 in arithmetic, and 1.89 vs. 1.07 in conduct.

Expectations were obtained from only 74% of the parents, even though interviewers went repeatedly to the homes of lower-class children to contact the parents. In advance of the interviewer's call, a note was sent home from school with children, explaining that an interviewer would come to the home a day or two hence and also what the purpose of the interview was. As many as three call-backs were used to try to reach lower-class parents and care was taken to send a black interviewer to see black parents and a white interviewer to see white parents.

2) Before their first report card children are exceedingly optimistic in reading and conduct. Their expectations in reading and conduct are significantly higher than their expectations in arithmetic ($p < .01$ for both paired t-tests).

3) Children's average expectations in all three areas remain remarkably constant over the first-grade year. The largest difference, that for conduct, is only 0.16 of a grade point.

Table 2.12. Means, standard deviations for first-grade cohort, lower-class school, 60% black

	Combined			Black			White		
	N	Mean	S.D.	N	Mean	S.D.	N	Mean	S.D.
Parents' expectations–T1									
Reading	105	2.33	0.81	62	2.37	0.77	43	2.28	0.85
Arithmetic	106	2.23	0.76	62	2.15	0.74	44	2.34	0.78
Conduct	106	1.89	0.59	62	2.08	0.49	44	1.61	0.62
Child's expectations–T1									
Reading	113	1.28	0.59	68	1.28	0.62	42	1.24	0.48
Arithmetic	113	1.74	0.62	68	1.65	0.48	42	1.83	0.70
Conduct	113	1.07	0.26	68	1.07	0.26	42	1.07	0.26
Child's expectations–T2									
Reading	119	1.32	0.70	71	1.28	0.59	46	1.30	0.76
Arithmetic	120	1.75	0.81	71	1.75	0.82	47	1.79	0.81
Conduct	120	1.23	0.51	71	1.24	0.49	47	1.21	0.55
Child's mark–T1									
Reading	72	3.15	0.85	43	3.16	0.84	29	3.14	0.88
Arithmetic	129	3.03	0.75	76	3.09	0.77	51	2.90	0.70
Conduct	129	1.93	0.62	76	2.03	0.61	51	1.77	0.59
Child's mark–T2									
Reading	127	2.59	0.89	78	2.69	0.90	49	2.43	0.84
Arithmetic	127	2.77	0.97	78	2.89	0.99	49	2.59	0.91
Conduct	127	1.72	0.73	78	1.81	0.74	49	1.59	0.71

Summary of changes over year

	Combined			Black			White		
	N	Mean	S.D.	N	Mean	S.D.	N	Mean	S.D.
Mark discrepance (T1 mark minus T2 mark)									
Reading	69	0.70	0.63	43	0.63	0.62	26	0.81	0.63
Arithmetic	121	0.22	0.74	74	0.18	0.73	47	0.30	0.75
Conduct	121	0.21	0.68	74	0.22	0.71	47	0.19	0.65
Expectation discrepance (T1 expectation minus T2 expectation)									
Reading	95	−0.04	0.87	61	0.00	0.82	34	−0.12	0.98
Arithmetic	96	−0.09	0.93	61	−0.13	0.90	35	−0.03	0.99
Conduct	96	−0.18	0.56	61	−0.18	0.50	35	−0.17	0.66
Mark-expectation discrepance T1 (T1 mark minus T1 expectation)									
Reading	60	1.87	1.02	39	1.77	1.04	21	2.05	0.97
Arithmetic	108	1.32	0.83	66	1.41	0.86	40	1.15	0.70
Conduct	108	0.84	0.58	66	0.92	0.62	40	0.68	0.47
Mark-expectation discrepance T2 (T2 mark minus T2 expectation)									
Reading	114	1.24	1.03	69	1.38	0.99	45	1.02	1.08
Arithmetic	115	0.95	1.23	69	1.09	1.25	46	0.74	1.20
Conduct	115	0.46	0.81	69	0.54	0.83	46	0.35	0.77

Table 2.12. (continued)

	Combined		Black		White	
	IQ correlations					
Average IQ	N	r	N	r	N	r
IQ[a]correlations with midyear marks						
Reading	71	.411[c]	43	.500[c]	28	.302
Arithmetic	121	.476[c]	73	.525[c]	48	.388[c]
Conduct	121	.236[b]	73	.157	48	.275
IQ correlations with year-end marks						
Reading	124	.484[c]	76	.462[c]	48	.494[c]
Arithmetic	124	.427[c]	76	.401[c]	48	.436[c]
Conduct	124	.191[b]	76	.006	48	.406[c]

[a]IQ scores are Primary Mental Ability scores.
[b]$p < .05$
[c]$p < .01$

4) Children's marks on the first report card are low. (The reading marks are particularly hard to evaluate at this time because teachers use different marking schemes.) The arithmetic marks average 3.03 and conduct marks average 1.93.

5) Children's marks improve significantly in all three areas over the first-grade year ($p < .01$ for all three paired t-tests). Improvement is largest in reading (0.56), next largest in arithmetic (0.26), and least in conduct (0.21).

White (N = 57) and Black (N = 86) Children in Cohort

1) White parents and black parents have comparable expectations for their first-grade children, except in conduct, where white parents look for a significantly better mark ($p < .01$). Expectations were obtained from 77% of white children's parents and from 72% of black children's parents. (The race of 5 children could not be ascertained.) Parents' expectations are uniformly lower than children's within each racial group.

2) Before their first report card, children of both races are highly optimistic about their forthcoming marks in reading and in conduct. Both races are noticeably less optimistic about marks to come in arithmetic, with whites on the average estimating an arithmetic mark 0.18 units lower than blacks (difference not significant).

3) Children's average expectations over the year are remarkably constant no matter what the race of the child.

4) Average reading marks are very close in the two races (3.14 vs. 3.16). Small differences (not significant) favor whites in arithmetic (2.90 vs. 3.09) and in conduct (1.77 vs. 2.03) (first report card).

5) Children's marks over the first-grade year improve more for whites than for blacks in both reading and arithmetic (for whites, 0.71 and 0.31 respectively, and for blacks 0.47 and 0.20 respectively). In conduct the changes are small (0.18 and 0.22) and close to one another.

Discrepances between Initial Expectations and the First Report Card

First, a word is needed about how marks are assigned in general, and in particular for reading. The report card that children take home contains the explanation below: "Your child's progress is being measured in terms of his progress in reaching standards or levels that are considered appropriate for his age or years in school." Marking is thus done with respect to grade level performance, comparing the child's progress with average progress of children his age. It is important to note that the child's ability is not weighed in, so a child with low ability is being measured against the same performance scale as the child with high ability. (In the middle-class school children were graded in terms of how their performance compared to their expected performance adjusted for ability level.)

Three different schemes were used for reporting marks in reading for this cohort: the number of Distar units completed, or the primer level (two series) of the book the child has completed. In the case of primer level, two different reading series were used. Since these series use the same letters, but the letters designate different levels of primers in the two series, the system is confusing. "P" in one system, for example, means a higher mark than "P" in the other.

To keep initial marks consistent with later marks, they were changed to a scale like that used for other subjects.

Close to half of the marks given (43%) in reading appear equivalent to a 4 (table 2.13). Most of the children (73%), however, expect the highest mark in reading. Only 5% expect a C, and one expects lower. There is a marked contrast between the marginal distribution of children's expectations (strongly skewed toward the high end) and the marginal distribution of marks given by the teachers (strongly skewed toward the low end). This difference leads to a highly significant asymmetry for children's expectations to exceed the marks received ($\chi^2 = 54.0, p < .01$).

Since no marks equivalent to A's are given, it may appear that our recoding of letter marks to numerical marks is faulty and the whole numerical scale should have been shifted one position lower. This is not the case, however. Both the teacher's comments on the students' report cards and the levels of student competence normally associated with the letter grades involved, suggest that the teachers did indeed view the students as displaying a range of competence markedly skewed toward

Table 2.13. Reading mark versus expectation time 1, lower-class integrated school

| | | Reading mark, time 1 | | | | | |
		1	2	3	4	Total	Percent
	1		10	13	21	44	73.3
Reading expectations, time 1	2		5	5	3	13	21.7
	3			1	2	3	5.0
	4						
	Total		15	19	26	60*	
	Percent		25.0	31.7	43.3		100.0

*One class is missing reading marks.

the low end. Such a rescaling would also have placed this set of marks completely out of line with those given at year end.

As it stands, not a single student has his performance exceed his expectation in reading and only 10% of the students were able to meet their expectations. (Seven percent would have been expected to do so by chance alone.) A large fraction of those who receive the lowest mark (21 out of 26, or 81%) expect the highest.

In summary the relationship between children's expectations and marks at the middle of grade one strongly reflects the pronounced positive skew in the expectation distribution. This produces an asymmetry in the relationship between marks and expectations. The children expect a higher mark than they receive (or conversely receive a lower mark than they expect). Students' expectations match the mark they receive with about the same frequency one would expect on the basis of chance.

Discrepances between Expectations and Report Cards at the End of First Grade

The agreement between children's expectations for reading and the mark they receive at the end of first grade is slightly (but not significantly) below what would be expected by chance (11% vs. 14%) (table 2.14). A relatively small proportion of the cases is involved, since the children's reading expectations are highly skewed toward high expectations (81% expect a 1; mean = 1.32), while the mark distribution is more nearly symmetrical (mean = 2.59). Of the 89% of the cases where the student's expectation does not match his mark, a significant majority, 92% ($\chi_1^2 = 71.5$, $p < .001$), expect a mark higher than the one they receive.

Table 2.14. Reading mark versus expectation time 2, lower-class integrated school

		Reading mark, time 2					
		1	*2*	*3*	*4*	*Total*	*Percent*
	1	7	43	32	10	92	80.7
Reading	2	3	5	2	5	15	13.2
expectation,							
time 2	3		2	1	1	4	3.5
	4		1	2		3	2.6
	Total	10	51	37	16	114	
	Percent	8.8	44.7	32.5	14.0		100.0

How Do Children's Expectations Change over the First-Grade Year?

The marginals for reading expectations sampled in the middle of the year and those sampled at the end are almost identical, with close to 80% of children expecting the highest mark possible on both occasions. *There is no shift downward*, for the same number move up as move down (15). Since 79% expect a 1 on both occasions, a high percentage of matches (62%) is expected by chance. The number of matches observed, 68%, is larger but not significantly larger. The lack of variance in both expectation distributions makes the question somewhat trivial.

Since about the same number of children get more optimistic as get more pessimistic, it appears that the marked discrepancy between the child's initial expectation and the first mark he received has had little impact. The expectations of children remain very high—close to 80% expect the highest grade! The effect of feedback will be discussed in detail in subsequent sections.

To sum up: There is very little difference in the expectations at midyear and year end in reading.

How Do Marks Change over the First-Grade Year?

The year-end reading mark shows 43% of the children falling in the lower two categories, getting 3's and 4's. About the same number (42%) were in the lowest category (4) for the first reading mark. The remainder at the second time point split about 1:3 between 1's and 2's respectively (table 2.15). About 30% had received 2's earlier, none received 1's. The marking scale has thus been altered at both ends with fewer children at the end of the year getting the lowest possible grade and a modest number (15%) receiving the highest possible grade.

Table 2.15. Reading mark, time 2, versus mark time 1, lower-class integrated school

		Reading mark, time 2					
		1	*2*	*3*	*4*	*Total*	*Percent*
	1						
Reading mark, time 1	2	8	13			21	30.4
	3	2	12			19	27.5
	4		4	16	9	29	42.0
	Total	10	29	21	9	69	
	Percent	14.5	42.0	30.4	13.0		100.0

By the end of the year the majority of children (57%) receive the two highest marks because so many 2's are given (42%). There is a significantly greater-than-chance degree of consistency in marks over the year (39%; $z = 2.38$, $p < .05$). Despite this greater-than-chance matching of midyear and year-end reading marks the majority of marks (61%) do not match at both times. All these mismatches have the year-end mark exceeding the midyear mark, which is not too surprising considering the pronounced skew toward lower marks that was present at midyear. (The asymmetry of matches is significant beyond the $p < .001$ level with $\chi_1^2 = 42.0$.)

What Is Impact of First Mark on Expectations Later?

Children's expectations at the end of the year are still exceedingly high—75% continue to look for the highest grade, and a very small percentage (10%) hope for the mark received earlier. This amount of agreement between expectations and earlier marks is well within the range of chance expectation (8%) (table 2.16). Over 90% still look for 1's and 2's, despite their teachers' having given no 1's and given only 30% 2's earlier. A very large proportion of those who received 3's and 4's still look for 1's and 2's (42 out of 47, close to 90%). The present analysis shows that feedback in the form of marks has little impact, for expectations over the year are remarkably similar.

In summary, *the first marks the children received seem to have had little effect on their expectations.* As noted previously, children's expectations are markedly skewed toward high expectations, while the teachers' mark distributions are not. This means that the large majority of children

Table 2.16. Reading expectation, time 2, versus mark time 1, lower-class integrated school

| | | \multicolumn{6}{c}{*Reading expectation, time 2*} |
		1	*2*	*3*	*4*	*Total*	*Percent*
	1						
Reading	2	14	5	1		20	29.9
mark,							
time 1	3	16	1	1	1	19	28.4
	4	20	5	2	1	28	41.8
	Total	50	11	4	2	67	
	Percent	74.6	16.4	6.0	3.0		100.0

receive negative feedback in the form of marks at midyear. A minority receive neutral feedback (mark equals expectation) and a rare few receive positive feedback (mark exceeds expectation). Expectations remain skewed despite the largely negative feedback.

The lack of any significant deviation from chance matching suggests that the midyear mark holds no special appeal for the children. There is *no special (beyond chance) tendency for children to "adopt" their midyear mark and turn it into a year-end expectation.*

The Effects of Feedback on Marks

As noted earlier, there is an increase in the average reading mark from midyear to end of year [3.15 ($N = 72$) vs. 2.59 ($N = 127$)]. In fact, as table 2.17 indicates, no child received a lower mark at the end of the year than he had at midyear. If, as could be the case, these initial reading marks are entirely uninterpretable by the child, one would expect no relation between improvement in marks and the midyear discrepance between expectation and mark. For the 57 cases where data are available this hypothesis is not contradicted, as shown by a χ^2 test on the collapsed table ($\chi^2_1 = 0.54$). The trend for the discrepant cases, however, in the noncollapsed table is suggestive. For 16 children with an earlier discrepance of 1, half improve (8) and half (8) stay the same; for 16 children with an earlier discrepance of 2, 63% improve; for 19 children with an earlier discrepance of 3, 74% improve. A trend such as this warrants attention, although it cannot be interpreted unless regression effects are allowed for.

Table 2.17. Reading expectation-mark discrepance earlier versus change in mark, lower-class integrated school

		Expectation-mark discrepance earlier		
		0–1	2+	
Year-end reading mark is *B,S*	Better	12	24	36
	Same	10	11	21
		22	35	57

Effects of Feedback on Expectations

If one looks closely at what happens to children's expectations at the end of the first-grade year in reading in relation to the discrepance earlier between expectation for the first mark and the first mark received, the following observations emerge. In 5 instances where the child's mark exactly equaled his expectations, 3 children's expectations later rose at the end of first grade, and 2 children's expectations remained the same. In 50 instances where the child's expectations exceeded his mark, expectations remained stable in 31 instances, rose in 8 instances, and declined in 11 instances. Thus, in only 22% of the cases, when the first mark was lower than the child hoped, does the child modify his hopes downward. Evidence disconfirming hopes does not lead to changing hopes. In no instance does the child's mark exceed his expectations! The changes in expectations for reading over the first-grade year in terms of the midyear mark-expectation discrepance is seen in table 2.18. The analysis is hindered by the lack of some midyear marks in reading. A rather small percentage (20%) registered an increase in expectations between midyear and end-of-year, and, of these, 3 out of 11 cases had received what he expected at midyear. The others had received less than they expected at midyear. Almost everyone did worse than he expected, and all of those whose expectations go down are recruited from this group. Overall, however, the table is not very satisfactory because of the small number (5) of persons falling outside the "worse" row.

For the cases where expectations changed, in all three areas *expectations tended to decline (nonsignificantly) more if there was an initial discrepance (overestimation) than if there was no initial disrepancy.*

Why Does Feedback Have Little Effect on Expectations?

What may be happening to account for the "lack of reality testing" in reading? Low marks had almost no effect on children's expectations.

Table 2.18. Change in reading expectations versus expectation-mark discrepance, lower-class integrated school

		Reading expectations go			
		Up	*Same*	*Down*	
	Better	0	0	0	0
Child earlier did *B,S,W* than he expected	Same	3	2	0	5
	Worse	8	31	11	50
		11	33	11	55

Perhaps the children do not know how they have been evaluated. The marks for reading as recorded on report cards are actually almost inscrutable. The authors were able to interpret these marks only after consultation with teachers and the principal. As mentioned earlier, three separate schemes were used for marking, which reflected progress in a given set of reading materials. None of the schemes coincides with the A, B, C, or 1, 2, 3 codes for other subjects on the report card. The Distar-units scheme reports the number of units completed. Only a person well versed in these instructional materials and in the general progress of first-graders in reading could readily interpret this scale. The other two scales are literal—P, PP, etc.—to indicate the book the child is currently reading. Again, only a person familiar with different genres of introductory reading texts could evaluate the child's progress. To complicate things further, the two series using P, PP, etc. use the same letters (e.g., P) to stand for two different levels of progress. A "Primer" level in one series is not equivalent to a "Primer" level in the other.

What children are receiving as feedback may therefore depend very little on recorded marks in reading. They may be relying almost exclusively on informal evaluations of the teacher given during classroom recitations. The Distar Program, interestingly enough, emphasizes lavish use of positive reinforcement: the teacher congratulating the child by shaking his hand, giving the child raisins or other small pieces of food, pinning signs on the child such as "I did well today," as well as the more usual types of reinforcement, like a steady flow of verbal praise and smiles. This exaggerated kind of informal positive feedback may kindle the very high expectations the children continue to register at the end of the year and swamp any negative feedback from report cards, especially since the report cards are essentially uninterpretable to children and parents.

Encouragement and positive feedback are certainly necessary to motivate children in day-to-day classroom efforts, but one wonders what effect the extreme dissonance between the teacher's classroom behavior and her forced use of an absolute level grade scale may eventually have. What happens to the child, for example, when later in the second or third grade he realizes what his earlier report cards actually signified and looks back upon a long series of low marks?

While the unintelligibility of marking schemes is a plausible explanation for the lack of a feedback effect in reading, the lack of feedback effects in arithmetic and conduct are less readily understood, especially as the year progresses. Here a plausible explanation for the lack of effect may lie in the informal positive feedback given by the teacher in daily classroom sessions outweighing the infrequent negative feedback on report card.

Race and Children's Expectations
before the First Report Card

There is almost no difference by race in expectations for reading. (About 60% of the children are black. Two teachers are white, two black.) Most of both races expect the highest mark, 80% of whites and 81% of blacks have this expectation. In arithmetic there is also little difference in expectations by race, although the few children (4%) who do have low expectations are all white. One-hundred percent of the blacks look for an A or B in arithmetic. The two distributions of conduct expectations by race are also almost identical, with virtually all (92%) in both groups looking for an A. Of the 8% who look for less than an A, all expect B's.

In sum: black and white children do not differ in their expectations.

Racial Differences in the Influence of Marks on Expectations

Both races receive marks at midyear and year end that are highly comparable. Both races remain overly optimistic about reading marks after receiving low marks at midyear. The percentage of children holding a year-end expectation that is two or more points above their midyear mark is 54% for whites and 68% for blacks. Since white children received slightly (not significantly) higher marks at midyear, these percentages seem quite in line with a statement that whites and blacks are identical in their adjustment of expectations to earlier marks. (The magnitude of the mark discrepance between the races was such as to give whites about 10% more 2's (the top mark assigned) and 6% fewer 4's than blacks.)

To sum up: blacks consistently display a greater probability of overoptimism at year end (i.e., year-end expectations exceed midyear mark by 2 or more points), but this difference is largely accounted for by the fact that blacks generally received slightly more, but not significantly more, low marks. (At year end about 80% of children expect 1's in reading and conduct, and 40% expect 1's in arithmetic, for both races.) *The conclusion is that the races do not differ in their response to first marks. The case base is small, however, and as more data become available the black children's disproportionate overoptimism may attain significance.*

DISCUSSION

The analyses just presented are lengthy and also at times fairly complex, as when changes in performance or expectations are studied as a function of prior differences in predictor variables. There are, nevertheless, many additional analyses not reported here because of space limitations, analyses dealing with parents' expectations, sex, self-esteem, sociometric standing, absences from school, and others (see Entwisle & Hayduk 1974). Here the aim was to present analyses that seemed most crucial to the causal interpretation of variability in children's expectations and marks. The reader is warned that subsequent analyses will undoubtedly lead to revisions in the preliminary findings reported here. Data for the middle-class school aggregate two successive first-grade classes (Cohort 1 and Cohort 2) and so allow fairly extensive analyses. Data for the lower-class school are more restricted, being based on a single cohort of first-graders. Since all black-white comparisons stem from this cohort, the reader should bear in mind that the findings with respect to racial differences are both limited and tentative.

School Differences

To give some notion of population differences in the two communities served by the middle- and lower-class schools, data from the 1970 U.S. Census for census tracts served by the schools are given in table 2.19. The lower-class school serves most of four tracts, the middle-class school most of three. In terms of median education of head of household, the social class composition of the two schools represents the customary definitions of middle class (some college) and lower class (high school or less). Income in the middle class commonly is over twice that of the lower-class community.

Several factors differ between schools besides social class. These factors are therefore confounded with class differences.

The middle-class school is white segregated, its regular staff is entirely white, its classes have no aides. The school building was recently enlarged and renovated. It has a large library, a cafeteria where hot food is prepared on site at noon, and a large playground. It is located in a quiet residential neighborhood of well-landscaped individual homes worth more than $30,000–$50,000 at current prices.

The lower-class school has about 60% black children, an integrated (roughly 50–50) staff, an aide in all kindergarten and first-grade classes. The school is set on a busy street corner in a densely populated urban residential area where traffic is very heavy. Nearby "row houses" are worth $6,000 to $20,000, depending on exact location and internal condition, and many have been turned into apartments for three or more families. Parts of the school building were erected before the turn of the century. The school has its own playground, with much play equipment and also a large gymnasium within the building and a large library. Hot lunches are delivered daily to the school. Many children in this school have family incomes low enough to qualify for free lunches under a federal program, as table 2.19 suggests. The school has the services of a social worker two days a week, a full-time guidance counselor, and "resource teachers" who help classroom teachers with reading instruction.

The two schools are very close to the same size, with three to four first-grade classes in each, depending on total enrollment. Staff quality in both schools is high and in both places there are many teachers who have taught at the school for several years. If anything, formal credentials of the staff in the lower-class school may be superior. Class size is about the same in the two schools.

Both schools have kindergartens with half-day sessions attended by many of the children who later enter first grade. Little study of these kindergartens has been undertaken so far, but one difference between schools very important for this research is that the lower-class school gives report cards to kindergarteners. We attempted to query kindergarteners about their expectations for report cards, but were unable to procure responses we felt were valid. In many cases the child would not respond at all; in other cases it was clear the child did not understand the nature of the task. Thus, the meaning of "first report card" may not be exactly the same from one school to the other.

The reader must be cautious in attributing differences to social class or to integration effects when there are so many other factors that also differ between schools. Fortunately, with some notion of intercohort differences available for the middle-class school, one has a benchmark to gauge the size of intraschool variability.

IQ Differences

There is a significant yet relatively small difference between average IQ's (PMA) of blacks and whites in the lower-class school (4.8 points—106.2 for whites and 101.4 for blacks). The IQ differences

Table 2.19. U.S. census data

Tract number	Middle-class school				Lower-class school				
	1	2	3	Ave.	1	2	3	4	Ave.
Median years school completed	12.4	13.6	12.9	13.0	10.2	8.4	10.2	8.5	9.4
Mean income	$13,294	$24,101	$17,036	$18,143	$8,573	$6,487	$ 8,073	$8,165	$7,825
Median value owner-occupied houses	$19,200	$30,600	$28,200	$26,000	$6,300	$6,000	$10,200	$5,800	$7,075
Percent black	0.0%	0.0%	0.2%	0.1%	63.7%	92.4%	7.3%	8.1%	18.46%
Percent of all families with income below poverty level	3.2%	1.1%	2.0%	2.1%	20.2%	36.2%	15.8%	14.2%	21.6%

between schools is also small, 115 for the middle-class school and 103 in the lower-class school. These two averages for first grade are significantly different but in second grade at the middle-class school (the only second grade for which there are data) the average IQ for Cohort 1 turns out to be 104 on the Stanford Test of Mental Maturity. School-to-school differences, then *are no larger than year-to-year differences between repeated tests of (approximately) the same* children in a single school.

IQ is a poor predictor of school performance in the early grades in the middle-class school. In first grade the highest correlation is around .20 at midyear. A correlation of this magnitude implies that only about 4% of the variance in performance is explained by IQ differences. Correlations at the end of the year between IQ and reading, arithmetic, or conduct diminish and are *nonsignificant in every way.*

The same pattern of correlations with IQ appears in second grade, with small but significant correlations at midyear giving way to nonsignificant correlations at the end of the year. Low correlations could be attributed to the relatively low reliability of the IQ measures (the year-to-year correlation between the different tests is .655), the low reliability of teacher's marks, or the relative restriction in range on both variables. Since, however, teachers in the middle-class school are supposed to assign marks with ability partialled out (i.e., by marking each child according to how his performance relates to his own ability), the small or nonsignificant correlations may also demonstrate that the teachers have successfully implemented the marking policies.

Correlations between IQ and marks are much higher in the lower-class school and remain significant throughout the year. For blacks, midyear correlations between IQ and marks are considerably higher (by about 0.20) than for whites, but they are not significantly higher. There are no significant correlations between IQ and conduct for blacks at either time (+.16 and +.01) but all other IQ-mark correlations are significant. The only statistically significant difference in IQ vs. mark correlations by race occurs for conduct marks at the end of grade one (.01 for blacks vs. .41 for whites).

The differences between sizes of correlations from school to school in first grade are striking. The pattern indicates that teachers are effectively implementing the different marking policies in the two schools. In the lower-class school children are supposed to be marked with reference to grade-level performance, and IQ is the strongest single predictor of this. Therefore a high correlation between IQ and first marks indicates the validity of the teacher's marks, given that marking policy.

The effects on children are quite another matter. Average IQ's are not very different in the two schools, but in the middle-class school a child is marked with IQ partialled out. As a consequence children can get different rewards in the two places for the same effort. If the middle-class child tries hard, he gets an A. If the lower-class child tries hard, he still may not get an A unless he also happens to be bright. The two policies with respect to marking could lead children to form very different perceptions of efficacy. Another implication of marking policies is that in the lower-class school, if the teacher is inept and the child reads below grade-level, the child pays an immediate penalty in terms of a poor mark. In the middle-class school, an inept teacher may have less damaging effects, because the child is not marked so much in terms of his performance, at least in the earliest grades.

Differences in marking practices of first-grade teachers in the middle-class school from one cohort to the next are surprisingly large, but nowhere near as large as interschool differences in marking practices. Full assessment of interschool differences, however, must await measurement of intercohort variability in the lower-class school as well.

Children's Expectations

In all three cohorts (two middle-class, one lower-class) correspondence between a child's expectations and his marks on his first report card is at chance levels. Children apparently have no genuine feeling for what marks they will get in any of the three areas.

On the average, children's expectations are too high, especially in the lower-class school. A natural question is whether this overestimation should be taken at face value or whether it comes about for some other reasons, perhaps because children do not understand the task or because they are unable to report accurately, or because they are loath to acknowledge anything less than high expectations to the interviewer.

Two kinds of supplementary evidence bear on the validity of verbally reported expectations, especially for middle-class children. First, in one classroom the expectation sampling procedure was carried out on two occasions one week apart. There was a high degree of concordance ($r=.76$) between answers on both occasions. Second, every first-grader in Cohort 2 of the middle-class school and all first-graders in the lower-class school were reinterviewed in depth in June 1973. At that time the interviewer did not ask for expectations at all but rather probed children's understanding of report cards by asking questions like the following: What are report cards? What do "reading" and "arithmetic" mean? What do the numbers "1," "2," etc. on the report card mean? The purpose was to see whether children's understanding of report cards and of the numerical grading system was clear enough so that the interviewer thought they could make a meaningful response in an "expectation interview."*

In the middle-class school, report cards are better understood (about 90% of children seemed to have a very good grasp) than in the lower-class school (about 70% of children seemed to have a good grasp). Both groups seemed to know what was at issue, however—that report cards were evaluations of how well they were doing in school. It is harder for an interviewer to get lower-class children to verbalize. As already mentioned, reports are issued in kindergarten in the lower-class school, so these children have had several more report cards by the end of first grade than middle-class children, although attempts to get lower-class kindergarten-ers' expectations were not successful. The confusing system of reporting reading progress in first grade in the lower-class school has already been described. This confusion may have interfered with lower-class children's and parents' understanding of the marking system in reading.

In both schools children differentiate between reading and arithmetic in giving their expectations. Expectations for reading exceed those for arithmetic, and there is a significant negative correlation between the two areas in both schools. Such differentiation is strong evidence of the validity of children's verbal reports. In both schools the negative correlation between expectations is in sharp contrast to the positive correlation between marks actually awarded in the two areas.

The average level of expectations was higher in the lower-class than in the middle-class school at the middle of first grade in both reading and conduct. Expectations for arithmetic were about the same. There was no difference between expectations of black children and white children in the same (lower-class) school for reading and conduct, but white children were less optimistic about arithmetic than black children.

The significant negative correlation between expectations in reading and in arithmetic in both schools strikes us as the strongest evidence for the validity of children's verbal reports of their expectations. Reliability over time, as in the one-week repeat elicitation, is encouraging, but could mean merely consistency on two occasions with no real understanding on the child's part at either time. Significant agreement from midyear to end-of-year can also be taken as an indicant of overtime reliability, but, again, could represent merely a recall and repetition of what was said earlier rather than a meaningful report.

---

*At the time of the initial interviews, when children guessed what they would get on their first report card, children were asked if they knew meanings of the relevant terms, etc. Only after the interviewer was satisfied that the child did understand was the interview continued. Also, of course, the plastic replica of the report card aided in specifying and defining the task. This later probing interview, undertaken by a different interviewer, served as a validity check.

The average overoptimism in children's expectations in the middle-class school must be interpreted in light of the considerable variability in children's expectations at midyear in first grade. A large percentage of children are overoptimistic, but a significant percentage are also overpessimistic, especially before the first report card. The variability in children's expectations is larger than variability in parents' expectations or in marks awarded by teachers.

The variability of children's initial expectations in the lower-class school is smaller than the variability of either marks or parents' expectations. This relatively small variability in children's expectations results from the extreme skewness (toward the highest mark) that is present in the children's expectations. By the end of first grade more cases of underoptimism begin to appear as expectations decline, but expectations still remain, on the average, well above marks and above parents' expectations.

As became clear from further analyses, the level of a child's expectations per se is relatively uninformative in predicting future change. Rather the discrepance between the child's expectations and rated performance is what accounts for change.

The observed lack of racial differences in expectation levels is surprising in some ways but not surprising in others. One might expect small differences between racial groups because the children are still very young. One might also look for small differences, as I did, because this school has been integrated for a number of years, and in considerable prior research on other topics in this same school I have found black children and white children to be very similar on other measures (rate of volunteering and the like). When black children are inducted into new or strange situations with white children—as when, say, children are moved abruptly from a segregated to an integrated setting for experiments—blacks may give evidence of low expectations for themselves (see Cohen & Roper 1973). These low expectations perhaps reflect the low expectations whites hold for blacks in unfamiliar situations, or the relatively more threatening nature of universities and scientists as perceived by black children. The observations for this research were made in a naturalistic rather than experimental setting and were rather unobtrusive.

The child's initial expectations seem independent both of his ability, his teacher's ratings of him, and his parents' forecasts for him. Yet since expectations do not change much, their initial level is important. At this time there is no satisfactory explanation for why lower-class children's expectations for reading are so much higher than middle-class children's (for parents the reverse holds true). At present we are observing day-to-day events in kindergartens in the two schools. This may uncover some cause for the difference.

Expectations over Time

Since expectations generally exceeded marks received at midyear in both schools, one would think that expectations would decrease over the first-grade year. Quite the opposite happens. In the middle-class school average expectation levels are higher at the end of first grade than at midyear. In the lower-class school expectations generally stayed at the same level (a moderate decline for conduct). In the lower-class school there is no difference, furthermore, between blacks and whites in how expectations change over the first-grade year.

Middle-class children get better at anticipating their marks over the first-grade year. In particular, they get better at not underestimating. There is highly significant agreement between children's expectations and the marks they receive in reading at the end of the year (not at midyear). For both arithmetic and conduct, agreement approaches significance only at the end of the year. Children there learn that teachers give no one the lowest mark and give few children the next-to-lowest, so children whose expectations were low at midyear modify their hopes upward. Children whose expectations were too high at midyear are less apt to modify them downward.

Of those middle-class children whose expectations and marks disagree, the majority have expectations that are too high in reading and conduct, but not in arithmetic. Arithmetic seems to be a topic that generates uncertainty (anxiety?) in first-graders. Teachers do mark harder in it than in other subjects. One might say that the feedback for arithmetic is culturally stereotyped, since more low marks are given in that area for no obvious reason. Children also arrive at school with a biased view of arithmetic, since there is a pronounced negative association between expectations for arithmetic and expectations for reading.

Lower-class children do not show significant matching of marks and expectations in any of the three areas at midyear or at the year end. Their high expectations—much higher than middle-class children's—are not modified over the year, despite hard marking by teachers—almost 50% get very low marks in reading on the first report card. The most prevalent finding is that expectations remain constant and, since most children start with high expectations, they are high also at year's end. Considerable negative feedback seems to be ignored, for lower-class children's expectations, if anything, increase rather than decrease. This is perplexing. One explanation might be that the children do not understand what they are doing when they report their expectations to the interviewers. Both the end-of-year depth interviews and the negative association between expectations in reading and arithmetic, however, argue against this simple explanation. Also, results to be discussed in greater detail below show that particular children whose marks increase are recruited from those who did worse than they expected at midyear, and their performance rises to equal expectations. Thus for certain children there is a causal role played by expectations.

The interpretation of the paradox may lie in the impact of day-to-day events rather than the impact of a relatively infrequent event like receipt of a report card. Reading marks were hard to understand (even for the researchers) and reports are given only twice, in November and March. The way reading is taught, though, leads to a high level of individual reinforcement in the classroom administered by both the teacher and the aide. Each spends part of every day in small group sessions with children, carrying out exercises related to reading. Children also spend part of every day doing individual written exercises related to reading. In these exercises there is a high rate of positive response by the adults, and comments are given in extremely positive terms, even if the child's performance has flaws, in order to encourage the child to keep trying. The use of continuous positive feedback, sometimes nonverbal in the form of raisins or M & M candies, is a characteristic of many of the reading programs developed for use with low achievers in recent years. In fact, children who are relatively poor performers may receive more encouragement than better performers, because they get so little self-generated reinforcement. Poor success at academic tasks may cause the teacher to subsidize the reinforcement of poor achievers to keep them working.

The upshot is that poor-performing children are receiving strong positive feedback face-to-face day after day, which contrasts sharply with the negative feedback they get in written form on two occasions during the school year. Persons of any age would be inclined to attend to massive positive feedback (especially when the positive feedback is direct, immediate, and unambiguous) and to discount rare pieces of negative feedback. The child's expectations, therefore, may be premised on what he perceives as the everyday behavior of his teacher and be little affected by the infrequent and ambiguous written reports. Lower-class children are probably also less able than middle-class children to appreciate linguistic usages involving mitigating terms (Bernstein 1970), so that the verbal comments teachers make may have a more positive impact than the teacher really intends.

It is hard to imagine how a young child can be brought to learn without considerable encouragement. The middle-class child, however, may be better at encouraging himself when he starts school. For one thing, his lower expectation level will let him experience subjectively defined success more often. If a child has very high expectations and his performance does not equal them, the contrast leads to negative reinforcement.

It may be dangerous to link heavy encouragement in the classroom with rigid marking practices, as is done in the lower-class school. At some point a child must experience severe dissonance when he contrasts his high subjective ideas of his own performance, reinforced by face-to-face interaction with the teacher, with the low marks he gets on report cards. In first grade dissonance may be minimal because marking practices are obscure. In later grades the dissonance may become less equivocal—imagine the feelings of the child who is strongly encouraged through the first three years of school when he reviews his report cards and it dawns on him that all his marks have been low or failing.

Discrepances between Marks and Expectations

The main purpose of this research is to uncover causal factors: do children's (or parents') expectations have causal impact on performance, and if so, how? Looking at average expectation levels one gets little feeling for how causal effects may occur. The following sections address the issue of causal sequences and examine in more detail what happens to children sequentially.

One might think that children with high marks are more astute and that they therefore are better at forecasting their marks. However, when expectation-mark agreement is stratified by mark received at midyear, middle-class children of all performance levels seem to formulate their expectations in the same way. Children receiving A's and those receiving D's show approximately the same distribution of expectations (as do those in between).

Another reasonable hypothesis might be that children with low expectations, more than children with high expectations, would manifest a high amount of agreement between forecasts and performance, because a poor performance is under the child's control. But middle-class children who forecast low marks, and they are relatively few in number, get about the same percentage of low marks as the class as a whole, so this line of reasoning also does not hold.

For lower-class children the data do not permit a meaningful analysis of expectation-mark agreement at first report card in terms of mark or expectation level because, as already remarked, the combination of exceedingly high child expectations with relatively low mark assignments severely restricts possible patterns of outcomes. Also with data for only a single cohort the case base is small.

By the end of first grade, in reading there is increased expectation-mark agreement for middle-class children (from about 55% to 80%). Change in marks and expectations seems related not to simple performance level or to simple expectation level, as already stated, but rather to the difference between performance and expectations. There are too few data for the lower-class school to allow definitive analyses, but in both arithmetic and conduct, those children whose marks do improve are disproportionately recruited from among those who earlier showed disagreement between mark and expectations. There is a tendency for both marks and expectations to change in a way to reduce expectation-mark discrepance.

Feedback effects will now be discussed for the middle-class school only. If a child did worse than he expected at midyear, his expectations at year's end tend to remain the same and his mark is brought into line. If he did better than he expected, he is very likely to modify his expectations upward and keep the mark the same. There is a consistent observation as well of the following types of cases: a child's mark remaining the same if his mark equaled what he expected, and a child's mark going down if he did better than he expected.

The majority of children, whether their midyear mark exceeded, equaled, or was below their expectation, can expect the same mark at year's end that they received at midyear, because there is great consistency in marks awarded. There is, nevertheless, a consistent (and significant for reading and conduct) observation of cases where marks move up, down, or remain stationary to agree with expectations. The data suggest that students' expectations causally affect the marks they receive, even if the degree of association is rather low.

Finding a causal role for expectations is one of the major achievements of this research. Only with data aggregated across two (middle-class) cohorts to supply an adequate number of cases for analysis could this effect emerge.

The data show that a child's cognitive state, his estimate of his own performance, is instrumental in changing that level of performance. Unfortunately, the data in the lower-class school are not yet extensive enough to allow an investigation of the same sort, but what data there are, as already stated, point to the same finding.

The other side of the coin must not be lost sight of, however. For all the children followed, the most likely outcome is for both expectations and marks to remain the same. In the middle-class school, where almost all children are awarded A's and B's and where expectation levels are high, but not inordinately high considering the high average performance level, the stability of expectations leads to high expectation, but not to an unrealistic cognitive state. In the lower-class school, where expectations also persist at high levels, if future analyses bear out present tendencies, several outcomes are possible. First the child may insulate himself from negative feedback—he may block out awareness of, or dissonance over, low marks—and so be hindered in monitoring his performance. Second, if there are downward shifts in expectations from time to time as the child becomes aware of low-level performance, serious limits could be imposed thereafter on aspirations.

We have shown so far that young children's expectations are high, resilient, and responsive mainly to positive feedback. More data are needed to see whether, if expectations are lowered, they are also resilient to change thereafter.

Implications and Future Research

An earlier review of reading models and language socialization noted "evidence is accumulating that socioeconomic status is a more crucial influence on reading performance than IQ" (Entwisle 1971). The present report looks not at linguistic factors or cognitive habits, as the earlier paper did, but at social factors or organizational (school) variables. The same conclusion can be stated here, however, with even more conviction. The average difference in IQ is not large between schools, but reading and arithmetic performance as rated by teachers differs by school. Experience suggests that there will be significant differences on standardized tests in reading and arithmetic between schools, when these children are tested later in their school careers. Informal classroom observation reveals very large differences in reading proficiency at the end of first grade.

We intend to investigate the present data much more thoroughly to gain insight into what may be responsible for these differences. Parents of lower-class children may be setting themselves up to administer negative reinforcement—by having higher expectations than their children can meet, they may be boxing themselves into a corner of not being able to be pleased with the child's performance. By marking on an absolute scale the teachers in the lower-class school may also be removing their ability to provide positive reinforcement. If a child is trying hard and sees no obvious result, i.e., no high mark, his effort must slack off. But by marking harder initially, teachers in the lower-class school are also leaving more room for improvement, however, and any marks that change do change in an upward direction.

Perhaps more important, by starting school with unrealistically high expectations the lower-class child may be setting himself up for punishment later. What is positively or negatively reinforcing depends on one's expectations. If one expects to win 50¢ and wins $5, this is positive, whereas if one expects to win $50 and wins $5 the same event may be negative. To get a low mark when one expects it may not lead to unhappiness. Most persons would agree, however, that to get a low mark when one expects a high mark is a punishing state of affairs. The high expectations noted for lower-class children in this research are reminiscent of the high self-esteem scores so many investigators have found for minority group or disadvantaged youngsters. These phenomena are undoubtedly adaptive for the individuals involved. How does this come about, especially since our data suggest that parents' expectations are lower? Social feedback may be very different in the two milieux.

The data already have some obvious implications for reading. First, the impact of parents on performance must be acknowledged. In both schools parents are able to forecast their children's performance with some accuracy, and are noticeably better than the child at forecasting his own performance. Other data indicate, in addition, that a parents' expectations are correlated with absences of his child during the year subsequent to when parents' expectations are sampled. This implies that time spent in school is less for children whose parents hold low expectations. As I puzzle over why ultimate reading performance in these two schools is so different, when average IQ, staff quality, and other factors appear so comparable, I am beginning to think that *sheer time spent effectively in learning to read* may hold the key. If a child spends less time because he is late or absent or if he effectively spends less time because he fails to use feedback to monitor his own performance, there may be less time for learning.

REFERENCES

Bernstein, B. 1970. "A sociolinguistic approach to socialization: With some references to educability," in F. Williams (ed.), *Language and Poverty*. Chicago: Markham Publishing Company, pp. 25–61.

Bikson, T. K. 1974. Minority speech as objectively measured and subjectively evaluated. Paper presented at the meeting of the American Psychological Association, New Orleans, September 1974.

Bloom, B H. 1964. *Stability and change in human characteristics*. New York: Wiley.

Cohen, E. G., and Roper, S. 1973. Modification of interracial interaction disability. *American Sociological Review* 37: 643–47.

Entwisle, D. R. 1971. Implications of language socialization for reading models and for learning to read. *Reading Research Quarterly* (Fall) 7(1): 111–67.

———. 1975. "Socialization of language: Educability and expectations," in M. Maehr and W. Stallings (eds.), *Culture, child and school*, forthcoming.

Entwisle, D. R., and Hayduk, L. 1974. Observational studies of Children's expectations. Part II of D. R. Entwisle, M. Webster, and L. Hayduk, *Expectation theory in the classroom* (Final Report, Office of Education grant OEG-3-71-0122). Baltimore, Md.: The Johns Hopkins University, June 1974.

Entwisle, D. R., and Webster, M. 1972. Raising children's performance expectations. *Social Science Research* 1: 147–58.

———. 1973. Research notes: Status factors in expectation raising. *Sociology of Education* 46: 115–26.

———. 1974*a*. "Raising children's expectations for their own performance: A classroom application," Chapter 7, in J. Berger, T. Conner, and M. H. Fisek (eds.), *Expectation states theory: A theoretical research program.* Cambridge: Winthrop Publishers.

———. 1974*b*. Expectations in mixed racial groups. *Sociology of Education* 47: 301–18.

Husèn, T. 1969. *Talent opportunity and career.* Stockholm: Almquist & Wilsell.

Kraus, P. E. 1973. *Yesterday's children.* New York: Wiley.

Lambert, W. E., and Tucker, G. R. 1972. The St. Lambert program of home-school language switch, grades K through five. (Mimeo.) Montreal: McGill University.

Rosenberg, M., and Simmons, R. A. 1971. *Black and white self-esteem.* Washington, D.C.: American Sociological Association Rose Monograph Series.

Rubovits, P. C., and Maehr, M. L. 1973. Pygmalion black and white. *Journal of Personality and Social Psychology* 25: 210–18.

Seaver, W. B. 1973. Effects of naturally induced teacher expectancies. *Journal of Personality and Social Psychology* 28: 333–42.

3 — *Paula Menyuk*

Relations between Acquisition of Phonology and Reading

It has been assumed that there are similarities between the processes involved in the acquisition of oral language comprehension and the comprehension of written language. The exact nature of these correspondences is at present largely a matter of speculation, although research in this area is flourishing and, hopefully, will lead to substantive findings that will elucidate the proposed similarities. It has also been assumed that the acquisition of comprehension of written language is dependent on the comprehension of oral language. This assumption is also being researched at present and has led to two distinct paths of investigation. The first is concerned with children who appear to deviate from the norm in terms of how they process oral language input and, therefore, possibly in what they know about language, as compared to children of comparable ages who presumably do not deviate from the norm in processing strategies. If a dependency between oral and written language comprehension is assumed, the researchers conclude that the oral language comprehension difference or deficit displayed by these children must also affect comprehension of written language. The other area of research is concerned with children who, because of differences from standard English in the structure of their spoken language (dialect variation or bilingualism), develop different structural categorizations of the language. These researchers conclude, again, that the dependency relation between oral and written language comprehension will create problems for these children, since the written language does not conform to the oral language with which they are familiar.

Although oral language comprehension entails not only comprehension of the phonology, or speech sound structure, of an utterance, and the same, of course, can be said of written language comprehension, this aspect of language processing has received the greatest attention in studies of the acquisition of reading for the following reason. It has been assumed that beginning readers approach the task by either (1) attempting to establish sound-symbol correspondences, and then synthesizing these segments into a whole recognizable word (the "sound out" method); or (2) attempting to match the symbol sequence of the word to the phonological sequence of a word (the "look-say" method). In either case it is assumed that reference is being made to a phonological representation, be it segment or word, or even, perhaps, syllable or phrase. The initial reference, therefore, for the beginning reader is presumed to be the phonological component of the grammar.

In this paper the beginning reader will be the focus of attention. Each of the assumptions outlined above concerning similarities between oral language and written language processing and the dependency of written language acquisition on oral language knowledge will be examined by reviewing studies that have addressed themselves to describing phonological acquisition, and those that have explored the correspondences and differences between phonological acquisition and reading acquisition. Finally, some tentative conclusions will be drawn concerning the relations between acquisition of phonology and reading by examining what the literature has had to say about the characteristics of good and poor readers.

DEVELOPMENT OF SPEECH PERCEPTION

There have been numerous studies of the maturation of the child's ability to differentiate between the speech sounds of his language and his ability to observe the phonological rules that govern speech sound sequences; that is, what are the permissible and impermissible phonological sequences in his language? Most of these studies, however, have dealt with the child's observation of distinctions and rules in the language he produces. For example, his distinction between the stop /t/ and the continuant /O/ has been noted as his ability to say both "thank" and "tank," not as his ability to indicate that he perceives the difference between "thank" and "tank." This latter ability presumably long precedes his productive distinction ability. Despite the fact that there have been few studies of speech sound perception per se, this is the ability that appears to be most germane to the question of similarity in the processing of speech and written language. It is the comprehension aspect of speech sound distinctions, therefore, that will be discussed rather than productive distinctions. Both the processes of speech perception and of reading comprehension have been described as involving reference to the articulatory gestures associated with speech production. In speech perception this view has been labeled "the motor theory of speech perception" (Liberman et al. 1967) and in reading as "subvocal articulation" while reading (Edfeldt 1960). Therefore, reference will be made to articulation as well as perception wherever it is pertinent.

Within the past five years there have been a number of studies that have examined the ability of infants to differentiate between acoustic stimuli that are speech-like. (Summaries can be found in Eimas 1974, and Morse 1974.) In these studies synthetic speech stimuli (stimuli that are generated by computer and have the acoustic characteristics of speech) are used, and the infant's habituation and dishabituation to different stimuli are are examined. In summary, it has been found that at one to two months of age infants distinguish between speech-like stimuli in a manner similar to that of adults. They will treat some acoustically different stimuli as being the same and other acoustically different stimuli as being different. The adult treats these stimuli in the same manner; categorizing some different stimuli as belonging to the same phonemic category, and, therefore, not perceiving the difference between them. Thus, it appears that the infant at a very early age observes potentially important speech sound distinctions. Also at this very early age the infant distinguishes between syllables that have rising and falling fundamental frequency contours and, thus, appears to be sensitive to those aspects of the signal that carry communicative information. The affective qualities of fundamental frequency differences, that is, friendly versus unfriendly voices, and male versus female voices, are presumably observed by infants from about three months on (Kaplan & Kaplan 1970), and at eight months of age the infant distinguishes between sentences that are read as statements and those read as questions (Kaplan 1969). The infant, therefore, before the stages at which recognizable words are produced, appears to be sensitive to both segmental and suprasegmental cues that are important in speech sound perception.

The infant can also discriminate differences in visual stimuli that are potentially useful for letter and word distinctions (Pick & Pick 1970) and, indeed, is a sophisticated visual perceiver at a very early age (Bower 1971). Clearly, a distinction must be made between the ability to perceive differences in acoustic and visual stimuli and the ability to categorize stimuli in a linguistically meaningful way. Despite the fact that the infant may be sensitive to acoustic differences that mark speech/sound distinctions, and, in fact, may initially be sensitive to all such possibilities (that is, the distinctions found within all languages of the world), the ability to observe differences in the speech sound composition of words and to relate them to particular objects and events in the environment does not appear until a later stage of development. Apparently the capacity to discriminate differences between speech sound stimuli, displayed at an earlier stage of development, is at this later stage recruited for a specifically linguistic use and is structured in a different way. It appears that a reorganization takes place at this later stage, in that speech sound discrimination operates on words, not segments of words, and that particular words (the topic of the message) and the overall prosody of the utterance are attended to (Menyuk 1974). It should be noted that these findings do not suggest that the capacity to discriminate between speech sound segments has disappeared, but, rather, that the capacity is not utilized at the beginning stages of word comprehension. At this stage the organization of language comprehension appears to be the following:

> phonological sequence = word = meaning
> meaning = semantic properties of the word plus intent
> intent = situation plus prosody of the utterance
> prosody = statement, emphatic and question

The hierarchy of decoding is from intent and meaning to phonological sequence. At no point is the child obviously making distinctions between the consonantal and vocalic segments of a particular phonological sequence.

Another developmental observation that leads to the conclusion that at the earliest stages children do not use the segmental distinctions they are capable of making is the observation that speech sound distinctions are acquired in a sequence during the linguistic stage, whereas, during the prelinguistic stage, in the research carried out thus far, there appear to be no distinctions that are easier for the infant to make than any other, that is, all distinctions are equally possible. In studies of speech sound differentiation, however, when words or word equivalents are employed, it has been found that children perceive some speech sound distinctions before others. Two researchers (Shvachkin 1973, and Garnica 1973) have examined children's speech sound differentiation at an early age, using the same experimental paradigm. Children were taught nonsense names for objects. Each nonsense name in a set contrasted either two or three consonants in initial position, with the remainder of the syllable being exactly the same, or contrasted the case in which an initial consonant was present in one instance and absent in the other. Shvachkin studied eighteen children over the age of ten to twenty-one months and found that the hierarchy of speech sound discrimination was similar to the hierarchy postulated by Jakobson and Halle (1956) for the sequence of acquisition of productive speech sound distinctions. Garnica, in her study of sixteen children, age seventeen to twenty-two months, observed over a four-month period, also found a hierarchy in the distinctions. However, although some general universal trends in ordering were observed in her population, there was considerable variation in the ordering observed with individual children. These studies indicate that (1) there is an ordering in the development of perceptual speech sound distinctions, and (2) the ordering is only partially universal, and may not be related to the ordering observed in productive distinctions. Perception may precede production, but it is not clear that the order of perceptual distinctions made matches the order in which productive distinctions are made. Indeed, some of the Garnica data is in direct contradiction to what has been found in studies of production. For example, although perception of the /w/ versus /y/ distinction appears to be an earlier acquisition than the labial versus non-nonlabial distinction, the inverse occurs in production. Furthermore, these studies do not make obvious the basis upon which perceptual distinctions are made in the development of speech sound perception when listening to ordinary language, since very little semantic information was provided in the task given the children.

Keeping in mind the reservations presented concerning the relation between the development of speech perception and production, it is nevertheless important to, at least briefly, look at speech production for two reasons. One is that although productions may be transformed realizations of perceptual categorizations and rules, they are obviously based on such categorizations and rules. Second, the motor theory of speech perception forces us to consider the role that production may play in perception. Shvachkin notes that at least some perceptual distinctions are only made after productive distinctions are accomplished. A number of studies examining the productive distinctions made by children (see Ferguson & Slobin 1973, for some examples) indicate a hierarchy of distinctions. These early distinctions seem to be motivated by two factors. The first is semantics. Children will create distinctions not in their own language to keep two words from being ambiguous, and they will observe an articulatory distinction with some words that are semantically important to them, while not observing the same distinction with words that are not. The second factor appears to be the constraints on the vocal mechanism in the maturing organism and the solutions that children come up with to encode as accurately as possible the words in their dictionary. An example of an early constraint is to limit a syllable to a CV. Final consonants may be reduced, weak syllables deleted, and initial consonant clusters reduced to a single consonant. However, distinctions are made between syllables usually in terms of the manner of articulation of the initial consonant and position of the vowel (back, front, high or low). The child appears to organize his production in terms of the features of syllables rather than the features of the segments in the syllable. Coarticulation effects can be observed in that both forward ("pop" for "pot") and backward ("tot" for "pot") assimilation occurs. This, again, indicates planning of articulation in terms of the syllable rather than the segment. Since many early utterances are monosyllables or reduplication of syllables, one can as easily hypothesize that organization occurs in terms of words rather than syllables. The question that remains is whether or not perception of phonological distinctions is also organized in terms of syllables or words rather than segments, despite Shvachkin and Garnica's findings.

In a study of the "psychological" reality of the phoneme (Savin & Bever 1970) it was found that whole syllable targets are responded to more quickly than single segment targets. That is, when subjects were asked to press a switch as soon as they heard the word "bat" or "sit," or when they heard the sound /s/ or /b/, they responded more quickly in the former context than in the latter. The conclusion drawn by the experimenters is that speech is not perceived by analysis of segments, then grouping these into syllables, then syllables into words, and so on, but that subjects analyze speech into syllables, and then identify phonemes in the syllable. A study by McNeill and Lindig (1973) led them to the following conclusion. In real speech processing it is normally meaning that is attended to; that is, the meaning of words and the relations between the words. However, any unit of speech (phoneme, syllable, word, and sentence) can be attended to and can be processed in commensurate amounts of time. The differences in response time to different units is a function of the context in which the unit is embedded; the linguistic level of the target, and the level of the search list. Thus, when the list and the target are on two different levels the subject must divide attention between two objects (for example, phoneme within a word). Response time increases as the difference in linguistic levels between target and search list increase, and is reduced when they are matched. The experimenters conclude by stating that "psychologically" no level has primacy over another. This, indeed, may be the case, but, clearly, both in real time processing and, it appears, in the ontogenesis of language, the organization of perception appears to be, first, analysis of meaningful units (words), and then, *if necessary,* analysis of the syllable into phonemes. Thus, the capacity to deal with all linguistic levels exists, and exists even in the very young child, but the frequency with which the different levels are used and, therefore, the accessibility of the levels in analysis probably varies. Phonemic analysis appears to be comparatively inaccessible, whereas syllabic analysis, which has been going on since the early period of word acquisition, appears to be a form of analysis with which the young child is quite familiar. Futher, there is increasing evidence that the acoustic cues to differentiation of speech sequences are encoded in a number of cues that certainly go beyond the bounds of a single segment (Stevens 1973).

Two other comments about the relation of speech perception and production are germane to the discussion of reading acquisition. A number of studies (Menyuk 1972*b*) examining children's identification and reproduction of initial consonantal segments (for example "pop," "top," "cop") and vowels in medial position (for example, "beel," "bill" and "bell") in minimally different words, at age three to four years indicate the following. On the whole, perceptual distinctions are made more successfully than reproductive distinctions, although there are some exceptions. However, it is not always the case that those sound differences that are best identified are also best reproduced. For example, the /p/, /t/, /k/ distinctions are among the easiest sounds to reproduce accurately, but are among the most difficult to identify in a set of minimally different words. The relation between perception and production of speech is far from a simple one-to-one relation. As has been stated previously (Menyuk 1972*a*), it may be that at some period of development speech sound distinctions are processed by reference to the articulatory mechanism, but it is at least questionable that this is the case during the period of acquisition of perceptual speech sound categorizations and rules. Also, when the child enters school he has not as yet established firm productive rules for consonant cluster sequences or morphological rules (Menyuk 1972*b*).

READING ACQUISITION AND PHONOLOGY

Reading has been described as involving the following processes: discrimination between and categorization of letters, segmental synthesis, and then translation into a phonological sequence (Gibson et al. 1962). If this is the case, then, immediately a distinction exists between processing strategies in the acquisition of speech and the comprehension of written language. As was described above, the process in speech perception appears to be one of coming to segmental analysis only if necessary, whereas, in acquisition of reading, presumably, segmental analysis is the first step—discrimination between and categorization of letters. There are, of course, suggestions in the literature that word recognition per se should be the beginning step in the acquisition of reading (Smith 1971). However, when the child begins to read, at approximately age five or six, he has had frequent opportunities to do segmental analysis in contextual situations where minimal pair distinctions must be made (for example, "Give me the mat" versus "Give me the bat"). As was stated previously, he is able to observe minimal pair distinctions in both words and nonsense syllables without any context other than picture or object. Thus, the child may be ready to engage in the process of synthesis by analysis

Table 3.1. Presumed hierarchy of processing

Speech perception	Written language comprehension
Word/s identification	Letter identification
Syllable identification	Syllable identification
Segment identification	Word identification

described above versus analysis by synthesis, although the latter is the usual process employed in phonological analysis of oral language. Table 3.1 indicates the hypothesized differences in the sequence of processing involved in the two tasks.

One other factor may mark a distinction between the processes of speech perception and written language comprehension. As was printed out previously, there appear to be differences in the sequence of acquisition of the perception and production of speech units. There is also evidence that the child makes no reference to the articulatory gestures that are associated with the production of speech sounds as he perceives speech. Indeed, when asked to simultaneously produce and identify a phonological sequence, production impairs identification (Menyuk 1972c). If reading acquisition requires the overt or subvocal articulation of phonological sequences, then the two processes (speech perception and reading) are, again, different from each other. It is not clear, however, that subvocal articulation is a requirement in reading. Some rather strong arguments have been presented that support the hypothesis that in reading, as well as in speech perception, reference is more frequently made to auditory images than to articulatory gestures (Conrad 1972).

Gibson (1972, p. 9) outlines some possible parallels between the processes of development of speech perception and written language comprehension. At the initial stages of development these parallels are pointed to: babbling with scribbling, segmentation (pauses) with segmentation (letters, white spaces), distinguishing features of phonemes with distinguishing features of letters, and learning a phonological rule system with learning an orthographic rule system. In addition, a parallel with intonation (stress), and categorical features of writing is suggested in that intonation distinguishes speech from other acoustic inputs, and certain features distinguish writing from other visual inputs on paper. Tying the processes of speech perception and reading together are abilities to transfer and a system of mapping rules, which is, of course, unique to the reading process.

Although some of the parallels drawn seem clear and obvious others are much less so. The infant, at a very early stage of development, distinguishes between speech and nonspeech and does so presumably using both suprasegmental (intonation and stress) and segmental features to make the distinction. He also actively engages in babbling, which provides feedback information. In comprehension of a written system the child at an early stage appears to distinguish between writing and other marks on paper and appears to do so by using both organizational information and segmental information (recombination of elements and repetitive regularity are suggested) to make the distinction. He also engages in scribbling, which may be assumed to provide some kind of feedback information.

Segmentation is required in both processes, however, as was indicated earlier, the process of segmentation appears to proceed from sentence (marked by intonation and stress patterns) to word and/or syllable, to phoneme in speech perception. In reading, however, information about segmentation is provided by separation of letters, then the white spaces between words, and then, one would presume, the sentence boundaries, marked by punctuation and capitalized letters. Categorization of segmental sequential features are required in both processes. The child must learn which features mark distinctions in the system in spite of transformations. With speech the child must learn that the different acoustic products of different speakers at different times should be categorized as being the same to obtain appropriate meanings. This is also true in understanding written systems within which different representations of the same letters and words are presented to the child. However, again, the unit upon which these decisions about categorization have to be made (letter versus syllable or word) appears to be markedly different. Both systems require knowledge of sequential rules. For example, the child learns the permissible consonant cluster rules at the beginnings and ends of words in both the speech and written system. Thus /str/ is possible as an initial sequence, whereas /smr/ is not, and /sts/ is a possible final cluster, whereas /sns/ is not. Writing systems, however, contain sequences impermissible in the system of phonological rules (ps,kn, etc., in initial position and gn, gh, etc., in final position). Information represented as a single element in writing (the /s/ in mats, bags, etc.) is differentiated in speech; and information represented as two elements in writing (ed) is represented as a single element in speech, and, in addition, in different ways (/t/, /d/, etc.). Although it is true that both systems require the ability to differentiate between and categorize segments, and the ability to observe sequential rules (this, of course, is not only true of phonological rules, but also of semantic and syntactic rules), the bases or units upon which differentiations, categorizations, and rule learning occur differ markedly in the two systems.

These differences in categories of representation create the possibility of difficulty in beginning reading, since it is presumed that a transfer and mapping procedure, from the written to the speech system, is required in learning to read. A many to one and a one to many relation exists between phonological and orthographic representations, as indicated in the few examples given. Thus, mapping rules may be simple in some instances and quite complicated in others. Some recent studies by Chomsky and Read (1971) of children's early writing reveal that children capture in their writing some phonological generalizations they have made before the time they enter school and are presented with the formal task of learning to read. Their translations indicate clearly that the orthographic representations they will encounter contradict the generalizations they have made. For example, vowel reduction in unstressed syllables is not preserved in writing ("palace" becomes "pals"). The nasal segment between vowel and stop is redundant, probably because nasalization of the vowel is the criterial distinction observed. Therefore, the nasal segment is not marked in writing ("hand" becomes "had," "bump" becomes "bup," etc.) Syllabic $/r/$ is encoded as such ("fern" becomes "frn," "girl," "grl," etc.). The child appears to be representing his phonological categorizations and rules as best he can with the symbol set that is available. It is clear from the examples given above that the symbol system the child is actually confronted with in learning to read does not best represent his phonological generalizations and rules. It should be added that, although groups of children appear to make similar generalizations about how to best represent their phonological knowledge in writing, it is not clear how universal these generalizations are. Regardless of this possible lack of universality, it is also clear from these findings that the categories and organization of the written system vary in important ways from the categories and organization of the phonological system, and, therefore, that mapping one system onto the other requires marked transformations.

All the correspondences between learning to comprehend speech and written language seem to lie in an area that might be called general perceptual abilities: the ability to perceive distinctive differences, categorize differences, and store them for further use. Learning to read, however, requires the additional tasks of transfer and mapping, which may in themselves be composed of several subcomponents. In addition, learning to read differs from comprehending language in a very important way. Children learn to understand and use language for highly significant reasons: to demand, question, and to organize their environment for themselves in useful ways. It is not only the structure and sequencing of oral and written language processing that may differ, but the functions they serve also widely differ. It has been suggested by Gibson (1972) that the motivation in acquiring comprehension of written material is to reduce uncertainty. Another motivation may be the need to comply with teachers' and parents' demands. It may be that for many children any

Table 3.2. Processing speech and written language

Process	Similarities	
	Speech	Written language
Feedback	Babbling	Scribbling
Discrimination	Speech versus nonspeech	Writing versus other visual representations
Categorization of units	Syllables	Letters
Meaning	Words and relations	Words and relations
	Differences	
Segmentation hierarchy	Word/syllable/phoneme	Letter to word
Categorical unit	Morpheme/syllable	Letter
Representation	One/many	Many/one
Mapping rules	Not required	Required
Motivation	Communication	Reduction of uncertainty

cognitive task imposes an intellectual challenge that they are anxious to meet and resolve. Therefore, what they are given to read doesn't matter. To successfully read is in itself sufficient motivation. It also may be that the motivation of intellectual challenge alone is insufficient for some or many children and that additional motivation must be provided to ensure acceptance of the challenge. Table 3.2 presents a summary of the correspondences and differences between the two processes that have been discussed above.

READING ACQUISITION AND LANGUAGE DIFFERENCE

Although dialect differences exist throughout this country, the dialect differences of the black and poor have been characterized as being separate and distinct from other variations and are often labeled as a separate language—Black English. Two other kinds of language difference exist in the population: knowledge of only one language different from English, and some form of bilingualism (other language plus English). A large number of those children who have difficulty in acquiring written language comprehension, although certainly not all, come from these populations. Several hypotheses have been presented to account for the difficulties these children encounter in acquiring written language comprehension. The first is that the transfer and mapping of written categories and rules to phonological categories and rules imposes enormous constraints on these children, since the written language, in structure, is so different from the structure of their spoken language. There are several arguments against this position: some of them logical, and others experimental. The first is that the orthography and the semantic and syntactic structure of sentences in written language matches no child's knowledge of the phonology and structure of his language. As we have seen, a translation of the written language into the child's spoken language appears to be required for all children. A counter argument might be that with these children their own language structure differs much more markedly from the text of readers than does the language structure of children who use standard English; a matter of degree.

A study (Melmed 1971) has been carried out with third-grade children who use Black English, which indicates the following: (1) differences exist in the phonological categorizations and rules of Black English and standard English speakers, and (2) Black English speakers show no significant inability to comprehend words that exemplify these differences when either reading orally or silently. When confusions do exist they are eliminated by increasing the syntactical and contextual clues in sentences and paragraphs. The conclusion reached in this study was that dialect differences in speech production and discrimination appear to have little relation to the comprehension of written language. Another study (Piestrup 1973) provides more clues as to why dialect differences may yet interfere in learning to read, because of attitudes toward these differences. This study was concerned with teacher styles in first-grade classrooms, and the product of six teaching styles was measured by reading scores and tests of dialect difference. Tests of homogeneity of regression showed no interaction between Black dialect and reading scores for teacher groups. It was found that involving children directly in reading, and mutuality of communication, with teachers and children sharing purpose and meaning in communication, were important factors in learning to read and achieving higher reading scores. The above study suggests that the most important factors in learning to read are: (1) meaningful communication between teachers and children, and (2) expectations of teachers concerning probable success. Therefore, either a direct approach is used in the teaching of reading, or indirect approaches are used, where attempts are made to either change the spoken language of the children or to make friends with them.

Another factor has been suggested (Savin 1972) to account for poorer reading performance of low SES as compared to middle SES children. Savin hypothesizes that whereas phonemic analysis is something that middle-class children are very familiar with, having often engaged in activities such as rhyming games, inner-city children come to school capable of using only a syllabic analysis of the speech they hear. Thus, words such as "cat" and "hat" are no more alike than "cat " and "dog," while a word such as "window" is clearly composed of "win" and "dow." It is interesting to note that in the previous study cited (Piestrup 1973), the more successful teachers frequently used rhythmic play and asked children to actively participate by listening to their own responses. However, even though middle-class children perceive "cat" and "hat" to be more alike than "cat" and "dog" it is, nevertheless, difficult for some of them to separate the /c/ and /h/ from the /aet/. Savin's findings are intriguing and certainly worthy of further exploration with all children, not only inner-city children. They provide insights into a possible hierarchy of analysis that may be required in successful reading acquisition: from syllabic analysis to observing similarities among syllables to phonemic analysis.

It seems logical to suppose that using one language creates enormous difficulties in learning to read another. Comparative unfamiliarity with the language to be read, as in the case of varying degrees of bilingualism, also may cause difficulty in learning to read the less familiar language. Again, however, it is not clear that difference in language alone can account for, and even importantly account for the difficulties that children may encounter. We shall point to one study that is presently ongoing and explore the possibilities that this study reveals. The study is being carried out in Montreal by W. Lambert, R. Tucker, and colleagues. Children from English speaking homes are being exposed to a totally French education. That is, they are learning to read, write, do mathematics, science, play games etc. in French, although their native language is English, and when they return to their homes, presumably English is the language spoken. In the primary grades French is the only language used in school. Tests of their abilities in various subject areas including, of course, reading, indicate that they are performing on a par with children who are being educated in their native language. This study clearly raises many questions about the difficulty of learning to read in a language other than one's native language. Many other factors outside of difference in language appear to affect success or failure of reading acquisition. Whether or not the other language is being imposed on the child, whether or not the other language is the dominant language (politically and socially), and, finally, the conditions under which the other language is introduced seem to be critical issues.

It is clear from the studies cited above that factors apart from language difference per se appear to play an important if not *the* important role in achieving written language comprehension. These factors fall into two categories: (1) attitudes and methods of teachers, and (2) language-processing strategies of children as they enter school, regardless of the language used. This latter factor seems to be one that can be accommodated to fairly easily, either by presenting the information in a form that they can easily handle (Savin suggests syllabically) or by providing material based on their own language experience (Serwer 1969). Both factors need a great deal more work.

DIFFERENCES BETWEEN GOOD AND POOR READERS

A sizeable proportion of children who have difficulties in learning to read are those described previously. However, a great deal of the literature is concerned with children who, presumably, have "perceptual deficits." They have either visual discrimination deficits that have been described as either orientation errors (b versus d) or sequencing errors ("was" versus "saw"). This difficulty presumably accounts for comparatively few children who have reading problems (Shankweiler & Liberman 1972). Other children are described as having difficulty in cross-modal associations, that is, presumably in transfer of auditory information to the visual mode or vice-versa (Goodnow 1971). Some poor readers are described as having auditory discrimination and blending problems (Chall et al. 1963, 1965). None of the children described thus far have been characterized as having an oral language problem. Their spontaneous speech appears to be commensurate with that of children without reading problems. Thus, presumably, on a connected discourse basis, these children do not appear to differ from children without reading problems, despite stated differences in auditory discrimination and blending.

On the phonological level these children do not display the same kinds of errors when reading a list of words as they do when listening to a list of words (Shankweiler & Liberman 1972). An analysis of their reading errors revealed that most were associated with the vowel (43%) and final consonants (32%). Initial consonants were read accurately. When listening, not only were errors much reduced (7% in listening versus 24% in reading) but also the error pattern was very different. When listening and reproducing, most errors occurred in initial and final consonants (equally distributed), while vowels were reproduced accurately. The explanation of the difference offered by the experimenters is that in speech perception segmental phonological analysis takes place "unconsciously" (for example, the similarity between "cat" and "hat" and the distinction between the initial segments when necessary). In reading, this segmental analysis must come to "conscious" awareness for transfer and mapping to take place. In the case of reading vowels the mapping task is particularly difficult, since written representation of the vowel varies widely from the phonological representation, in that there is a many-to-one and a one-to-many relation between written vowels and spoken vowels. Again, the difficulty pointed to is the distinction between the processing required in speech perception and written language comprehension.

Differences in "general" cognitive abilities between good and poor readers have also been discusssed as a cause. General cognitive abilities appear to be defined in the literature as an ability to conserve or an ability to understand abstract representations of relations. For example, a study examining the comprehension and reproduction of representations of action relations that varied in abstractness was carried out with first-grade problem and average readers, third- to fifth-grade problem readers, and head start children (Denner 1970). Children were asked to engage in (1) an "enactive task" (clap your hands, jump over a block), (2) identify pictographs (stick figures) as representing an activity after practice, (3) identify logographs (simple line drawings) as representing an activity after practice, and (4) to read sequences of logographs. The groups did not appear to differ in their ability to carry out task 4. Average first-grade readers exceeded all other groups in their ability to carry out task 4. However, third- to fifth-grade problem readers did better than head start children and first-grade problem readers. The sentence per se was understood, but the abstract representation of the sentence caused difficulty. One can see the analogy between the above task and reading acquisition, since children must learn to relate abstract written representations to phonological sequences. However, it seems insufficient to say that abstractness of representation causes difficulty, since inner-city children who were experiencing difficulty in learning to read were found to succeed in reading when given abstract ideographic symbols to read, which stood for familiar lexical items (Rozin et al. 1970).

At the level of reading sentences aloud the following observations have been made about good and poor readers. Good readers chunk items within a string, and, therefore, pauses occur after a number of words rather than after every word, as is the case with poor readers. Good readers, of course, make fewer errors and only stop and go back when a word does not fit into the context of what they are reading. Poor readers read as if they were given a list, that is, one word at a time (Clay & Imlach 1971). Good readers use their knowledge of the semantic and syntactic rules of the language to chunk items, to predict items, and to correct errors. The process is called psycholinguistic guessing (Goodman 1973). Poor readers are unable to or do not use this information. It is difficult to see how contextual information can be used if the analysis of each word takes an inordinate amount of time. Given the constraints of short-term memory, the information obtained at the beginning of the sentence can no longer be used to chunk, or to predict, or to verify items that appear later in the string. It seems logical to suppose that degree of knowledge of the structure of the language will play an important role at what might be called, for at least some children, the second stage of reading; reading for meaning of phrases and sentences. However, it is difficult to see how this second stage can be reached until word analysis has been accomplished by some strategy (whole-word, or syllabic, or phonemic analysis and storage). It is possible that different factors play different roles at varying stages of the development of written language comprehension, and that different children experience difficulty at the word analysis or message unit stage, or both. Studies that have come up with the finding that the perception and production of language by good and poor readers is commensurate have not really carefully probed this question. Regardless of dialect difference or language difference, children at some stage of development begin to understand first conjoined and then embedded sentences. As part of a recent study, children who were experiencing difficulty in reading were asked to decode conjoined ("The boy hit the girl and ran away") and embedded sentences ("The boy who hit the girl ran away"). At an age far beyond that at which children have been normally found to understand the relations in both types of sentences, these children still experienced difficulty in understanding embedded sentences.*

Throughout this discussion it has been assumed that the phonological representations of children with reading problems do not differ in any marked way from the phonological representations of other children in their linguistic community who read well. The difficulty thus far seems to be in the transfer and mapping of information from visual representation to the speech code.

There is still another group of children who clearly evidence differences in their phonological representations at either the perceptual or productive level, or both. Some of these children have by the time they reach first grade apparently resolved this difficulty. Others continue to show marked differences in language development well into the school years. These children may be called aphasic, since, although there is no hard evidence of neurological abnormality, there are apparently "'soft signs." In addition, they have no difficulty in peripheral visual and auditory processing and usually are within the normal range on nonverbal tests of intelligence.

We have carried out some studies (Menyuk & Looney 1972a, 1972b) of the language processing of these children at ages of approximately four to ten years and concluded that their primary difficulty was one of short-

*Personal communication—Nathalie Badian (doctoral dissertation).

term memory for language sequences. They could accurately repeat sentences of varying structure if sentence length was limited to three items. If this length was exceeded, sentences were recoded into more immature forms, but meaning was preserved. Thus, "He didn't go to school," might be recoded into "He no do go school." Both recodings are examples of how younger children might produce these utterances, but the latter is more advanced than the former. In both instances of recoding, the semantic intent of the utterance (negation and relations) is preserved. With these children, in an examination of their phonological recoding, it was also found that there were two subgroups. One group of children recoded phonological representations in a manner similar to that of younger children (/t/ for /s/, /f/ for /O/, etc.) whereas others displayed unique phonological rules and segments (/x/ for all strident sounds in initial position and ϕ in final position, etc.). A significant correlation was found between number of errors in sentence recoding and number of errors in phonological recoding. It was also found that morphological markers were almost never preserved ("bees" becomes "bee," "played" becomes "play," etc.), whereas, final stridents and clusters were preserved in some way if they were within the word stem ("nose" becomes "nosh"). In addition to their multiple oral language problems, all of the children in the population who were of school age were experiencing difficulty in learning to read.

Most of the results described above pertain to the reproduction of language not perception. Tallal and Percy (1973, *a* and *b*) have studied the nonverbal auditory perception of these children and children developing language normally. There is a significant difference in the ability of the two groups in rapid auditory sequences that are pure tones and speech syllables. However, the performance of the aphasic children improved when time for processing increased either by increasing the stimulus duration or increasing the interstimulus interval. There was, however, a limit to this effect. They were still significantly inferior to their normal controls on stimulus patterns of four and five elements, despite the increased stimulus duration or interstimulus interval. It is interesting to note that in both exact sentence recoding and in memory for meaningless acoustic stimuli a sequence of three categories appears to be a comfortable limit. In sentence processing, however, unlike acoustic or syllabic processing, these children use semantic and syntactic cues to decode and re-encode messages. If these children still have enormous difficulty in segmental analysis, but appear to be able to compensate to some extent with semantic-syntactic cues, then a radically different approach to teaching them reading, which takes into account both limitations on processing time and the amount of information to be processed, seems crucial.

There is, of course, the possibility of differences among these children in speech-processing abilities. Menyuk and Looney (in preparation) compared the speech-sound categorization of these children and children who are developing language normally in an identification and reproduction task. The language-disordered children were divided into three groups by their therapists: language, language and articulation, and articulation problems. The mean age of the normal group was three years and six months and of the language-disordered group six years and three months. The task required minimal pair distinctions among members of speech sound sets. In comparing the four groups of children (articulation, language and articulation, language problems and normal) it was found that one group was quite comparable in pattern of performance to normal children, while the other two groups varied. Table 3.3 indicates those sets in which errors occurred at a frequency greater than 10% for each group.

The groups may be characterized as follows: the articulation group seems to have primarily an expressive problem, with markedly different productive phonological categorizations than normally developing children; the language and articulation group has both an expressive and receptive problem, with markedly different perceptual and productive categorizations; and the language group a problem of delayed development in both performances. That is, their perceptual and productive categorizations resemble those of much younger children. A possible prediction might then be that the articulation group will experience no particular difficulty in learning to read (that is, if subvocal articulation plays no part in learning to read) and the language group some difficulty because of the delay in establishment of phonological representations and acquisition of syntactic structures. The language and articulation group would experience the most difficulty, not only because of delay in development but also because of different language-processing strategies that require significantly greater amounts of time for resolution of stimulus characteristics and/or place constraints on the amount of information that can be processed. It should be remembered that the studies necessary to substantiate the proposed relations have not, as yet, been carried out.

One might ask why this population should be of concern to people in the field of reading? There may be a number of children who by the time they reach school age show no overt oral language disorder (the language-delayed group) but have still not yet reached the level of linguistic competence of most other children. They, indeed, might not be ready to read in a very real sense and when confronted by the task will fail. There may be other children who show some signs of a language disorder and, in addition, have difficulty in learning to read. These children may or may not be seen by a speech clinician in their schools. With these latter

Table 3.3. Sets within which errors occur at frequency greater than 10%

	Task Identification				Task Reproduction			
Groups	Artic.	L/Artic.	Lang.	Normal	Artic.	L/Artic.	Lang.	Normal
		s/f/sh			s/f/sh	s/f/sh		
		w/r/l	w/r/l	w/r/l	w/r/l	w/r/l	w/r/l	w/r/l
		b/d/g	b/d/g	b/d/g	b/d/g	b/d/g	b/d/g	b/d/g
p/t/k	p/t/k	p/t/k	p/t/k	p/t/k	p/t/k			

children both oral language and written language may suffer because of differences in the language-processing strategies of these children. In summary, there may be some children who are experiencing difficulty in learning to read because of either delay in language development *or* differences in language-processing strategies, as well as those who are experiencing difficulty for the reasons cited earlier.

SOME CONCLUSIONS AND SUGGESTIONS

The processes of speech perception and of written language comprehension appear to be inverse to each other in sequence of analysis during acquisition; speech perception proceeds from meaning to analysis whereas written language comprehension presumably proceeds from analysis to meaning, at least at the beginning stages. Furthermore, analysis of speech appears to take place at an unconscious level, in units of syllables, and phonemic analysis only takes place when required, as in the case of niminal pair distinctions in ambiguous contexts. Conscious awareness of phonemic segments is presumably required in the acquisition of written language comprehension. Successful readers appear to spend comparatively little time at this stage of development and very quickly begin to use their knowledge of superordinate structures, such as phrase and sentence, and only return to phonemic analysis of a word when their preliminary pass at the data is not verified by the meaning of the phrase or sentence. Unsuccessful readers, on the other hand, seem to spend a great deal of time at the preliminary stage, and in some instances never achieve the stage of reading for meaning.

Many possible causes have been cited to account for the differences between good and poor readers. One is language or dialect difference. However, since orthographies are neutral concerning these differences, and transformation of the written symbols to speech symbols is required in all instances, this does not seem to be a satisfactory explanation. Evidence is available that indicates that language difference per se cannot account for difficulties in reading. Speech discrimination and reading comprehension studies of these groups indicate almost no correlation between the two performances within dialect-different groups. Another suggestion is that low SES children are not ready for the phonemic analysis required and they segment speech in terms of syllabic units. Therefore, their initial exposure to written material should be organized into written syllabic-speech correspondences not letter-sound correspondences. Evidence from other studies suggests that other factors, such as meaningfulness of material to be read, and attitudes and techniques of teachers play, perhaps, the more important role in reading acquisition by these children. Within language-similar groups many causes have been cited to account for failure in reading: cognitive differences, developmental delay, differences in processing both written and speech information, difficulty in seeing relations between abstract representations and meaning, problems in visual discrimination, auditory discrimination, and blending. However, oral language competence differences are seldom cited as a possible cause, except where oral language differences are clear and extreme. The suggestion has been made here that such differences may exist at both the phonological representation level and the semantic-syntactic level which are not obvious. These differences might cause difficulties at the first stage of reading and/or the second stage, since a transfer and mapping procedures between written symbols and language is required.

It is clear that any combination of factors could account for a child's difficulty in learning to read. We have yet to discover the strategies used by successful readers. It seems entirely possible that they use a variety of reading acquisition strategies and are successful because that particular strategy (or strategies) works for them. An experimental approach, which might lead to a better understanding of successful versus unsuccessful strategies, is to carry out a prospective study. That is, observe the discrimination, categorization, sequencing, and translation behaviors of children before they have been exposed to formal teaching of reading, and then follow them through the first grade and determine which repertoire of behaviors in which settings leads to the greatest success in reading.

REFERENCES

Bower, T. 1971. The object in the world of the infant. *Scientific American* 225: 30–38.

Chall, J., Roswell, F., Alshan, L., and Bloomfield, M. 1965. Language: visual auditory and visual-motor factors in beginning reading. Paper presented at Annual Meeting of the Amer. Research Association, Chicago.

Chall, J., Roswell, F., and Blumenthal, S. H. 1963. Auditory blending ability: A factor in success in beginning reading. *The Reading Teacher*, pp. 113–18.

Chomsky, C. 1971. Invented spelling in the open classroom. Harvard Graduate School of Education.

Clay, M., and Imlach, R. 1971. Juncture, pitch and stress as reading behavior variables. *J. Verbal Learning and Verbal Behavior* 10: 133–39.

Conrad, R. 1972. "Speech and reading," in J. Kavanagh and I. Mattingly (eds.), *Language by ear and by eye*. Cambridge: M.I.T. Press, pp. 205–40.

Denner, B. 1970. Representational and syntactic competence of problem readers. *Child Develop.* 41: 881–87.

Edfeldt, A. W. 1960. *Silent speech and silent reading*. Chicago: Chicago University Press.

Eimas, P. 1974. "Linguistic processing of speech by young infants," in R. Schiefelbusch, and L. Lloyd, (eds.), *Language Perspectives*. Baltimore: University Park Press, pp. 55–74.

Ferguson, C., and D. Slobin (eds.), 1973. *Studies of child language development*. New York: Holt, Rinehart and Winston, pp. 4–167.

Garnica, O. 1973. "The development of phonemic speech perception," in T. Moore (ed.), *Cognitive development and the acquisition of language*. New York: Academic Press, pp. 215–21.

Gibson, E. 1972. "Reading for some purpose," in J. Kavanagh and I. Mattingly, *Language by ear and by eye*. Cambridge: M.I.T. Press, pp. 3–19.

Gibson, E., Pick, A., Osser, H., and Hammond M. 1962. The role of grapheme-phoneme correspondence in the perception of words. *Amer. J. Psych.* 75: 554–70.

Goodman, K. 1973. Theoretically based studies of pattern of miscues in oral reading performance. Final Report, Project No. 9–0375. Kent State University.

Goodnow, J. 1971. Matching auditory and visual series: Modality problem or translation problem. *Child Develop.* 42: 1187–1202.

Jakobson, R., and Halle, M. 1956. *Fundamentals of language*. The Hague: Mouton.

Kaplan, E. L. 1969. The role of intonation in the acquisition of language. Doctoral dissertation, Cornell University.

Kaplan, Eleanor L., and Kaplan, G. A. 1970. "The prelinguistic child," in J. Eliot (ed.), *Human development and cognitive processes*. New York: Holt, Rinehart and Winston, pp. 358–81.

Liberman, A. M., Cooper, F. S., Shankweiler, D. P., and Studdert-Kennedy, M. 1967. Perception of the speech code. *Psych. Review* 74: 431–61.

McNeill, D., and K. Lindig, 1973. The perceptual reality of phonemes, syllables, words and sentences. *J. Verbal Learning and Verbal Behavior* 12: 419–30.

Melmed, P. 1971. Black English phonology: The question of reading interference. Monogr. of the Language Behavior Research Laboratory, Univ. of California, Berkeley.

Menyuk, Paula. 1974. Early development of receptive language: From babbling to words. In R. L. Schiefelbusch and L. L. Lloyd (eds.), *Language perspectives*. Baltimore: University Park Press, pp. 213–36.

_____. 1972a. Some studies in the child's acquisition of phonology. G. Fant (ed.), Internatl. Symposium on Speech Communication Ability and Profound

Deafness. Washington, D. C.: Alexander Graham Bell Association for the Deaf, pp. 173–82.

_____. 1972*b*. *The development of speech*. Indianapolis, Indiana: Bobbs-Merrill.

_____. 1972*c*. Speech sound categorization within sets. Quarterly Progress Reports, Res. Lab. of Elec., M.I.T., No. 105, pp. 119–23.

Menyuk, P., and Looney, P. In preparation. Speech sound categorization by children with and without language disorders.

_____. 1972*a*. A problem of language disorder: Length versus structure. *J. Speech and Hearing Research* 15: 264–79.

_____. 1972*b*. Relationships among components of the grammar in language disorder. *J. Speech and Hearing Research* 15: 395–406.

Morse, Phillip. 1974. "Infant speech: A preliminary model," in R. Schiefelbusch and L. Lloyd, (eds.), *Language perspectives*. Baltimore: University Park Press, pp. 19–54.

Pick, H., and Pick, A. 1970. "Sensory and perceptual development," in P. Mussen (ed.), *Manual of child psychology*. New York: John Wiley and Sons, pp. 773–848.

Piestrup, A. 1973. Black dialect interference and accommodation of reading instruction in first grade. Monogr. of the Language Behavior Research Laboratory, University of Calif., Berkeley.

Rozin, P., Poritsky, S., and Sotsky, R. 1971. American children with reading problems can easily learn to read English represented by Chinese characters. *Science* 171: 1214–67.

Savin, H. 1972. "What the child knows about speech," in J. Kavanagh and I. Mattingly (eds.), *Language by ear and by eye*. Cambridge: M.I.T. Press, pp. 319–26.

Savin, H. B., and Bever, T. G. 1970. The non-perceptual reality of the phoneme. *J. Verbal Learning and Verbal Behavior* 9: 295–302.

Shankweiler, D., and Liberman, I. 1972. "Misreading: A search for causes," in J. Kavanagh and I. Mattingly (eds.), *Language by ear and by eye*. Cambridge: M.I.T. Press, pp. 293–318.

Shvachkin, W. Kh. 1973. Development of phonemic speech perception in early childhood. Translated in C. Ferguson and D. Slobin (eds.), *Studies of child language development*. New York: Holt, Rinehart and Winston, pp. 91–127.

Smith, F. 1971. Phonology and orthography, reading and writing. The Ontario Institute for Studies in Education.

Stevens, K. N. 1973. The potential role of property defectors in the perception of consonants. Paper presented at the Symposium on Auditory Analysis and Perception of Speech. Leningrad.

Tallal, P., and Percy, M. 1973*a*. Defects of non-verbal auditory perception in children with developmental aphasia. *Nature* 241: 468–69.

_____. 1973*b*. Developmental aphasia: Impaired rate of non-verbal processing as a function of sensory modality. *Neuropsychologia* 11: 389–98.

4

Paul Satz
Janette Friel
Fran Rudegeair

Some Predictive Antecedents of Specific Reading Disability: A Two-, Three- and Four-year Follow-up

The present chapter is addressed to a longitudinal review (years 2 and 3) and follow-up evaluation (year 4) of the predictive validity of a developmental neuropsychological test battery that was administered to an original population (N=497) of white boys at the beginning of kindergarten in 1970 in Alachua County, Florida. The children represented virtually all of the white male population (96%) enrolled in the 20 schools (14 urban, 6 rural) in 1970. In addition, the chapter is addressed to a three-year cross-validation follow-up on an additional sample of 181 white boys who were tested at the beginning of kindergarten in 1971 with the same battery to forecast reading achievement at the end of grade 2 (1974).

The purposes of this research project are twofold: (1) to test a theory (Satz & Sparrow 1970; Satz, Rardin, & Ross 1971; Satz & Van Nostrand 1973) that purports to identify the predictive antecedents (i.e., precursors) of developmental dyslexia (specific reading disability) several years before the disorder is clinically evident and (2) to evaluate the mechanism that is postulated to underlie and influence later developmental changes in this disorder.

The present chapter is addressed to the first objective (i.e., early detection) because not enough time has elapsed in the longitudinal project

Research supported in part by funds from The National Institute of Mental Health, Behavioral Sciences Research Branch (MH 19415).

(four years) in order to investigate the developmental course of this disorder after the reading disability has been diagnosed and confirmed. However, preliminary data on developmental changes within the first three years (K–G2) are reported in a recent paper (Satz, Friel, & Rudegeair 1974).

The present research springs from the need for an early and valid detection or "warning system" that could be administered before the child begins formal reading—at a time when his central nervous system may be more plastic and responsive to change and when he is less subject to the shattering effects of repeated academic failure. The need for early detection research in the field of childhood reading disorders has long been recognized, but has been marked by a paucity of well-controlled long term longitudinal studies (Critchley 1968; Money 1962; Eisenberg 1966; Gallagher & Bradley 1972; Kline 1962; Ames 1968; Satz 1973). The advantages of an early identification and remediation program are highlighted by the recent survey by Keeney and Keeney (1968). It was shown that "when the diagnosis of dyslexia was made in the first two grades of school nearly 82 percent of the students could be brought up to their normal classroom work, while only 46 percent of the dyslexic problems identified in the third grade were remediated and only 10 to 15 percent of those observed in grades five to seven could be helped when the diagnosis of learning problems was made at those grade levels" (Strag 1972, p. 52).

Experimental studies with humans and infrahumans also suggest that the child may be more responsive to environmental stimulation (e.g., remediation) during that period in which the brain is maturing and when behavior is less differentiated (Caldwell 1968). Bloom (1964) has shown that variations in the environment have their greatest quantitative effect on a characteristic (e.g., speech) at its most rapid period of change (i.e., ages 2–10) and the least effect at the least rapid period of change (i.e., ages 11–15). Infrahuman studies also suggest that organization can be strongly modified only when active processes of organization are under way and that when facilitated, they progressively inhibit attempts at reorganization (Scott 1968).

Despite the obvious advantages for an early intervention thrust, they must be based on a valid and efficient detection procedure, especially when the detection measures are applied during preschool and before formal reading instruction is commenced. Within such a prevention context, certain types of prediction errors are crucial to the utility of an "early warning" system—e.g., the false positive and negative signs. To initiate an intervention program for test-classified high-risk children in kindergarten may be fruitless if the majority of true high-risk children are missed by the tests (i.e., false negatives). Equally serious and perhaps more risky is the case where an intervention program is based on erroneously test-classified positives (high-risk) who in three years would have become average to superior readers without remediation (i.e., false positives). These prediction errors can occur with tests, despite an apparent demonstration of validity via more simplified descriptive univariate tests of significance (e.g., t-test, Chi-square). In other words, the experimental validation of an early detection battery must incorporate a multivariate design in which multiple measurements are made on the same subjects over time with sufficient temporal separation between the initial test probe (e.g., kindergarten) and the criterion reading assessment in later years (e.g., grades 1–3). This type of design should utilize a longitudinal framework based preferably on a total population rather than smaller sample of children to offset the potential attrition effects over time and to provide more reliable base–rate estimates of reading disability in the designated population. Further, the selection of a more homogeneous population (e.g., white boys) provides an opportunity to obtain a higher at-risk group for later reading disability (i.e., dyslexia) without confounding sex, race, or cultural variables (Bentzen 1963; Satz 1973). A final methodological requirement, essential to the evaluation of an early detection battery, concerns the use of a separate group of children upon which to cross-validate the predictive validity of the tests administered to the standardization population—and for the same interval of time between the initial probe and the reading criterion assessment.

Failure to incorporate the preceding methodological factors into an early detection study would surely limit if not invalidate the results. A review of the current early detection literature reveals an alarming disregard of these problems and a scathing indictment of the area (Gallagher & Bradley 1972).

An equally serious problem in the early detection literature concerns the lack of a theoretical framework in which to conceptualize the nature of the disorder—namely, dyslexia—and its antecedent precursors. Without a testable theory one is bound to be restricted in the selection of a test battery that purports to identify the potentially high-risk child. Although a theory represents a framework in which to organize diverse sets of data—often seemingly unrelated—it's ultimate validation must rest on empirical verification over time. In the present context, a theory that postulates the precursors of developmental dyslexia before the child begins formal reading can only be evaluated empirically within a longitudinal framework. Further, if support for the theory can be replicated and cross-validated in later years, then information is available for application (i.e., early intervention) and for further understanding of this complex disorder of childhood (i.e., etiology and mechanism).

The preceding theoretical rationale reflects some of the basic assumptions that underlie all behavioral research (Lindgren & Bryne 1971, pp. 18-19):

1. All behavior is caused—that is, it is determined by and is the necessary consequence of antecedent events.

2. The causes of behavior are multiple.

3. The causal factors leading to the variance in the behavior being studied must be identified, if valid principles or generalizations are to be developed.

4. The principles or generalizations that govern causal factors or account for variations in behavior are simpler than the original data on which they are based.

5. The test of whether principles or generalizations are valid is whether they can be used to predict behavior.

Theory

The theory that provides the methodological and conceptual framework for the current longitudinal research has been discussed in previous papers (Satz & Sparrow 1970; Satz, Rardin, & Ross 1971; Satz & Van Nostrand 1973). Briefly, it postulates that developmental dyslexia reflects a lag in the maturation of the brain, which delays differentially those skills that are in primary ascendancy at different chronological ages. Consequently, those skills that during childhood develop ontogenetically earlier (e.g., visual-perceptual and cross-modal sensory integration) are more likely to be delayed in younger children who are maturationally immature. Conversely, those skills that during childhood have a later or slower rate of development (e.g., language and formal operations) are more likely to be delayed in older children who are maturationally immature.

The theory is compatible with those developmental positions that postulate that the child goes through consecutive stages of thought during development, each of which incorporates the processes of the preceding stage into a more complex and hierarchically integrated form of adaptation (Hunt 1961; Piaget 1926; Bruner 1968). Thus, it is predicted that those children, during preschool, who are delayed developmentally in skills that are in primary ascendancy at this stage, will eventually fail in acquiring reading proficiency. It is predicted, however, that these children will eventually catch up on these earlier developing skills, but will then lag on those more cognitive-linguistic skills that have a slower and later ontogenetic development (Thurstone 1955; Bloom 1964). In other words, the theory predicts that the nature of the disorder will vary as a function of the chronological age of the child.

More specifically, the lag in brain maturation is postulated to delay the acquisition of those developmental skills that have been shown to be crucial to the early phases of reading—namely, learning to differentiate graphic symbols (Gibson 1968) or the perceptual discrimination of letters

(Luria 1966). Both authors recognize an orderly and developmental sequence in which the early phases of reading are characterized by processes of perceptual discrimination and analysis. In this early phase the child must discriminate the distinctive features of letters (e.g., break vs. close, line vs. curve, rotation and reversal) before he can proceed to later phases that require more complex phonetic and linguistic analysis. Smith (1971) also recognizes the importance of learning the distinctive features of written language in the beginning phases of reading, but cautions that fixation at this level will retard the syntactic process of fluent reading.

The theory, in summary, conceptualizes developmental dyslexia as more than a reading disorder per se. That is, the disorder is explained as a delay in those crucial early sensori-perceptual and later conceptual-linguistic skills that are are intrinsic to the acquisition of reading and that are triggered by a lag in the maturation of the cerebral cortex. (The lag mechanism, being unobservable at the present time, is treated as a hypothetical construct.) In other words, dyslexia (specific reading disability) is seen as a disorder in central processing, the nature of which varies with the chronological age of the child. This delay in central processing is not meant to imply damage, loss of function, or impairment. Such terms are more compatible with a disease model, which often implies a static developmental-acquisition course. With respect to early detection of high-risk children; the theory predicts that delays in those developmental skills that are in primary ascendancy during preschool (i.e., kindergarten) are more likely to forecast later problems in reading by grades 2 and 3.

Current Objectives

The following section is divided into two parts, the first of which reviews the second- and third-year predictive follow-up of those children (N=497) who were tested at the beginning of kindergarten in Alachua County (1970) and for whom independent criterion reading measures were obtained at the end of grade 1 (1972) and grade 2 (1973). The results of these two follow-up studies are reported elsewhere in detail (Satz & Friel 1974; Satz, Friel, & Goebel, in press).[1] The second part of this section is addressed briefly to two recent unpublished studies: the first subpart concerns the fourth year predictive follow-up of this original population of boys (N=497) for whom independent reading measures were obtained at the end of grade 3 (1974); the second subpart concerns a three-year cross-validation of the weights derived from the standardization population (1970, N=497) to an additional sample of 181 white boys who were tested at the beginning of kindergarten (1971) with the same battery to forecast reading achievement at the end of grade 2 (1974).

REVIEW STUDIES (Part I)

Second-Year Follow-up (1970–1972)[2]

During the spring term of 1972 (grade 1) independent reading measures were obtained for 95% of the boys who were tested at the beginning of kindergarten in 1970 (N=473). This figure represents an attrition rate of only 5% during the two-year interval. The reading measure, which was completed by the individual classroom teachers (within and outside Alachua County), was adapted from the standard grade report for grades 1–3 of Alachua County, Florida. On this basis, children were classified into four dichotomous reading groups, which can be seen in the column totals of Table 4.1: *Severe* (N=18), *Mild* (N=55), *Average* (N=339), and *Superior* (N=61). These frequencies indicate a 15% incidence of reading disability at the end of grade 1 (73/473), with an incidence of only 4% in the *Severe* group (18/473). These incidence figures, which were based on preliminary reading assessment in our population (grade 1, 1971), were later shown to be premature when assessed at the ends of grades 2 and 3 (see following sections).

Despite the tentative nature of this reading measure, the developmental tests given in 1970 (n=19) correctly predicted 84.4% of the children into four discrete reading groups (Satz & Friel 1974). These results, based on a multiple discriminant function analysis (4 group), can be visualized in Table 4.1 by comparing the test predictions ($+$, $-$) in the rows (1970) against the criterion outcomes (n=4) in the columns (1972). For valid positives the tests correctly predicted all of the 18 *Severe* cases (V_p=100%) and 39 of the 55 *Mild* cases (V_p=71%). For valid negatives, the tests correctly predicted 284 of the 339 *Average* readers (V_n=84%) and 58 of the 61 *Superior* readers (V_n=95%). In other words, the predictive accuracy was largely confined to the extreme reading groups, with overlap error largely confined to the *Mildly Disabled* and *Average* reading groups. In terms of overall hit-rate, the tests correctly predicted 399 (18 + 39 + 284 + 58) of the 473 Ss or 84.4% of the standardization population.[3]

Predictive Ranking of Tests

A stepwise regression analysis was then computed to determine the ranking of the predictor variables in terms of their criterion discrimination. Table 4.2 presents the ranking of the most accurate variables, along with their cumulative hit frequencies and factorial loadings. Inspection of this table reveals that the *Finger Localization Test* ranked highest (76%), followed cumulatively by the *Recognition-Discrimination Test* (77%), *Day of Testing* (79%), and the *Alphabet Recitation Test* (82%). The

Table 4.1. Predictive classification of *S*s into criterion reading groups (1972)[a] based on discriminant function composite scores (1970)

Composite test scores		Criterion groups			
		Severe	*Mild*	*Average*	*Superior*
+	N	18	39	55	3
	%	(100)	(71)	(16)	(5)
−	N	0	16	284	58
	%	(0)	(29)	(84)	(95)
	T	18	55	339	61

[a]Criterion = Classroom Reading Level (end of grade 1)
(N_T = 473).

remaining variables contributed an additional increment of less than 3 percent to the total hit-rate of 84.4%. This table (Table 4.2) also shows that three of the most discriminating variables loaded on Factor I, which has previously been defined as a general measure of sensori-perceptual-motor-mnemonic ability (Satz & Friel 1973).[4] In the original factor analysis, four factors emerged (principal axis solution and orthogonal rotation to varimax criterion): *Factor I*—tests of sensori-perceptual-motor-mnemonic ability (30.7% common variance); *Factor II*—kindergarten teacher evaluations (16% common variance); *Factor III*—tests of conceptual-verbal ability (13.4% common variance); and *Factor IV*—tests of motor dominance and laterality (7.7% common variance). Factor I is felt to tap those skills that are in primary ascendancy during preschool years (i.e., kindergarten). As such, the results were felt to lend preliminary support for those developmental precursors postulated to underlie and forecast subsequent reading achievement (Satz & Van Nostrand 1973). When the means and standard deviations were examined for each of the kindergarten measures (1970) it was observed that those children destined to reading problems at the end of grade 1 (1972) were lagging behind the to-be good readers on most of the developmental tests—but particularly on the Factor I tests. In fact, on the Beery Developmental Test of Visual-Motor Integration (Factor I), the high-risk reading group (*Severe* and *Mild*) revealed almost a twelve-month lag between their chronological age (65.8 months) and performance age (54.4 months). By contrast, the low-risk reading group (*Average* and *Superior*) virtually matched their chronological and performance age on this test (66.4 months vs. 66.5 months, respectively).

Table 4.2. Discriminative ranking and cumulative classification of tests by factor loadings based on discriminant function composite score[a]

Ranked variables	Factor	Cumulative % correct
1. Finger localization	I	76.1
2. Recognition-discrimination	I	77.2
3. Day of testing		79.1
4. Alphabet recitation	I	81.6
5. Residual tests	I-IV	84.4

[a]Criterion = Classroom Reading Level (end of grade 1).

Third-Year Follow-up (1970-1973)

Despite the encouraging preliminary findings in the two-year follow-up (Satz & Friel 1974) the interval of an additional year provided an opportunity to obtain more objective and stable measures of reading achievement in this population at the end of grade 2 in 1973 (Satz, Friel, & Goebel 1975). It was also felt that the availability of more objective reading measures by grade 2 (spring) would provide more valid estimates on the incidence of reading problems in this population (white boys) and a comparison of the differential incidence of reading disability, if any, between grades 1 and 2. Furthermore, with more objective reading measures, independently assessed, it was felt that a more rigorous evaluation of the predictive validity of the kindergarten tests could be made (K–G2), including their discriminative ranking.

With this objective in mind, two different methods of reading assessment were obtained at the end of grade 2 (1973). The first method was again based on the classroom reading level which was filled out by the individual teachers both within and outside Alachua County, Florida. Reading forms were returned for 458 of the original 497 Ss, which represents 92% of the population three years later (attrition=8%). Subjects whose reading was assessed at levels 0–4 (No Readiness through Primer) were designated as the *Severely Disabled* readers. Those assigned level 5 (First Reader) comprised the *Mildly Disabled* reading group. Subjects reading at levels 6 and 7 (Second Readers) were designated as *Average* readers, and those reading above that level comprised the *Superior* reading group.

The second criterion reading measure was based on Classroom Reading Level and the Monroe's Iota Word Test. This combined reading measure afforded the advantage of incorporating both the teacher's assessment of reading, based on nearly a year's interaction with the child, and an independent, individually administered, objective reading test. Both of these measures were obtained on 419 of the original population (85%).[5] After converting the raw scores on each measure to T-scores ($\overline{X}=50$, $s=10$), the distribution was dichotomized again into four reading groups (*Severe, Mild, Average,* and *Superior*).

Criterion I Analysis

The first four-group discriminant function analysis (Program DS-CRIM) was computed on Classroom Reading Level in order to compare the predictive validity of the tests (1970) against a similar type of reading criterion at the end of grade 2 (1973). The results of this analysis can be seen in Table 4.3 by comparing the test prediction (+, -) in the rows (1970) against the criterion outcomes ($n=4$) in the columns (1973). Before discussing the predictive hits, it can be seen that the incidence of reading disability (columns) increased substantially between grades 1 and 2 (1972-73): *Severe* ($N=54$), *Mild* ($N=66$), *Average* ($N=270$), *Superior* ($N=68$). This criterion distribution reveals a 26% overall incidence of reading disability [(54+66)/458] and an incidence of 12% in the *Severe* group (54/458). Compared to grade 2 (1972), this represents a three-fold increase in the frequency of *Severe* cases (1973).

To further assess the validity of this criterion measure (i.e., Classroom Reading Level), scores on the Gates–MacGinitie, which was administered to the *total* population of children in grade 2 (spring) in Alachua County, were averaged for each of the reading groups. Vocabulary recognition scores on this test were compatible with the results of Classroom Reading Level [*Severe* (-12.3 mos.), *Mild* (-6.5 mos.), *Average* (+7.9 mos.), and *Superior* (+18.8 mos.)]. In other words, the *Severe* group was well over a full grade level behind in reading (where academic year=10 mos.). In contrast, the *Superior* group was almost two years ahead in terms of grade level and month of testing. Moreover, the *Mild* group was only six months behind grade level, whereas the *Average* reading group was approximately eight months ahead.

Table 4.3 also reveals the predictive hits. For valid positives, the tests correctly predicted 48 of the 54 *Severe* cases, ($V_p=89\%$) and 47 of the 66 *Mild* cases ($V_p=71\%$). For valid negatives, the tests correctly predicted 196 of the 270 *Average* readers ($V_n=73\%$) and 64 of the 68 *Superior* readers ($V_n=94\%$). Once again, the predictive accuracy of the tests was largely confined to the extreme reading groups, with overlap error largely confined to the *Mildly Disabled* and *Average* reading groups. In terms of overall hit-rate, the tests correctly predicted 355 (48 + 47 + 196 + 64) of the 458 Ss or 78% of the population.

Table 4.3. Predictive classification of children into criterion reading groups (1973)[a] based on discriminant function composite scores (1970)

Composite test scores[b]		Criterion groups			
		Severe	Mild	Average	Superior
+	N	48	47	74	4
	%	(89)	(71)	(27)	(6)
−	N	6	19	196	64
	%	(11)	(29)	(73)	(94)
	T	54	66	270	68

[a]Criterion = Classroom Reading Level (N_T = 458).
[b]Program = DSCRIM, Multiple Discriminant Analysis (4 group predictions collapsed), prior probabilities set equal.

Predictive Ranking of Tests

A stepwise regression analysis was then computed to determine the ranking of the predictor variables in terms of their criterion discrimination. Table 4.4 presents the ranking of the most accurate variables, along with their cumulative hit frequencies and factorial loadings. Inspection of this table reveals that the *Finger Localization Test* ranked highest (71%), followed cumulatively by the *Alphabet Recitation Test* (76%), *Recognition-Discrimination Test* (77%), and *Day-of-Testing* (77%). The remaining tests contributed an additional increment of less than 1% to the total hit-rate of 78%. This table (Table 4.4) again shows the same four variables that ranked highest in the two-year follow-up (grade 1, 1972), three of which, in both studies, loaded on Factor I (Table 4.2). This finding again strengthens the validity of sensori-perceptual-motor-mnemonic abilities in forecasting subsequent reading achievement levels.

Criterion II Analysis

This analysis was based on the predictive accuracy of the tests ($n=19$) given at the beginning of kindergarten (1970) to the combined criterion of Classroom Reading Level plus IOTA Word Recognition at the end of grade 2 (1973). These results can be seen in Table 4.5 by comparing the test predictions (+, −) in the rows (1970) against the criterion outcomes ($n=4$) in the columns (1973). First, the criterion outcomes in the columns revealed an even higher incidence of reading disability: *Severe* ($N=67$), *Mild* ($N=77$), *Average* ($N=214$), and *Superior* ($N=61$). Although based on a smaller number of Ss, this criterion assessment revealed a 34%

Table 4.4. Discriminative ranking and cumulative classification of tests by factor loading based on stepwise discriminant function composite scores[a,b]

Ranked variables	Factor	Cumulative % correct
1. Finger localization	I	70.5
2. Alphabet recitation	I	75.5
3. Recognition-discrimination	I	77.3
4. Day of testing		76.9
5. Residual tests	I-IV	77.7

[a]Criterion = Classroom Reading Level.
[b]Program = BMD07M, Stepwise Discriminant Analysis (4 group), prior probabilities set equal.

overall incidence of reading disability [(67 + 77)/419] and an incidence of 16% in the *Severe* group (67/419)—which is four times higher than was observed at the end of grade 1 (1972).[6]

The validity of this combined reading criterion was further assessed by computing the mean scores of the Gates–MacGinitie for each of the four reading groups. Vocabulary recognition scores on the Gates were in essential agreement with the reading groups based on Classroom Reading Level and the IOTA [*Severe* (–12.1 mos.), *Mild* (–10.7 mos.), *Average* (+3.3 mos.), and *Superior* (+16.3 mos.)]. In other words, the *Severe* group was over a full grade level behind in reading, and the *Superior* group was over a year and a half ahead in terms of grade level and month of testing. Moreover, the *Average* reading group was essentially at grade level.

The predictive hits can also be seen in Table 4.5. For valid positives, the tests correctly predicted 61 of the 67 *Severe* cases (V_p=91%) and 51 of the 77 *Mild* cases (V_p=66%). For valid negatives, the tests correctly predicted 146 of the 214 *Average* readers (V_n=68%) and 59 of the 61 *Superior* readers (V_n=97%). Once again, the total hits (61 + 51 + 146 + 59 = 317/419 or 76%) were largely confined to the extreme reading groups.

For purposes of brevity, the stepwise regression analysis also revealed the same discriminative ranking of tests that was found in the second- and third-year follow-up studies using Classroom Reading Level as the criterion. The *Finger Localization Test* ranked highest, followed cumulatively by the *Alphabet Recitation Test, Recognition-Discrimination Test*, and *Day-of-Testing*. Three of these four variables each loaded significantly ($r \geqslant .37$) on Factor I.

Table 4.5. Predictive classification of children into criterion reading groups (1973)[a] based on discriminant function composite scores (1970)

Composite test scores[b]		*Criterion groups*			
		Severe	*Mild*	*Average*	*Superior*
+	N	61	51	68	2
	%	(91)	(66)	(32)	(3)
−	N	6	26	146	59
	%	(9)	(34)	(68)	(97)
	T	67	77	214	61

[a]Criterion = Classroom Reading Level and IOTA Word Recognition (N = 419).
[b]Program = DSCRIM, Multiple Discriminant Analysis (4 group predictions collapsed), prior probabilities set equal.

Two additional findings emerged from this third-year follow-up that merit attention for educators. First, it was found that an abbreviated sample of the nineteen tests yielded virtually the same predictive accuracy as the full battery. Selection of this abbreviated battery (seven test and one nontest variables) was based on empirical evaluation of the highest ranking tests in each of the stepwise regression analyses across the years.[7] After separate discriminant function (Program DSCRIM) and stepwise regression analyses were computed against the combined reading criterion (grade 2, 1973), it was found that eight of the tests given in 1970 detected almost all of those children destined to extremes in the reading distribution at the end of grade 2 (i.e., *Severe* and *Superior* groups). Also, the same three Factor I tests again ranked highest (*Finger Localization, Alphabet Recitation,* and *Recognition-Discrimination*). This finding, which minimizes both time and cost factors associated with test administration without sacrificing accuracy, greatly increases its applicability for educators concerned with large-scale early screening assessment.

The second finding of possible interest to educators concerned the utility of this test battery (abbreviated or standard) to provide a decisional basis upon which to initiate or withhold treatment for an individual child, based on his test scores at the beginning of kindergarten. This decisional process, which was prompted by the consistently high predictive accuracy in the extreme reading groups across years, is determined by computing the conditional probability of the differential test signs (+, −). These conditional probability values are based on the inverse probabilities of the test signs (valid and false positives and valid and false negatives) and the base rates of reading competency in this population (Meehl & Rosen 1955; Satz, Fennell, & Reilly 1970). To compute the conditional probabilities for each of the test signs, the (+) and (−) rows in Table 4.5 were subdivided (on the basis of the original four-group DSCRIM analysis) to generate four levels of test decisions [(++), (+), (−), (− −)]. Table 4.6 reveals this 4×4 contingency table in which test signs (and decisions) are represented by rows and the outcomes are represented by columns. This table thus allows the educator to determine the probability that a given child is destined to reading disability or competency in three years, given that his test scores fall in the (++), (+), (−), (− −) range. As such, it also provides him with the likelihood that intervention should be instituted or withheld.

The results of this analysis which can be seen in table 4.6, indicate that with a severe high-risk composite sign (++), the decision to *initiate treatment* would have been correct in 82% of the cases; further, this treatment decision would have included 50 of the 67 potential *Severe* cases (75%) and none of the potential *Superior* readers in the intervention program. By contrast, the decision to initiate treatment, given a less severe high-risk composite sign (+), would have been correct only 44% of the time. In other words, extension of treatment services to this group would have yielded only 11 more of the potential *Severe* cases and 33 of the potential *Mild* cases, but it would also have involved treatment for 55 children who would have not needed it (false positives). Thus, initiation of treatment for this composite test sign (+) would have resulted in treating more children who didn't need it than did.

This table also shows that the decision to withhold treatment (NT) would have been correct 77% of the time, given a mild low-risk sign (−) and 96% of the time given a very low-risk sign (− −). The only risk, given a mild low-risk sign (−) is that treatment would have been withheld for a small number of potentially *Severe* ($N=5$) and *Mild* ($N=23$) reading cases. This decision risk, however, would have been virtually eliminated by adopting a more conservative no-treatment policy based on very low-risk signs (− −).

The latter findings, in summary, illustrate the potential usefulness of a detection procedure which, while brief and economical to administer, can also generate the conditional outcome probabilities (i.e., reading level) for an individual child during kindergarten. Within this framework, educators could base their treatment strategies on a number of factors, including the incidence of severe high-risk children in the school, available resources, and the risks associated with intervention (false-positive errors) vs. nonintervention (false-negative errors). If treatment resources were limited and the number of high-risk children was large, then surely a

Table 4.6. Probability of decision risk (treatment/no treatment) associated with differential composite test score predictions to third-year reading level[a]

Composite test scores[b]		Criterion groups					
	Decision	Severe	Mild	Average	Superior	Ratio correct	P
+ +	T	50	18	15	0	68/83	.82
+	T	11	33	53	2	44/99	.44
−	NT	5	23	84	11	95/123	.77
− −	NT	1	3	62	48	110/114	.96
	Total	67	77	214	61		

[a]Criterion = Classroom Reading Level and IOTA Word Recognition (N_T = 419).
[b]Program = DSCRIM, Multiple Discriminant Analysis (4 group), prior probabilities set equal.

conservative decisional strategy should be adopted for treatment [i.e., (++) only]. With respect to the present study, this treatment strategy would have been correct for 82% of the cases; moreover, it would have detected or included 75% of the potential *Severe* cases in the treatment program and *none* of the potential *Superior* readers!

On the other hand, if multiple treatment resources were available, educators might choose to adopt a more liberal intervention policy, given the present utility table, i.e., [(++) and (+)]. While this strategy would pick up most of the potential *Severe* cases, it would also entail considerable efforts and time for many children who would not have needed such help (i.e., false positives). But then again, these latter children, through intervention, may have eventually become superior readers.

It should be apparent that the final decision to initiate treatment or not should be made by the educator who has to consider a multiplicity of factors. The utility table presented in this section merely simplifies this decisional task by generating the likelihood probabilities and risks for either decision (*T* or *NT*) in each individual case.

These outcome probabilities, while generated by the test signs and base rate incidence of reading disability in the population, are of little use to educators if the predictive validity of the tests cannot be replicated across years within *S*s or cross-validated across years on additional *S*s. The following section is addressed to this problem.

NEW STUDIES (Part II)

Fourth-Year Follow-up (1970–1974)

In view of the high predictive accuracy of the developmental tests in the second- and third-year follow-up studies (grade 1, 1972 and grade 2, 1973, respectively), the question was raised as to whether the accuracy would attenuate as the test-criterion interval increased to four years. After all, an interval of this length would seemingly increase the number of uncontrolled environmental, growth, and treatment factors that could produce changes in criterion group membership and thus lower the predictive accuracy of the tests given in 1970. In fact, by the end of grade 3 (year 4, 1974), it was learned that the vast majority of the *Severe* cases were receiving remedial help in the schools. With this knowledge it also became necessary to determine whether the incidence of reading problems decreased between the third and fourth follow-up years and if not, to determine whether the same *S*s again fell in the same criterion groups.

Classroom Reading Level was again used to assign *S*s into the four discrete reading criterion groups at the end of grade 3 (1974). These reading forms, which were independently filled out by the individual classroom teachers, were completed for 459 of the original 497 *S*s (1970). This figure represents almost 93% of the original population now residing in Florida, the United States, and abroad.[8] The obtained reading distribution can be seen in the column totals of table 4.7: *Severe* (N=55), *Mild* (N=93), *Average* (N=234), and *Superior* (N=77). This distribution reveals a 32% overall incidence of reading disability [(55 + 93)/459] and an incidence of 12% in the *Severe* group (55/459). These frequencies can be more easily visualized in figure 4.1 by comparing the longitudinal changes in the incidence of reading disability (based on Classroom Reading Level) from the end of kindergarten (1971) to the end of grade 3 (1974). Inspection of this figure reveals an *increasing* incidence of overall reading disability from grades 1–3, but with a leveling off in the *Severe* reading group between the ends of grades 2 and 3 (1973–74). In other words, the increase in overall reading disability in the last follow-up year (grades 2–3) was due to an additional increase (N=27) in the number of *Mild* reading cases. It should be kept in mind that this increasing incidence of reading problems across years has occurred despite the equally increasing intervention of the schools to provide remediation for these disabled readers (*Severe* and *Mild*).

Of particular interest are the changes in reading disability between the ends of grades 2 and 3 (1973–74). These changes can be visualized by comparing the column totals in tables 4.3 and 4.7. The totals in the *Severe* group remained essentially unchanged (grade 2, N=54; grade 2, N=55).

Table 4.7. Predictive classification of children into criterion reading groups (1974)[a] based on discriminant function composite scores (1970)

Composite test scores[b]		Criterion groups			
		Severe	Mild	Average	Superior
+	N	50	64	71	5
	%	(91)	(69)	(30)	(06)
–	N	5	29	163	72
	%	(09)	(31)	(70)	(94)
	T	55	93	234	77

[a]Criterion = Classroom Reading Level (*N*=459).
[b]Program = DSCRIM, Multiple Discriminant Analysis (4 group predictions collapsed), prior probabilities set equal.

However, there were *S* changes within groups. Of the 54 *S*s in the *Severe* group (grade 2), 38 remained in grade 3. Of the 16 *S*s who changed from the *Severe* group, 10 were reassigned to the *Mild* group in grade 3, and 6 to the *Average* reading group. Despite these changes in the *Severe* group between grades 2 and 3, there were an additional 17 *S*s who were reassigned to the *Severe* group in grade 3 from the remaining groups in grade 2 (1973). Further, 13 of these 17 *S*s came from the *Mild* group and 4 from the *Average* reading group.

Figure 4.1 also shows that there was a 6% increase in the incidence of overall reading disability between the ends of grade 2 and 3 (1973–74). This increase was due to the reassignment of 27 additional cases to the *Mild* group (grade 3), 10 of whom came from the *Severe* group (grade 2), and 17 of whom came from the *Average* reading group (grade 2).

The next question was whether this reassignment of *S*s into different criterion groups (grades 2–3), plus the uncontrolled treatment intervention in the schools, would lower the predictive accuracy of the tests given, in 1970 (*n*=19). To answer this question, a four-group discriminant function analysis (Program DSCRIM) was again computed on the test scores (1970) against the criterion reading membership (1974). These results can be seen in table 4.7 by comparing the test predictions (+, –) in the rows (1970) against the criterion outcomes in the columns (1974). For valid positives, the tests correctly predicted 50 of the 55 *Severe* cases (V_p=91%) and 64 of the 93 *Mild* cases (V_p=69%). For valid negatives, the tests correctly predicted 163 of the 234 *Average* readers (V_n=70%) and 72 of the 77 *Superior* readers (V_n=94%). Once again, the predictive accuracy of the tests was high, particularly in the more important extreme groups, despite an interval of almost four years from test probe to criterion determination. In terms of overall hit-rate, the tests correctly predicted 349 (50 + 64 + 163 + 72) of the 459 Ss or 76% of the population.[9] This hit-rate is almost identical to the results of the third-year follow-up (grade 2, 1973). Of particular importance is the fact that the tests continued to show greater accuracy for those children destined to extremes of the reading distribution in later years. It is these children that educators must identify, hopefully during primary grades, in order to institute more effective programs for future growth and development. In this context, the potentially gifted child should be given the same consideration as the

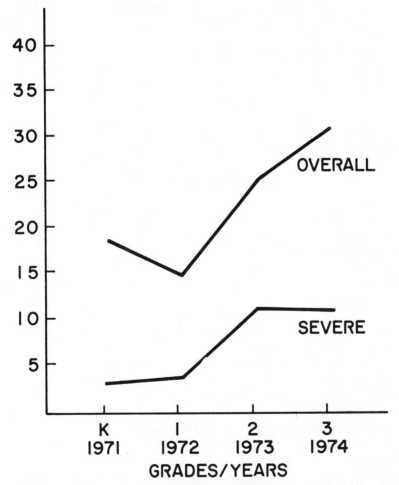

Fig. 4.1. Follow-up changes in incidence (%) overall reading disability (severe and mild) and severe reading disability in population from end of grades K-3 (1971–74).

high-risk child. To stifle creativity or achievement in a gifted child by improper placement or lack of stimulation is almost as negligent as the failure to identify and help the immature child at a critical time in his delayed development.

Predictive Ranking of Tests

A stepwise regression analysis was also computed to determine the ranking of the predictor variables in terms of their criterion discrimination. Table 4.8 presents the ranking of the most accurate variables, along with their cumulative hit frequencies and factorial loadings. Inspection of this table reveals that the *Finger Localization Test* ranked highest (70%), followed cumulatively by the *Alphabet Recitation Test* (74%), *Recognition-Discrimination Test* (77%), and *Dichotic-Listening Test* (*Total Recall*) (77%). The remaining tests contributed an additional increment of less than 2% to the total hit-rate of 78.2%.[10] This table (table 4.8) again shows that three of the same tests ranked highest in predictive discrimination across each of the follow-up years. Further, that each of these tests have loaded on Factor I. In the present study, all of the four top-ranking tests loaded on Factor I, which again buttresses the significance of this factor in forecasting subsequent reading achievement.

Cross-Validation: Third-Year Follow-up (1971–1974)

The following section summarizes the results of the final and major evaluation of the predictive test battery given at the beginning of kindergarten in 1970. Despite the high predictive accuracy that was demonstrated across each of the follow-up years (grades 1–3) for both the standard and abbreviated test batteries, the results must be interpreted as only tentative until replicated on an independent group of children with the same time interval between test probe and criterion determination. This methodological requirement must be met, notwithstanding the high predictive validity and internal consistency (predictive ranking) of the tests across follow-up years.

In the present study, it was decided to cross-validate the test weights (lambdas) derived from the third-year follow-up of the standardization population (grade 2) against a new sample of children, who were tested at the beginning of kindergarten in 1971 and whose criterion reading scores were obtained three years later at the end of grade 2 (1974).

This cross-validation sample included 181 *S*s, who represented the total population of white kindergarten boys enrolled in five of the largest elementary schools in Alachua County (based on the 1970 census). They were individually tested, under identical conditions to the standardization population in 1970, in a mobile testing laboratory with four assessment

Table 4.8. Discriminative ranking and cumulative classification of tests by factor loadings based on stepwise discriminant function composite score[a,b]

Ranked variables	Factor	Cumulative % correct
1. Finger localization	I	70.4
2. Alphabet recitation	I	74.1
3. Recognition-discrimination	I	76.5
4. Dichotic listening (Total)	I	77.0
5. Residual tests	I-IV	78.2

[a]Criterion = Classroom Reading Level.
[b]Program = BMD07M, Stepwise discriminant analysis (4 group), prior probabilities set equal.

modules. The only difference in this new sample was the fact that the children were all selected from urban schools.

This additional sample was followed for three years until they reached the end of grade 2 (1974), at which time reading assessments were made. For comparison purposes to the third-year follow-up study (standardization group), two types of reading assessment were again employed: Criterion I (Classroom Reading Level) and Criterion II (Classroom Reading Level plus IOTA Word Recognition).

Criterion I Analysis

This analysis was based on the test scores of the cross-validation group during kindergarten (1971), multiplied by the individual lambda weights derived from the standardization discriminant function analysis (grade 2), against the criterion of Classroom Reading Level assessed at the end of grade 2 for the cross-validation group (1974). Reading measures were obtained on 175 of the original 181 Ss, or 96% of the sample. The resulting distribution of reading groups can be seen in the column totals of table 4.9: *Severe* (N=18), *Mild* (N=25), *Average* (N=92), and *Superior* (N=40). This distribution reveals a 25% overall incidence of reading disability [(18 + 25/175)] and an incidence of 10.3% in the *Severe* group (18/175). These percentages are almost identical to the figures obtained with the standardization population at the end of grade 2 (1973) [reference table 4.3 and figure 4.1].

The predictive hits of the abbreviated test battery (n=8) can be seen in table 4.9. For valid positives, the tests correctly predicted 16 of the 18 *Severe* cases (V_p=89%), but only 9 of the 25 *Mild* cases (V_p=36%).

Table 4.9. Predictive classification of cross-validation sample into criterion reading groups (grade 2, 1974)[a] based on discriminant function weights of standardization population (1970–73)

Composite test scores[b]		Criterion groups			
		Severe	Mild	Average	Superior
+	N	16	9	28	3
	%	(89)	(36)	(30)	(7)
–	N	2	16	64	37
	%	(11)	(64)	(70)	(93)
	T	18	25	92	40

[a]Criterion = Classroom Reading Level (*N*=175).
[b]Abbreviated Test Battery.

However, for valid negatives, the tests correctly predicted 64 of the 92 *Average* readers (V_n=70%) and 37 of the 40 *Superior* readers (V_n=93%). These detection outcomes are virtually the same as with the standardization population for the second, third, and fourth follow-up years (grades 1–3). That is, the tests were again more predictive of the extreme groups in the reading distribution (i.e., *Severe* and *Superior*). In terms of overall hit-rate, the tests correctly predicted 126 (16 + 9 + 64 + 37) of the 175 *S*s, or 72% of the sample. This predictive accuracy, based on weights derived from a different population and with a test-criterion interval of nearly three years, lends convincing support for the intrinsic validity of the tests. In fact, the overall hit-rate was even higher when the full test battery was employed (H_T =76%); however, the full battery failed to detect as many severe high-risk children. In other words, its false-negative rate was higher than its false-positive rate.

Predictive Ranking of Tests

A stepwise regression analysis was computed on the full battery to see if the discriminative ranking of the tests remained essentially the same for this cross-validation sample of children. The results can be seen in table 4.10. The *Finger Localization Test* ranked highest (66.9%), followed cumulatively by the *Embedded Figures Test* (68.2%), the *WISC Similarities Subtest* (70.9%), and the *Finger Tapping Test* (*Total*) (71.5%). The remaining tests contributed an additional increment of less than 6% to the total hit-rate of 77.5% (using uncross-validated weights). It is interesting to note that the *Finger Localization Test* again ranked highest in terms of criterion discrimination; however, the following rankings varied from the

Table 4.10. Discriminative ranking and cumulative classification of tests
by factor loadings based on discriminant function composite score[a,b]

Ranked variables	Factor	Cumulative % correct
1. Finger localization	I	66.9
2. Embedded figures	I	68.2
3. Similarities	III	70.9
4. Finger tapping (total)	IV	71.5
5. Residual tests	I–IV	77.5

[a]Criterion = Classroom Reading Level (N_T=175).
[b]Program = BMD07M, Stepwise Discriminant Analysis (4 group), prior
probabilities set equal.

standardization studies in terms of tests and factorial loadings. Although
the two top ranking tests were again associated with Factor I, the next
two were associated with Factor III (*Similarities*) and Factor IV (*Finger
Tapping Test*). This change in discriminative ranking must reflect subtle
differences in the composition of the cross-validation group as compared
to the standardization population. One difference already mentioned was
the selection bias in favor of urban schools. A second difference might
relate to the expected discrepancy between a sample (N=181) and a
population (N=497). Regardless of the reason for this difference, it does
suggest that the differential discriminability of the tests will vary, in part,
as a function of the population or sample selected. However, if the battery
consists of at least eight tests, the overall hit-rate should not be affected.

Criterion II Analysis

This analysis was based on the test scores of the cross-validation group
during kindergarten (1971), multiplied by the individual lambda weights
derived from the standardization discriminant function analysis (grade 2),
against the *combined* criterion of Classroom Reading Level and IOTA
Word Recognition assessed at the end of grade 2 for the cross-validation
group (1974). The IOTA was individually administered to those children
who still resided in Florida and Georgia by the end of grade 2. For this
reason, criterion information was available on only 151 of the original 181
Ss (83%). Inspection of the column totals in table 4.11 reveals a 40%
overall incidence of reading disability in this sample [(25 + 36)/151] and
a 16% incidence in the *Severe* group (25/151). The higher overall
incidence in this sample may simply reflect sampling bias due to the
smaller N. However, the percentage of *Severe* cases (16%) was identical to

Table 4.11. Predictive classification of cross-validation sample into criterion reading groups (grade 2, 1974)[a] based on discriminant function weights of standardization population (1970–73)

Composite test scores[b]		Criterion groups			
		Severe	Mild	Average	Superior
+	N	19	19	16	1
	%	(76)	(53)	(27)	(3)
–	N	6	17	44	29
	%	(24)	(47)	(73)	(97)
	T	25	36	60	30

[a]Criterion = Classroom Reading Level and IOTA Word Recognition (*N*=151).
[b]Abbreviated Test Battery.

the standardization group (Grade 2) for the *combined* reading criterion (table 4.5).

The predictive hits against this additional criterion can also be seen in table 4.11. For valid positives, the tests correctly predicted 19 of the 25 *Severe* cases (V_p=76%) and 19 of the 36 *Mild* cases (V_p=53%). For valid negatives, the tests correctly predicted 44 of the 60 *Average* readers (V_n=73%) and 29 of the 30 *Superior* readers (V_n=97%). In other words, the tests correctly predicted 111 (19 + 19 + 44 + 29) of the 151 Ss or 74% of the cross-validation sample. Again, the accuracy was largely confined to the extreme groups (*Severe* and *Superior*). This hit-rate of 74%, based on the lambda weights from a different standardization group and with a test-criterion interval of nearly three years, provides additional support for the predictive validity of these kindergarten measures. In fact, the shrinkage in this cross-validation analysis was only 2% when compared to the hit-rate for the third-year standardization follow-up, using this combined criterion (table 4.5).

For purposes of brevity, the stepwise regression analysis (full battery) revealed essentially the same discriminative ranking of tests for this combined reading criterion as for Classroom Reading Level (table 4.10). The *Finger Localization Test* (Factor I) again ranked highest, followed cumulatively by the *Embedded Figures Test* (Factor I), *WISC Similarities Subtest* (Factor III), and *Socio-economic Level* (Factor II). The only change in this ranking was the substitution of *Socioeconomic Level* for the *Finger Tapping Test*. However, the discriminative ranking of tests changed somewhat between the standardization group and the cross-validation group analyses. This change may well reflect sampling differences between the two groups. Nevertheless, the *Finger Localization Test* (Factor I) retained its primary ranking across the follow-up years and groups, lending further support to the validity of this factor as a precursor to later reading disability.

CONCLUDING REMARKS

The preceding discussion has focused on the predictive accuracy of a developmental-neuropsychological test battery that was given to a total population of white boys during kindergarten (1970) in order to forecast their reading achievement in subsequent years. This was accomplished by assessing reading in this population independently at the end of grades 1, 2, and 3 (1972–74). The results, based on systematic evaluation at yearly follow-up periods, revealed that performance on these tests during kindergarten was extremely predictive of the child's reading group membership in later grades—particularly those children destined to become *Severely Disabled* or *Superior* readers. Also, it was shown that this accuracy was largely accounted for by a small number of tests that consistently ranked highest in predictive discriminability. These latter tests represented measures of sensori-perceptual-motor-mnemonic skills, which were postulated to be in rapid development during preschool years and crucial to the early phases of reading. It was also shown that these predictive tests could be applied in educational settings as detection procedures for early intervention decisions. A utility matrix was presented to illustrate this concept of statistical decision theory. Finally, it was shown that the test weights derived from the standardization population (K–G2) held up under cross-validation for a separate group of children who were followed for three years (K–G2).

These findings, in summary, lend substantial support to the validity and utility of an early detection or "warning system" that could be administered economically before the child begins formal reading—at a time when his central nervous system may be more plastic and responsive to change—and at a time when he is less subject to the shattering effects of repeated academic failure. One of the real tragedies in our educational system has been the tendency to institute the intervention program only after the reading disability has become clinically manifest, at which time secondary behavioral and psychological problems are often confounded with the underlying handicap (De Hirsch & Jansky 1966). It may be that these secondary problems serve to exacerbate if not reinforce the vicious cycle of frustration and failure for the child.

This problem of delayed intervention is probably based on multiple factors including limited diagnostic and treatment resources and, sometimes, the naively optimistic view that the slow starter will eventually catch up if left alone. The incidence changes across years in the present study should provide a sobering contrast to this view. The incidence of overall reading disability has continued to increase yearly in our longitudinal population despite the increasing intervention efforts of the schools during this same time period (reference figure 4.1). Furthermore, although the incidence of *severe* reading disability seems to have plateaued between grades 2 and 3, it has never decreased—again, despite the remedial programs for these children in the schools.

The high predictive accuracy of the test battery (standard and abbreviated) has two interesting implications concerning the nature of this disorder—namely, dyslexia. First, the fact that these kindergarten tests assessed a variety of developmental skills that were shown to forecast subsequent reading competency suggests that the disorder is the consequence of antecedent events that are present in the child as early as kindergarten—and most probably before. Second, the fact that these antecedent factors comprised nonreading skills suggests that dyslexia is more than a reading disorder per se. This latter finding is most compatible with those theories that conceptualize dyslexia as a disorder in central processing (Chalfont & Scheffelin 1969).

One instructive point to be drawn from these comments is that faulty methods of instruction in the schools cannot be singled out as the primary cause of reading failure today (Furth 1972). The results of the present study indicate that there are precursors that are reflected in the behavior of the child—at least as early as kindergarten—which forecast reading competency before formal reading instruction or remediation is commenced. This statement, however, is not meant to exclude an interaction between the child's readiness and the type of instruction involved. Certainly, faulty instruction will serve to intensify the problems of a high-risk child. This point has never been disputed.

But what are these precursors or antecedents that forecast future reading competency? In the present context, they seemed to reflect a general developmental readiness in perception, cognition, language, and memory. There was no one particularly striking function or skill area that stood out. For those children destined to become severely disabled readers in four years, their performance during kindergarten was depressed or delayed on almost all of the developmental tests—especially on the most discriminative predictors (i.e., Finger Localization, Recognition-Discrimination, Alphabet Recitation). In this respect, the precursors suggest some type of developmental unreadiness or immaturity. For example, during kindergarten assessment, this group of severely high-risk children could only recite parts of the alphabet, their visual-motor integration on the Beery was approximately ten months behind their chronological age. Similar delays in somatosensory integration, perceptual discrimination, auditory discrimination, and verbal-cognitive processing also characterized the performance of these severe high-risk children.

By contrast, those children destined to become superior readers in three or four years were advanced on almost all the developmental tests given in kindergarten. This comparison can be quickly visualized by inspection of table 4.12, which presents the means for each of the tests in the Abbreviated Battery for each of the reading groups at the end of grade 2. The potential superior readers were advanced in terms of visual-motor, perceptual, somatosensory, and language development—and they were intellectually much brighter (IQ = 113 vs. 92). In fact, those children destined to superior reading levels in four years were advanced developmentally, whether compared within Ss (to their chronological age) or between Ss (to other reading groups). In fact, table 4.12 shows that as one moved from the *Severe* group to the *Mild, Average,* and *Superior* reading groups, that overall performance increased in linear additive increments. There was no special pattern (nonlinear) that characterized any of the groups, except an increasing developmental integration in perception, cognition, language, and memory as one proceeded from the high- to the low-risk groups.

This latter finding should dispel any premature attempts to explain specific reading disability as a primary lag or defect in one particular modality or function (e.g., auditory sequencing, or memory, etc.). The problem is unfortunately not that simple, particularly when viewed within a longitudinal framework. Yet, considerable controversy continues to exist concerning the nature of the disorder—namely, dyslexia and it's etiology. All too often these terms are used interchangeably or are poorly defined. Similar problems could occur in the present study if one were to treat the developmental precursors as causal antecedent events. At best, the precursors represent phenotypic behavioral expressions of events intrinsic to the child that are probably mediated by more basic brain mechanisms. Hence, the elusive and complex nature of the problem.

At present, the concept of a developmental readiness seems to represent the most parsimonious and least pernicious way to describe these behavioral differences (precursors) that characterize children destined in later years to extremes in the reading distribution. This concept, which has long been proposed by others (De Hirsch & Jansky 1966; Critchley 1968; Money 1962) is certainly compatible with the theory proposed in this paper (Satz & Van Nostrand 1973). However, the present results do not permit a test of the mechanism that is postulated to underlie this disorder—namely, a lag in the maturation of the cerebral cortex (Satz & Van Nostrand 1973). This formulation must still be treated as a hypothetical construct, the mechanism of which is neither observable nor directly

Table 4.12. Means and standard deviations of abbreviated test battery (grade K) for reading groups (combined criterion, grade 2)

Tests	Criterion groups			
	Severe (N=67) Age=65.9[a]	Mild (N=77) Age=65.6	Average (N=214) Age=66.4	Superior (N=61) Age=67.0
1. Finger localization	26.2 (7.1)	31.1 (8.0)	35.9 (7.6)	39.5 (5.2)
2. Alphabet recitation	14.0 (8.8)	17.5 (8.5)	22.2 (6.8)	25.3 (6.9)
3. Recognition-discrimination	6.9 (2.9)	8.9 (3.0)	9.9 (2.6)	11.6 (2.0)
4. Peabody IQ	92.0 (16.5)	100.2 (12.3)	106.4 (14.9)	113.1 (12.1)
5. Beery (VMI)[b]	56.3 (7.5)	60.7 (8.1)	66.5 (9.3)	71.4 (10.8)
6. Auditory-discrimination	1.1 (.5)	1.1 (.5)	1.3 (.4)	1.5 (.3)
7. Dichotic listening (total)	57.6 (13.7)	63.0 (14.5)	68.1 (14.2)	76.4 (13.9)
8. Socio-economic status	1.7 (.4)	1.8 (.4)	1.9 (.3)	2.0 (0.0)

[a]Age in Months.
[b]Score in Months.

measurable at the present time. However, the formulation has some heuristic value in that it postulates that this lag mechanism retards the acquisition of those developmental skills that are in primary ascendancy during preschool and that are crucial to the early phases of reading. This statement, which is conceptualized in developmental-behavioral terms, is subject to more direct test and evaluation. The theory is also explicit with respect to this concept of a developmental lag. First, it states that the precursors of this disorder can best be explained in developmental terms, without recourse to terms such as damage, impairment, or dysfunction. Second, that this lag in brain maturation will delay the acquisition of the different stages of thought that unfold during the developmental process. This latter position is critical to the second objective in our longitudinal project—namely, developmental changes in this disorder over time. However, not enough time has elapsed in the project to determine the nature of these developmental changes, if any, from ages five to eleven.

The theory nevertheless states that this lag in brain maturation (genetic or otherwise) will delay the acquisition of the developmental stages in thought for the dyslexic child. In this context, the disabled reader is expected to be constantly lagging behind his normal age control. In younger years, the pattern will involve those skills that are in primary ascendancy at that age (e.g., perceptual, cross-modal integration). In later years the pattern will change as the dyslexic child eventually catches up on the earlier developing skills—now only to be lagging on those crucial later-developing cognitive language skills that unfold from the preceding stages of concrete perceptual operations. If the dyslexic child fails to catch up on these more cognitive-language skills that develop in later childhood—when the brain is reaching full maturation—then more permanent delays in language and reading skills are predicted (Satz & Van Nostrand 1973).

Evaluation of this part of the theory will not be completed until the children reach eleven years of age in 1976 (grade 5). The test of a developmental lag hypothesis, however, will be possible because of the repeat administration of the tests at three-year intervals since kindergarten (K, G2, and G5). Preliminary evaluation between grades K and G2 (Satz, Friel, & Rudegeair 1974) provided some initial support for this hypothesis of delayed acquisition. Only time will determine whether these preliminary findings are replicable. If so, they should provide additional knowledge concerning the precursors and developmental course of this disorder over time. This should bring us one step closer to the major questions of etiology and prognosis. These questions can and must be answered if we are to prevent or reduce the large number of human casualties that needlessly result when academic problems begin so early in life.

NOTES

[1]Nineteen variables derived from the kindergarten battery were utilized in these studies. A detailed description of each variable is reported elsewhere (Satz & Friel 1973). They consist of (1) *Day of Testing* (2) *Age,* (3) *Handedness*, (4) *Finger Tapping Total*, (5) *Peabody Picture Vocabulary Test*, (6) *Recognition-Discrimination*, (7) *Embedded Figures*, (8) *Verbal Fluency*, (9) *Beery Developmental Test of Visual-Motor Integration*, (10) *WISC Similarities Subtest*, (11) *Alphabet Recitation*, (12) *Right-left Discrimination*, (13) *Finger Localization*, (14) *Auditory-Discrimination,* (15) *Dichotic Listening, Right Channel Recall,* (16) *Dichotic Listening, Left Channel Recall,* (17) *Auditory-Visual Integration*, (18) *Behavioral Checklist* and (19) *Socio-economic Status.*

[2]A preliminary one-year follow-up to the end of kindergarten is reported in a separate study (Satz & Friel 1973).

[3]This hit-rate was based on a standard computer generated cutting line (Satz 1966); however, the hit-rate increased to 91% when an adjusted cutting line was employed (reference Satz & Friel 1974).

[4]*Day of Testing*, which also loaded on Factor I, was excluded as a factorial variable because of its low correlation coefficient with this factor ($r \leqslant .37$).

[5]Fewer *S*s were included in this combined criterion than the Classroom Reading Level group, since the IOTA was administered to only those *S*s who still resided in Florida or Georgia at the end of grade 2, whereas, the teacher questionnaires were distributed throughout the United States and abroad.

[6]A 34% overall incidence of reading disability, using this more refined composite reading criterion, is approximately what would be expected for a male population. If the national incidence is approximately 20%, with a sex ratio of 4:1 in favor of boys, then the incidence should increase to 32% in a male population.

[7]The abbreviated battery comprised the following: (1) *Peabody Picture Vocabulary Test*, (2) *Recognition-Discrimination Test*, (3) *Beery Developmental Test of Visual-Motor Integration*, (4) *Alphabet Recitation Test*, (5) *Finger Localization Test*, (6) *Auditory-Discrimination Test*, (7) *Dichotic Listening Test (Total R and L Recall)*, and (8) *Socioeconomic Status*.

[8]This figure (*N*=459) is almost identical to the available population in the third-year follow-up (*N*=458).

[9]Similar discrimination between groups was observed for the abbreviated battery (*N*=8) in this four-year follow-up.

[10]The slight discrepancy in total hit-rate between DSCRIM and BMDO7M is believed to reflect computational differences between the two programs.

REFERENCES

Ames, L. B. 1968. "Learning disabilities: The developmental point of view," in H. R. Myklebust (ed.), *Progress in learning disabilities: Volume one.* New York and London: Grune and Stratton, pp. 39–74.

Bentzen, F. 1963. Sex ratios in learning and behavior disorders. *American Journal of Orthopsychiatry* 23: 92–98.

Bloom, S. 1964. *Stability and change in human characteristics.* New York: John Wiley and Sons.

Bruner, J. S. 1968. "The course of cognitive growth," in N. S. Endler, L. R. Boulter, and H. Osser (eds.), *Contemporary issues in developmental psychology.* New York: Holt, Rinehart and Winston, pp. 476–94.

Caldwell, B. M. 1968. "The usefulness of the critical period hypothesis in the study of filiative behavior," in N. S. Endler, L. R. Boulter, and H. Osser (eds.), *Contemporary issues in developmental psychology.* New York: Holt, Rinehart and Winston, pp. 213–23.

Chalfont, J. C., and Scheffelin, M. A. 1969. Central processing dysfunctions in children: A review of research. NINDS Monograph No. 9, U.S. Department of Health, Education and Welfare.

Critchley, M. 1968. Dysgraphia and other anomalies of written speech. *Pediatric Clinics of North America* 15: 639–50.

De Hirsch, K., Jansky, J., and Langford, W. S. 1966. *Predicting reading failure.* New York: Harper and Row.

Eisenberg, L. 1966. "The epidemiology of reading retardation and a program for preventive intervention," in J. Money (ed.), *The disabled reader: Education of the dyslexic child.* Baltimore: The Johns Hopkins Press, pp. 3–20.

Furth, H. G. 1972. Symposium on current operation, remediation and evaluation: Dallas, Texas. Meeting report. *Journal of Learning Disabilities* 5: 650–52.

Gallagher, J. J., and Bradley, R. H. 1972. "Early identification of developmental difficulties," in I. J. Gordon (ed.), *Early childhood education.* Chicago: University of Chicago Press, pp. 291–303.

Gibson, E. J. 1968. "Learning to read," in N. S. Endler, L. R. Boulter, and H. Osser (eds.), *Contemporary issues in developmental psychology.* New York: Holt, Rinehart and Winston, pp. 291–303.

Hunt, J. McV. 1961. *Intelligence and experience.* New York: Ronald Press.

Keeney, A. H., and Keeney, V. T. 1968. *Dyslexia: diagnosis and treatment of reading disorders.* St. Louis: C. V. Mosby Co.

Kline, C. L. 1972. The adolescents with learning problems: How long must they wait? *Journal of Learning Disabilities* 5: 262–71.

Lindgren, H. C., and Bryne, D. 1971. *Psychology: An introduction to a behavorial Science.* New York: John Wiley and Sons.

Luria, A. R. 1966. *Higher cortical functions in man.* New York: Basic Books.

Meehl, P. E., and Rosen, A. 1955. Antecedent probability and the efficiency of psychometric signs, patterns or cutting scores. *Psychological Bulletin* 52: 194–216.

Money, J. (ed.). 1962. *Reading disability: Progress and research needs in dyslexia.* Baltimore: Johns Hopkins Press.

Piaget, J. 1926. *Judgment and reasoning in the child.* New York: Harcourt and Brace.

Satz, P. 1966. A block rotation test: The application of multivariate and decision theory analysis for the prediction of organic brain disorder. *Psychological Monographs* 80: (21, whole no. 629).

——. 1973. Left-handedness and early brain insult: An explanation. *Neuropsychologia* 11: 115–17.

Satz, P., Fennell, E., and Reilly, C. 1970. The predictive validity of six neurodiagnostic tests: A decision theory analysis. *Journal of Consulting and Clinical Psychology* 34: 375–81.

Satz, P. and Friel, J. 1973. "Some predictive antecedents of specific learning disability: A preliminary one-year follow-up," in P. Satz and J. Ross (eds.), *The disabled learner: Early detection and intervention.* Rotterdam, The Netherlands: Rotterdam University Press, pp. 79–98.

——. 1974. Some predictive antecedents of specific reading disability: A preliminary two-year follow-up. *Journal of Learning Disabilities* 7: 437–44.

Satz, P., Friel, J., and Goebel, R. 1975. Some predictive antecedents of specific reading disability: A three-year follow-up. *Bulletin of the Orton Society* 25: 91–110.

Satz, P., Friel, J., and Rudegeair, F. 1974. "Differential changes in the acquisition of developmental skills in children who later became dyslexic: A three-year follow-up," in D. Stein, J. Rosen, and N. Butters (eds.), *Plasticity and recovery of function in the central nervous system.* New York: Academic Press, pp. 175–202.

Satz, P., Rardin, D., and Ross, J. 1971. An evaluation of a theory of specific developmental dyslexia. *Child development* 42: 2009–21.

Satz, P., and Sparrow, S. 1970. "Specific developmental dyslexia: A theoretical formulation," in D. J. Bakker and P. Satz (eds.), *Specific reading disability: Advances in theory and method.* Rotterdam, The Netherlands: Rotterdam University Press, pp. 17–39.

Satz, P., and Van Nostrand, G. K. 1973. "Developmental dyslexia: An evaluation of a theory," in P. Satz and J. Ross (eds.), *The disabled learner: Early detection and intervention.* Rotterdam, The Netherlands: Rotterdam University Press, pp. 121–48.

Scott, J. P. 1968. "Critical periods in behavioral development," in N. S. Endler, L. R. Boulter, and H. Osser (eds.), *Contemporary issues in developmental psychology.* New York: Holt, Rinehart and Winston, pp. 213–23.

Smith, F. 1971. *Understanding Reading: A psycholinguistic analysis of reading and learning to read.* New York: Holt, Rinehart and Winston, pp. 15–27.

Strag, G. A. 1972. Comparative behavioral ratings of parents with severe mentally retarded, special learning disability, and normal children. *Journal of Learning Disabilities* 5: 52–56.

Thurstone, L. L. 1955. *The differential growth of mental abilities.* Chapel Hill, North Carolina: University of North Carolina Psychometric Laboratory, #14.

5

Marcel Kinsbourne

Looking and Listening Strategies and Beginning Reading

INTRODUCTION: THE READING PROCESSES

Reading is a sophisticated and widely disseminated human skill. Its acquisition and its fluent exercise must be considered separately. How fluent readers operate is a question for students of human information processing (Simon 1967, 1971; Venezky & Calfee 1970). Existing experimental findings that give insight into adults' fluent reading are incomplete but not negligible (e.g., Posner, Lewis, & Conrad 1971). But insight into reading acquisition is trivial in comparison. How children learn to read is a question for developmental psychologists. We have some idea about how reading can be taught (Bond & Dykstra 1967; Chall 1967), but practically no certainty about how it is learned (Singer & Ruddell 1970; Williams 1971). For this reason, the present study of reading acquisition cannot be based on existing models, but must construct its own model on the basis of common-sense notions.

We consider the acquisition of each of the mental operations that are necessary for beginning reading as marking a stage in one of a set of parallel developmental sequences (Elkind, Horn & Schneider 1965). A child who is insufficiently advanced along any one of the relevant developmental sequences is not ready to read. If he has reached the requisite stage, then, if given the opportunity, he will acquire information (Chomsky 1965) and thus accumulate the data base requisite for the next level of reading instruction. This level will call for new operations, some of which are possibly related to different developmental sequences. Whether progress continues depends on the degree of development of these new operations. But further progress along the previously useful developmental sequences is not necessarily relevant. For reading, many processes must function at beyond a criterial level of efficiency. If one operation is inadequately efficient, it limits further improvement of overall reading performance. Once it matures, it ceases to be "performance limiting." In this case, efficiency greater than criterial is redundant, because once an operation ceases to limit further development of the overall reading skill it will idle, while waiting for some other operation that has now become performance-limiting to run its slower course. For instance, a reader rapidly shifts his gaze from point to point on a page of print as soon as he has comprehended the contents of each glance. Faster gaze shifts than that leave material incompletely understood and defeat the purpose of the exercise. If he is to improve his reading still more, he must first refine another skill, such as the storing of the contents of each glance, or the comprehension of the material.

Any one of the operations that interact to support beginning reading is potentially "performance limiting." That is, its unavailability could prevent a child from reading. At a given developmental stage, the same operation probably sets the ceiling on overall performance for most children. But some otherwise normal children are limited with respect to operations that are available to most of their peers. The identity of the defective operations can differ from child to child. It is operationally useless to treat "backward readers" or "dyslexics" as though these labels implied that all such children necessarily have the same limitation on performance. With any such child, the performance-limiting operation has to be identified anew. To do this we need to assess, one at a time, the efficiency of each mental operation that is necessary for beginning reading. The efficiency of the operation should be treated as a continuous variable up to a criterial performance level sufficient to allow the child to achieve the level of reading expected of him. Efficiency of an individual operation in excess of this is irrelevant; it neither explains present achievement nor predicts future achievement. If we can determine the stage a child has reached for each mental operation necessary for reading, we will be able to specify the particular processing problem that besets a particular child. We will then know in which operations he is up to expectation for his age and in which he is lagging. Then we will know at which level he should be taught and from what type of instruction he can benefit. In this way we can use his particular spectrum of competencies to the utmost.

It is clear that adverse or impoverished environments can result in failure to translate competence into performance. This underachievement can at times be corrected by normalizing the environment. But whether competence itself can be generated by external influences is not known. Many ambitious and demanding remedial educational programs assume that it can. But so far the *full use of existing competence and the generating of new competence* have been confounded, and we do not even know how to tease them apart. Our analytic approach, if successful, should at last make it possible to answer questions of this type in a rational rather than a blindly empirical manner.

COMPETENCE AND PERFORMANCE IN BEGINNING READING

The literature does not contain an experimentally validated model of beginning reading. We therefore simply looked at what is required of a beginning reader and listed the operations that seem to be involved. The outcome has face validity. If subsequent evidence shows this to have been misleading, then our conclusions may be quite wrong.

Given a model of beginning reading, it is not unduly difficult to develop appropriate tests or to collect the necessary data. The problem is to find an external reference point against which to validate the conclusions. We are attempting to measure competence, and competence alone does not guarantee performance in the classroom. There are many environmental and emotional reasons why some children underachieve. A child who reaches criterion on all our measures might nevertheless fail to read. This may be because our inventory is perhaps after all not exhaustive, and he is lacking on some relevant operation that has eluded us. Or it may be that noncognitive factors prevent him from putting his competence to use. So while we can expect to find that the reading failure of some children is consistent with failure to reach criterion on one or more of our tests, we cannot necessarily expect the converse—reading success just because of adequate test performance. The tests will underpredict reading failure. It is true that a child who falls short of one or more test criteria will be found to be an unsuccessful reader if the model is valid. But even this need only hold for achievement at the time of testing. It is not necessarily correct to predict failure on the basis of defective test scores. Hazardous as it is to use test results to account for present reading performance, it is more so still to predict, say, from the beginning of the school year to achievement at the end (let alone from preschool to school age, as attempted by De Hirsch, Jansky, & Langford 1965). The developmental psychologist works against a shifting (unpredictably ascending) baseline of mental development and brain maturation. Some children whom we judge immature at initial testing early in the school year will mature prior to the end of the year, when the standardized achievement test is given, and perform better than expected. Incorrect (false-positive) prediction of a learning failure is particularly undesirable, as one would hardly wish to hold back or otherwise complicate the education of a child who would have performed adequately had events been allowed to take their natural course. Yet if, in order to avoid this, we use a very conservative set of criteria to predict learning failure, then as a corollary we reduce our yield of correctly predicted failing children, perhaps to the point of making the whole exercise impractically inefficient. To make matters still worse, the various reading achievement tests themselves are discrepant and apt to classify children quite differently (Jerrolds, Callaway, & Gwaltney 1971). Also, the quality of instruction determines whether the child fully realizes his increasing potential. Even the correlation of reading achievement with a general psychometric measure expressed as mental age is substantially greater with skilled teaching (Gates 1937).

We have not solved this problem. Perhaps it is insoluble. It may also be the wrong question to ask. Although in the data presentation that is to follow, the predictive value of our tests is discussed, they probably should not be used quite in this way. Rather, the test should serve as an immediate guide to teachers, telling them a particular child's learning requirements.

THE MODEL AND THE TESTS

The reading process has visual, auditory, and associative components. Therefore, the analytical test battery also has visual, auditory, and associative components. In the visual mode, a distinction is drawn between simultaneous discrimination (both forms being shown at the same time) and recognition (successive discrimination, with one form only viewed at a time), and allowance is made for the fact that the reverse is not true. The three visual dimensions involved in reading—form, orientation, and sequence—are incorporated into separate tests in an order that represents a developmental sequence (for discrimination) established by our earlier work; that is, a child first becomes able to discriminate form, then orientation, and finally sequence. In each of the six tests in the visual portion of the test battery, the situation is complicated only to the extent needed to simulate beginning reading successfully. Thus, the visual displays consist of no more than three items, and they differ along the dimensions of form, orientation, and sequence to an extent that is at least as salient as are corresponding differences among letters. We use unfamiliar forms to avoid potentially misleading prior associations. Also, letters could be aversive to those children who have already experienced repeated failure in learning to read. To avoid complicating the findings by nonvisual variables, we hold the response constant right through the visual component: a simple sameness/difference judgment is called for. At each trial, the child is given

Table 5.1. Visual component

	Form	*Orientation*	*Sequence*
Discrimination (simultaneous presentation)	Items = 24	Items = 8	Items = 16
	Same = 12	Same = 4	Same = 8
Recognition (successive presentation)	Different = 12	Different = 4	Different = 8
	Singles = 4	Singles only	No singles
	Pairs = 8	No pairs	Pairs = 4
	Triads = 12	No triads	Triads = 12

knowledge of results. The auditory component aims at evaluating children's readiness to learn by the phonics method. It isolates the purely auditory aspect of phonics instruction. Children must know the words in question, at least to the point of being able to sound them out (e.g., repeat them). But this is not enough. They must, in addition, be able to break them up into their constituent phonemes, for purposes of spelling, and construct them by blending constituent phonemes, for reading. The tests therefore, begin by assessing word repetition, then evaluate the child's ability to match words, prior to a comparable exercise using a word to a phoneme. If a child can match a phoneme to a whole word, and also can hold three phonemes separately in mind at a time, he is ready to be tested on his ability to analyze and synthesize (blend) three-letter words.

The auditory part of the battery includes two tests in which the child is simply asked to repeat a pair of speech sounds (word pairs and phoneme-word pairs, respectively). In a third, he is asked to judge whether two words are the same or different. The fourth auditory test is matching a phoneme with a word in which it appears, and the fifth is repetition of a three-phoneme series. These two tests were known to be most difficult and, therefore, put last.

Children do not necessarily process letter groups in the way they process individual letters. Notoriously, they search inefficiently (Nodine & Lang 1971) and incompletely (Vurpillot 1968) and fail to take note of some letters, perhaps basing an impulsive guess on the letters they did notice. By simulating the letters of words with groups of nonsense forms, we could assess an individual child's propensity to close his search prematurely. The same incomplete search characterizes young children's listening habits (Blank 1968), and, again, the tests are designed to detect it.

Table 5.2. Auditory component

	Word-Word	Word-Phoneme	Phoneme-Phoneme-Phoneme
Repetition	Trials = 36*	Trials = 36	Different = 24
	Same = 12	Same = 12	Same = 12
	Different = 24	Different = 24	Different = 24
Matching	Trials = 36	Trials = 24	
	Same = 12	Same = 0 .	
	Different = 24	Different = 24	

*Three attempts allowed for each item.

The associative portion of the battery consists of two paired-associate learning tasks. In one, sets of shapes are drawn from the visual tests and nonsense words from the auditory tests. This simulates the whole-word method of teaching reading. In the other associative test, children first associate each single shape with a phoneme, then build up the complete three-letter word, thus simulating the phonetic approach to teaching reading. In this way, we determine the relative ease with which a given child is able to learn on the basis of these contrasting methods of reading instruction (Bond 1935; Fendrick 1935). The materials are not presented in the manner usual in verbal learning experiments, in which the full set is serially displayed time and again; instead, they are presented in a cumulative manner (Jung 1964; Kinsbourne 1970). New items are phased in one by one only after the child has securely learned the previous items. If a mistake is made, the item is repeated. If two mistakes are made, the schedule regresses to the previous step (Moore & Goldiamond 1964). The two paired-associate learning tests are too difficult for the first-graders, as might be expected from the fact that they are only beginning to be able to read. Data from these tests has not yet been analyzed. Therefore, associative skills will not be discussed in this paper.

The components of the test batteries are summarized in tables 1, 2, and 3.

The tests were set up as a miniature teaching exercise. Each test is graduated in difficulty. Whichever the type of mental operation involved, the early items within a test utilize gross differences along the dimension in question, so as to focus attention and illustrate what is required by grossly obvious instances. The sequence in which one test follows another similarly reflects a hierarchy of difficulty. Easier tests introduce the child

Table 5.3. Association component

"Whole Word" Method:

Eight pairings of three shape sequences with CVC nonsense words (central shape and
    central vowel held constant).
Total testing time = 8 minutes.

"Phonics" Method:

Eight pairings of single shapes with individual phonemes (consonants).
Total testing time = 8 minutes.

---

to concepts that will be useful to him at later, more difficult stages. This
arrangement is particularly useful for children of low socioeconomic
status, of which our sample is largely composed. We try to compensate
for these children's lack of "test-wiseness" and of competitiveness in the
test situation by incorporating a learning element rather than entirely
relying on what they can already do at the start.

Convenient as it would be to test groups at a time, we decided on
individual administration. The time involved (some forty minutes per
child for visual and auditory tests) did not seem excessive. It is difficult to
test visual recognition of shapes and repeating of words on a group basis.
Also, the group situation is less compelling of children's attention and
might permit casual responding. As the tests are intended for general use
by teachers, they were given by undergraduates and technicians trained in
this testing but not otherwise expert in test administration. For the same
reason, no attempt was made to equate sex and color of tester and child.
If the tests are not robust enough to withstand such noncorrespondence,
they would be of limited use anyway.

Two hundred seventy-five entering first-graders drawn from a low
socioeconomic level public school system were tested. A longitudinal
design seemed desirable (Rohwer 1972) and was implemented as follows.
At successive six-month intervals, randomly selected samples are retested,
so that at the fourth retest, two years after the initial sample, each child
would have been retested once. The retesting was done in conjunction
with Metropolitan reading and arithmetic achievement testing. We will
present some preliminary highlights.

THE FINDINGS

Beginning reading is decoding visual symbols into their auditory-
verbal referents. Grapheme-phoneme correspondence is the critical unit
(Gibson, Pick, Osser, & Hammond 1962). The first step in decoding is to

discriminate the visual symbols sufficiently to be able to choose correctly between members of the set of alternatives. This is done by attending to the distinctive features (Gibson, Schapiro, & Yonas 1968) that may reside in the form, orientation, or sequence of the written material. What limits children's ability to make such discriminations?

Guttman scaling showed that visual discrimination of form was easier than of orientation, and sequence discrimination was hardest (coefficient of reliability, 0.84). Contrary to certain claims (Benton 1962; Frostig 1961), Dr. Daniel Rosof and I, in a previous developmental study of visual aptitude of children aged three through seven, found that the ability to make visual discriminations of form and orientation well enough to be in a position to distinguish letters from one another reaches a ceiling early; this level of discrimination ability is available to normal children well before grade school entry. Suchman (1967) came to a similar conclusion about visual form, using an oddity paradigm to evaluate the discriminatory ability. Further training in visual discrimination will further improve children's mastery of this skill, but will not help them learn to read. For instance, using the Frostig program to train children in visual discrimination improves their ability to discriminate Frostig's stimuli, but not their ability to read (Buckland 1969; Rosen 1965). Nevertheless, on entering, first-graders were far from perfect on the present measures of discrimination skills. This is because, whereas the early study used only single items for matching, the present study included pairs and sets of three. Children who could correctly judge a single form to be "different" from another one failed to observe this difference when the two forms were included in a multi-item display. It seems that incomplete search, leading to erroneous "same" judgments, limits the ability of entering first-graders to discriminate groups of visual shapes.

In discrimination of orientation, erroneous "same" judgments are far more prevalent than erroneous "different" ones, especially for mirror-image reversed pairs. Of the errors, most were made for mirror-image reversed pairs, fewer for inversions, still fewer for inverted reversals, and fewest for rotations. In our earlier study, the identical hierarchy in error incidence held for all ages (although overall efficiency steadily improved with age). The hierarchy of salience of the various orientational distinctive features remains the same; search through that hierarchy goes further with increasing age (and among developmentally more mature children at a given age). When normal young children make orientation errors in beginning reading and writing, mirror-image reversals are by far the most prevalent (Davidson 1935).

A comparison of six- and seven-year-old children's simultaneous and successive discrimination ability for mirror image shapes (Kinsbourne, unpublished) illustrates the effect of children's task orientation of the manner in which they process information. One group of children was given a pair of square brackets ([ ]) as a set for successive discrimination, another group received the same two brackets for simultaneous discrimination (randomly to the left and right of each other), and both were trained to criterion. Not only did the "successive" group learn significantly faster but also there was subsequently better transfer from successive to simultaneous than vice versa. The results may be understood as follows. In simultaneous discrimination, subjects can mistakenly adopt hypotheses based on positional cues or on configurational cues (cf., Sutherland 1961). In the successive case, such misleading options are not available, and the child is not presented with more salient but irrelevant dimensions that can distract him from the relevant orientational cues. The learning that results is more specific and therefore more useful in transfer. Interestingly enough, Stein and Randler (1974) using similar stimuli, have recently presented evidence that location change is more salient than change in orientation for five- to seven-year-old children. Pick (1965), Pick, Pick, and Thomas (1966), Williams and Ackerman (1968), Samuels (1969), and Williams (1969) found that children taught to memorize shapes or letter groups better learn to discriminate than the children trained without a memory component. In the light of our experiment, we interpret this result as due to the greater salience of relevant visual distinctive features when stimuli are presented in isolation for memorizing than when they are presented in displays for simultaneous comparison. Applied to beginning reading instruction, we infer that children would most readily learn letters or letter groups if these are presented singly for successive comparison with displays that differ from them by single cues; in this way, attention is focused without distraction on the crucial aspect of the array, one at a time. Another way of focusing attention on orientation is by manually tracing the figure (Jeffrey 1958; Koenigsberg 1973; Stein & Mandler 1974).

The recognition test in each case followed a simultaneous discrimination test for the identical material, because failure to recognize is hard to interpret in terms of memory processes if the materials have not first been shown to be discriminable. An effort to ensure that children entered upon each recognition test on a par as regards acquaintance with the test forms was made by use of specific feedback after each discrimination trial. If two figures differed, the child was shown in which aspect of the figures the difference resides. If the two figures were identical, the child was systematically shown that this was so. Directing attention to these distinctive features helps children encode the figures in a manner stimulating subsequent remembering.

Indeed, if that is achieved, the instruction to memorize may be redundant. Appel et al. (1972) found that preschoolers and even many first-graders did no better in remembering a list if asked to memorize than if merely asked to look. The instruction to memorize is only effective over and above mere inspection if it induces subjects to inspect the material more analytically and more comprehensively. Appel et al (1972) found better recall after instruction to memorize than merely to look with fifth-graders, and the latter also showed more clustering by word category after the "memorize" instruction. We would suppose that entering first-graders have not yet developed the selective attentional skills needed to encode spontaneously just those aspects of a figure that best serve as retrieval cues for recall, or, in the present situation, other members of a recognition set. Quite possibly, the unelaborated instruction to memorize has little meaning for first-graders. However, the fact that a person's cerebral maturation is not sufficiently advanced to enable him spontaneously to hit upon an optimal strategy does not imply that such a person would be unable to put such a strategy to use if instructed in it. This is the responsibility of the teacher in the early grades. When teaching the letters, the teacher should focus attention on distinctive features (Gibson 1969). When teaching words, he should emphasize invariances in letter groupings. Neither the whole word nor the phonics method does this, and this defines the early role of linguistic approaches to teaching for those children who show themselves able to profit by them.

Guttman scaling for the three recognition tests shows recognition of orientation to be easiest, then form, then sequence (coefficient of reproduction is 0.81). This order of difficulty deviates from that established for discrimination and recognition in our earlier study. In that study, children matched a sample for orientation to one of an ensemble of either four or eight alternatives. Now Kinsbourne and Hartley (1969) have shown that preschoolers find it far easier to match for orientation one-to-one than to pick out a corresponding item from an ensemble. Children's search through a display is apt to be incomplete and the response therefore fallible. In the present study, a one-to-one match only was required in the case of orientation, whereas, some of the tests of form recognition used multiple item displays. Also, a preceding discrimination test had cued the children in to orientation (Jeffrey 1958), a normally not very salient perceptual dimension (Caldwell & Hall 1969). These are possible reasons why recognition scores were relatively higher for orientation than form. The error pattern on the orientation recognition test corresponded closely to that on the discrimination test. This suggests that those aspects of a visual display that engage attention in simultaneous comparison are the same as those that achieve priority in encoding for purposes of successive comparison. It follows that we can improve children's ability to remember orientation by teaching them what cues to look for in the initial inspection. Thus, children's main difficulty with the forms is the registering of the information into memory; with orientation it is attending to the relevant cues. The forms had many features, salient, but heavily loading memory. Orientation is a single cue, but it is not salient.

Recognition of sequence proved to be the hardest of the visual tests. Again, the error pattern resembles that of discrimination of sequence. However, the earlier study revealed that the error patterns of six-year-olds do not correspond to those of younger children. The younger children as often make errors by failing to notice difference to the left of the display as to the right, and often they judge identical sequences to be different. The six-year-olds ignore the right end of the display far more often than the left—they have picked up the left to right reading habit—and they hardly ever call identical sequences "different" (i.e., they adopt a consistent search strategy). Again, the results suggest that children who are unready for beginning reading fail in discrimination and in recognition of sequence not primarily because of inadequate processing but because their attention is not expediently distributed across the sequence. Again, the educational implications are clear. Samuels and Jeffrey (1966) taught beginning readers a vocabulary of highly discriminable words by the whole-word method. After rapid initial learning, they found that the children transferred the verbal responses to other words with the same first or last letter. There had been incomplete search through the sequences initially.

Learning to read involves the committing to memory of much detailed information about both widely applicable rules (Gibson 1970) and specific instances. The organization of memory is incompletely understood, but it is possible to sustain a distinction between access and storage processes. Once information is entered into the memory store, there is no evidence that attrition of that information is greater in poor than in good readers at a given age (Schuell & Kennel 1970). If poor readers have inferior visual memory (Anderson & Samuels 1970; Benton 1962; Lyle & Goven 1968; Money 1966; Rabinovitch 1962; Samuels & Anderson 1972), it is probably because they, like the retardates studied by Zeaman and House (1964), less efficiently use the allotted time for encoding because they waste time on irrelevant cues, which then are ineffective when the time comes to retrieve the information. The general similarity in error pattern of performance on each of the three simultaneous and the corresponding one of the three successive discrimination tests suggests that the ingredient that makes for success in discrimination and recognition is the same. If children are instructed to memorize, they may not know how to generate an efficient encoding strategy (Tenney 1973). But if well chosen materials are presented, memory might improve, even without explicit instruction to memorize.

Not only do beginning readers rely unduly upon the most salient visual cues to the detriment of other relevant information available in the printed words but also, if given the opportunity, they will base their responses upon visual dimensions that bear only incidental relationship to the words they are reading. Samuels (1968, 1970) found it easy to teach a vocabulary of words printed in different colors; but when the color cues were faded out, the responses were lost. In this case, irrelevant cues were deliberately inserted by the researcher. But often such cues appear inadvertently on the cluttered page of the reading manual, and the children are led into mistaken hypotheses. Redundant contextual and pictorial cues should be avoided (Biemiller 1970).

Among the auditory tests, Guttman scaling reveals the following sequence of relative difficulty (at a 0.9 coefficient of reliability): phoneme-word repetition, word-word repetition, word-word matching, phoneme-phoneme-phoneme repetition, and word-phoneme matching.

The repetition tasks are easier than the matching tasks. This bears out an earlier unpublished study of consonant-vowel-consonant word-pair matching (in collaboration with Dr. Steven Levy). Errors on word-pair matching were found usually to consist of spurious "same" judgments, usually due to ignoring a terminal consonant difference (Blank 1968). When subjects were asked to repeat the second word as well as match both on the same trial, performance improved. The instruction to repeat alerted children to listen to all parts of each word and, incidentally, this improved their performance on word matching. The improvement was due to the fact that terminal consonant errors now occurred at a lower rate that was equal to that of the unchanged low initial consonant error incidence. These results are particularly significant in that they show children may be helped without explicit instructions about what they should do.

Experience with word-pair matching is particularly important for word-phoneme matching, which represents the beginnings of phonemic word analysis for use in phonics. When an earlier version of this test was given to entering first-graders, in collaboration with Dr. Linda Lohr-bauer, children of low socioeconomic status behaved virtually randomly. The comparable children of the present sample, although they experienced much more difficulty on this than on any of the other four auditory tests, scored better, presumably because the preceding tests familiarized them with the test vocabulary and test structure and eased them into the mental set required by the more exacting word-phoneme matching tests.

That phoneme-word repetition would be easier than word-word repetition could be predicted from our earlier study with Levy. The two words, differing in one phoneme only, are less distinctive than the phoneme-word pair, and what chiefly contaminates children's ability to respond to speech sounds is inadequate listening rather than a limitation in decoding or encoding of individual sounds.

The children's scores on the battery of eleven tests as a whole account for no more than 20% of the variance in end-of-year Metropolitan reading achievement. This is contributed primarily by two relatively easy tests: discrimination of visual form and word-word repetition. Each is the first test administered in its modality (visual and auditory), and the results might reflect task orientation and attentiveness as much as the cognitive processes involved. However, each test taps what we regard as fundamental operation within its modality. Visual discrimination, including sets of two and three items, necessitate used systematic search through the displays to locate the difference when present. Word-pairs repeating involved on some trials the repetition of different but very similar sounding words, necessitating systematic and exhaustive listening. The ability to attend in an orderly and analytic manner may be the primary prerequisite for beginning reading. Possibly children who lack it will show their deficiency even in these simple initial tests. To assess the battery's ability to classify correctly failing and succeeding readers, we arbitrarily fix a cut-off point of a 1.5 grade-equivalent Metropolitan reading score as the upper limit of poor readers. Twenty-six of these are predicted by our tests. Of the 185 "good readers," 50 are predicted failures. With cutoff adjusted to minimize false-positive predictions, only 8% such errors occur, but then only 48% of nonreaders are correctly predicted. Four tests suffice to generate this result—the two mentioned above, plus phoneme-word repetition and recognition of orientation.

Factor analysis reveals first an auditory factor, than a visual discrimination factor, and a visual recognition factor.

An analysis of the results of the six months retests suggests which factors make for efficiency in learning to read (and why the task of prediction is so complicated). The sample happened to contain sixteen children who, by our test criteria, would be predicted to fail in reading. Eight of them, indeed, fell short of the 1.5 grade-level Metropolitan test cut-off point, but the other eight performed in what we have defined as the normal range. The two groups were found not to differ on either the visual or the auditory test components at initial testing. At the retest six months later, both groups performed much better in both modalities. The extent of improvement in the visual modality was comparable for both. In the auditory modality, however, the children who turned out to be adequate readers did much better than those who read poorly, as predicted. These findings suggest that continued improvement on visual skills did not substantially facilitate reading achievement at the first-grade level. What made the difference was the extent of improvement in the auditory set of tests.

Analyzing this further, we find that only word-word matching gave an anomalous result. The other four tests all yielded substantial differences between the eight good and the eight poor readers. Most powerful was the difference on the word-phoneme matching task. This is intelligible in the context of reading instruction using phonics. One cannot be sure that improved auditory processing was the cause and better reading was the effect. Nor is it certain that the differential improvement in auditory skills was due to differential brain maturation as opposed to some experiential difference. However, it seems at least possible that the reason eight children did better than predicted was that in the interim they experienced a maturational spurt in listening skills (these being skills that are at a premium in first grade).

Generally speaking, the results so far show that entering first-graders low in socioeconomic status often lack competence in some basic prereading skills, notably recognition of sequence and word-phoneme matching. The difficulty seems not to reside in inadequate power of information processing, but rather in the way children deploy their attention when looking or listening. Children are apt to fail to attend exhaustively to all points on a given dimension, to all dimensions when more than one is represented, and to all items of a multiple display. The appropriate teaching approach would therefore be to permit the child to focus his attention correctly by simplifying the situation to the utmost and avoiding all distractions or capacity overload until he acquires the basic concept. Then the stimulus may be complicated in stages, but always with knowledge of results and backtracking if errors creep in.

As reading skill advances, there is a shift in the nature of the cognitive processes that is crucial for improvement (Singer 1970). When a child is backward in reading, the nature of his errors represents the grade level at which he is functioning rather than his age or any relevant pathology. Learning-disordered children studied on the original visual battery (with Dr. Dan Rosof) fell into two groups: (1) those functioning at first- or second-grade level, almost all of whom failed to achieve a criterion of two standard deviations below the mean on one or more of the tests, and (2) those who, although retarded in reading for their age, were reading above second-grade level and showed little such dramatic failure on our battery. Interestingly, the subtest most successful by far in distinguishing backward orders at early-grade level from controls was retention of orientation. This is perhaps indicative of the beginning reader's difficulty in detaching his attention from more salient to less salient visual attributes. The preceding discrimination of orientation test, with concentration on each trial, serves to switch the normal child into the dimension of orientation. The perceptually immature child still fails to detach from often visual dimensions. The children picked out by this subtest were not necessarily ones that make many reversals in reading and writing. Correspondingly, Sidman and Kirk (1974) report that children with reading problems who had ceased to have a reversal tendency still had undue difficulty in delayed matching and sample by orientation. Lyle and Govan (1968) found good readers superior in visual memory as compared to poor readers, but for a given disparity in reading skill, the difference as regards memory was less among nine-year-olds than seven-year-olds. The same was true of orientation errors, i.e., a greater disparity in the seven-year-old group. Again, on the word-phoneme matching procedure (with Dr. Lohrbauer), sixteen failing readers showed a mean incidence of errors greater than that of normal children of similar socioeconomic status half way through first grade. The incidence of errors was unrelated to the children's chronological age, WISC verbal mental age, or percentage delay in Wide Range Reading Aptitude (WRRA) score. However, children with a WRRA age below 2.5 made significantly more errors. The reading grade level of a backward reader is symptomatic of the limiting factor on his performance. In the early-grade levels the limitation is in perceptual learning, but it is not so at higher-grade levels. In the hierarchy of reading-related skills (Gagné 1970), perceptual learning occupies the lowest, most basic level and is prerequisite for the rest.

USES OF THE TEST RESULTS

We have seen that the ability to predict future progress in reading on the basis of a sampling of present efficiency on a set of reading-related procedures is unavoidably limited both by false-positive and false-negative errors. False-negative errors arise from the fact that noncognitive variables affect reading acquisition, so that children who are cognitively ready may, nevertheless, fail to perform at the level expected on the basis of their competence. This tendency to underpredict is offset by a tendency to overpredict. False-positive predictions arise from children's propensity to make cognitive gains to a highly variable and unpredictable extent between test and retest. Reading-readiness tests can yield information only about the child's state of readiness at the time of testing. If the test battery is analytic, its proper use is to define the tested child's immediate learning requirements at once. For this reason, the composition of the battery should be determined not by the subsets of reading-related tasks that best predict a long-term outcome, but rather by the best available and most comprehensive inventory of components of beginning reading. No doubt some component operations cause more children trouble than do others; but individualized instruction allows appropriate treatment of the child who, because his difficulty is not that of the majority, tends to be labelled dyslexic, instead of having his particular learning requirements met by appropriate measures.

The chief purpose of prediction is as a warning device to alert educators that an ongoing program will not satisfy a particular child's learning requirements. If the testing inspires immediate appropriate adjustments of the program, then the main goal is fulfilled, and prediction becomes irrelevant. The details of the program depend on each child's pattern of reading-relevant strengths and weaknesses and should be based on these rather than on unrelated sensorimotor activities (Delacato 1959; Frostig & Home 1964; Kephart 1960, Manolakes et al. 1967). Our research does, however, permit some generalizations about its optimal form.

Groen and Atkinson (1966) point out that the reading researcher has the opportunity to specify the instructional medium, to control presentation rate and sequence, and to modify both in relation to the child's learning history (make them "response sensitive"). Our work suggests that the medium should incorporate no more than the minimal number of display units that satisfy the immediate instructional goal. Motivating devices should be clearly separated from the message, visual or auditory, that is being studied. The sequence of presentation should conform to the developmental sequence in which children normally acquire control over the cognitive operation in question, and the rate should be determined by the student's performance. Both rate and sequence are further controlled by the child's learning history; the information presented to the child should never greatly exceed the amount of information he has already mastered. This necessitates a recursive program based on responses and knowledge of results. Such a program can be implemented either by a teacher or by programmed instruction. While there is scope for ingenuity in discovering and developing strategies for reading acquisition, the outstanding strategic problem seems to be premature closure of looking and listening, in favor of decisions that will necessarily be incompletely substantiated and therefore often in error. There are, in principle, two ways in which this can happen. The child suspends attending because he has done all he is capable of; extra time would not help. Or, the child responds impulsively, rather than first picking up all the information available to him. Such a child would do better if persuaded to take more time (Kagan, Pearson, & Welch 1966). For many children, impulsive responding must first be overcome, before perceptual strategies can be developed (Odom, McIntyre, & Neale 1971).

When we account for inadequate reading readiness in terms of inadequate deployment of attention rather than deficit in basic information processing, we do not imply that this is always simply due to inexperience and could be easily swept aside by informed instruction. Cognitive development between ages five and seven puts a wide range of new operations within the child's reach (White 1965). The older child, however inexperienced, will spontaneously hit upon successful ways of deploying his attention that the younger child seems unable to generate. Continued brain maturation underlies this change, as it underlies the strengthening of basic ability to process information. Older children may behave like younger ones, if their relevant cerebral mechanisms are subject to developmental lag (Kinsbourne 1972; Lyle & Goyen 1968). Speculatively, we can even identify the change with maturation of the left cerebral hemisphere (Satz & Sparrow 1970). However, when a child fails to hit upon a strategy spontaneously, he might still be able to use it if shown how (Samuels 1969, 1972) and thus achieve his educational goal.

RELATIVE CONTRIBUTIONS OF
THE CEREBRAL HEMISPHERES

Dr. Margy Gatz and I studied the ability of children and of right-handed patients with right- and with left-cerebral-hemisphere lesions to copy geometric figures. In brief, we could identify the predominant error patterns of kindergarteners as similar to those typical of the left-sided lesion cases, while the first- and second-graders failed in ways similar to the right-side-lesioned cases. From our previously published work (Warrington, James, & Kinsbourne 1967), we know that a left-hemisphere lesion tends to make it hard for patients to analyze the model and plan an action sequence in accordance with the desired outcome (although they have no difficulty in recognizing what the model represents). Instead, the patient takes a holistic view (which the intact right hemisphere provides) and then represents what seem to him to be the essentials (e.g., open vs. closed, number of enclosed areas) in a simplified, topologically correct manner. Though verbal mediation is often involved, the left hemisphere's analytic contribution is by no means limited to verbal processes. Its contribution to beginning reading relates to attentional rather than specifically linguistic strategies. The child who is as yet unready to read may have a similar difficulty as regards the written word. He cannot pick out the distinctive features (of form, orientation, and sequence) that he needs to know in order to choose correctly from among alternative reading responses. In listening he has the same problem in analyzing a word sound into phonemes. Further instruction in first and second grade enables him to use left-hemisphere-based ability, perhaps because he learns to use verbal mediation to summarize his analysis and formulate his plan. While he as yet lacks this ability, the teacher can provide it for him by exemplifying the strategy and having him learn it by rote. Instances of "reading" by very young children (and autistic children) may be so explained. But the child will be unable to generalize from the experience. Thus, whatever his sight vocabulary, he will be deficient in new-word attack.

Once the child's left hemisphere is mature enough to allow him to analyze a word or figure, his next task is to articulate the accurately analyzed and reproduced components into a spatially well-organized whole. This ability becomes available in the course of cerebral maturation (Gottschalk, Bryden, & Rabinovitch 1964) with left-to-right directionality on each line, right-to-left and downward refixation from line to line. It may be classified as similar to processes regarded as subserved primarily by the right cerebral hemisphere and selectively unavailable to some right-cerebral-lesioned patients. The children now have to await further development of their right hemispheres. Once the spatial skills have matured to the necessary extent, the spatial organization of reading is no longer performance-limiting, and the rest of the work is truly linguistic, and again referable to the left cerebral hemisphere.

It would follow that children who have delayed left-hemisphere maturation would present in first grade, difficulty in selective looking and listening, while children with right-hemisphere immaturity would present in about third grade, with disorganized overview of the printed page. But the left hemisphere is also destined to subserve linguistic processes, and if its lag in maturation persists, the children who initially were immature in attention will in the higher grades be immature in linguistic processes. Thus, the reading difficulty will persist, although the nature of the limitation on performance would change over time.

REFERENCES

Anderson, P. H., and Samuels, S. J. 1970. Visual recognition memory, paired-associate learning, and reading achievement. Paper presented to American Education Research Association Annual Convention, Minneapolis.

Appel, L. F., Cooper, P. G., McCarrell, N., Sims-Knight, J., Yussen, S. R., and Flavell, J. H. 1972. The development of the distinction between perceiving and memorizing. *Child Development* 43: 1365-81.

Benton, A. L. 1962. "Dyslexia in relation to form perception and directional sense," in Money, J. (ed.), *Reading disability.* Baltimore: The Johns Hopkins Press.

Biemiller, A. 1970. The development of the use of graphic and contextual information as children learn to read. *Reading Research Quarterly* 6: 75-98.

Blank, M. 1968. Cognitive processes in auditory discrimination in normal and retarded readers. *Child Development* 39: 1091-1101.

Bond, G. L., and Dykstra, R. 1967. The cooperative program in first-grade reading instruction. *Reading Research Quarterly* 2: 5–142.

Brooks, L. R. 1971. The constitution of verbal descriptions to visual memory in nursery school children. *Project Report, U. S. Office of Education.*

Buckland, P. 1969. The effect of visual perception training on reading achievement in low-readiness first-grade pupils. Doctoral dissertation, University of Minnesota.

Caldwell, E. C., and Hall, V. C. 1969. The influence of concept training on letter discrimination. *Child Development* 40: 63–71.

Chall, J. 1967. *Learning to read: The great debate.* New York: McGraw–Hill.

Chomsky, N. 1965. *Aspects of the theory of syntax.* Cambridge, Mass.: M.I.T. Press.

Davidson, H. P. 1935. A study of the confusing letters B, D, P and Q. *Journal of Genetic Psychology* 47: 458–68.

DeHirsch, K., Jansky, J. J., and Langford, W. S. 1966. *Predicting reading failure: A preliminary study.* New York: Harper and Row.

Delacato, C. H. 1959. *The treatment and prevention of reading problems.* Springfield, Illinois: Charles C Thomas.

Elkind, D., Horn, J., and Schneider, G. 1965. Modified word recognition, reading achievement and perceptual de-centration. *Journal of Genetic Psychology* 107: 235–51.

Fendrick, P. 1935. *Visual characteristics of poor readers.* New York: Teachers College, Columbia University.

Frostig, M. 1961. A developmental test of visual perception for evaluating normal and neurologically handicapped children. *Perceptual and Motor Skills* 12: 383–94.

Frostig, M., and Home, D. 1964. *The Frostig program for the development of visual perception.* Chicago: Follett.

Gagné, P. M. 1970. *The conditions of learning.* New York: Holt, Rinehart, and Winston, 2nd edition.

Gates, A. J. 1937. The necessary mental age for beginning reading. *Elementary School Journal* 37: 497–508.

Gibson, E. J. 1969. *Principles of perceptual learning and development.* New York: Appleton.

_____. 1965. Learning to read. *Science* 148: 1066–72.

Gibson, E. J., Pick, A., Osser, H., and Hammond, M. 1962. The role of grapheme-phoneme correspondence in the perception of words. *American Journal of Psychology* 75: 554–70.

Gottschalk, J., Bryden, M. P., and Rabinovitch, M. S. 1964. Spatial organization of children's responses to a pictorial display. *Child Development* 35: 811–15.

Groen, G., and Atkinson, R. C. 1966. Models for optimizing the learning process. *Psychological Bulletin* 66: 309–20.

Jeffrey, W. E. 1966. Discrimination of oblique lines by children. *Journal of Comparative and Physiological Psychology* 62: 154–56.

Jerrolds, B. W., Callaway, B., and Gwaltney, A. 1971. A comparative study of the three tests of intellectual potential, three tests of reading achievement, and the discrepancy scores between potential and achievement. *Journal of Educational Research* 65: 168–72.

Jung, J. 1964. A cumulative method of paired-associate and serial learning. *Journal of Verbal Learning and Verbal Behavior* 3: 290–99.

Kegan, J., Pearson, L., Welch, L. 1966. The modifiability of an impulsive tempo. *Journal of Educational Psychology* 54: 359–65.

Kephart, N. C. 1960. *The slow learner in the classroom.* Columbus, Ohio: Merrill.

Kinsbourne, M. 1970. Optimal learning conditions for fast and slow learners. Paper presented to the American Association for Mental Retardation, Washington, D. C.

———. 1973. Minimal brain disfunctions as a neurodevelopmental lag. *Annals of the New York Academy of Sciences* 205: 268–73.

Kinsbourne, M., and Hartley, D. 1969. Distinctive feature analysis in children's perception of simple shapes. Paper presented to the Society for Research in Child Development.

Koenigsberg, R. S. 1973. An evaluation of visual versus sensorimotor methods for improving orientation of discrimination of letter reversals by preschool children. *Child Development* 44: 764–69.

Lyle, J. G., and Goyen, J. 1968. Visual recognition, developmental lag, and strephosymbolia in reading retardation. *Journal of Abnormal Psychology* 73: 25–29.

Manolakes, G., Weltman, R., Scian, M. J., and Waldo, L. 1967. *Try tasks 1, 2, and 3.* New York: Noble and Noble.

Money, J. 1966. "On learning and not learning to read," in Money, J (ed.), *The disabled reader.* Baltimore: The Johns Hopkins Press.

Nodine, C. F., and Lang, N. J. 1971. Development of visual scanning strategies for differentiating words. *Developmental Psychology* 5: 221–32.

Pick, A. D. 1965. Improvement of visual and tactual form discrimination. *Journal of Experimental Psychology* 69: 331–39.

Pick, A., Pick, H., Jr., and Thomas, M. 1966. Cross-model transfer and improvement of form discrimination. *Journal of Experimental Child Psychology* 3: 279–88.

Posner, M. I., Lewis, J. L., and Conrad, C. 1972. "Component processes in reading: A performance analysis," in Kavanagh, J. F., and Mattingly, I. G. (eds.), *Language by ear and by eye.* Cambridge, Mass.: M.I.T. Press.

Odom, R. D., McIntyre, C. W., and Neale, G. S. 1971. The influence of cognitive style on perceptual learning. *Child Development* 42: 883–89.

Rabinovitch, R. D. 1962. "Dyslexia: Psychiatric considerations," in Money, J. (ed.), *Reading disability.* Baltimore: The Johns Hopkins Press.

Rohwer, W. D., Jr. 1972. Decisive research: A means for answering fundamental questions about instruction. *Educational Researcher* 1: 5–11.

Rosen, C. I. 1965. A study of visual perception capabilities of first grade pupils and the relationship between visual perception training and reading achievement. Doctoral dissertation, University of Minnesota.

Samuels, S. J. 1968. Relationship between formal intralist similarity and the vonRestorff effect. *Journal of Educational Psychology* 59: 432–37.

———. 1970. Interaction of list length and low stimulus similarity on the vonRestorff effect. *Journal of Educational Psychology* 61: 57–58.

———. 1972. Effect of distinctive feature training on paired-associate learning. *Journal of Educational Psychology* 64: 164–70.

———. 1969. The effect of simultaneous versus successive visual discrimination training on paired associate learning. *Journal of Educational Psychology* 60: 46–48.

Samuels, S. J., and Anderson, R. H. 1973. Visual recognition memory, paired associate learning, and reading achievement. *Journal of Educational Psychology* 65: 160–67.

Samuels, S. J., and Jeffrey, W. E. 1966. Discriminability of words and letter cues used in learning to read. *Journal of Educational Psychology* 57: 337–40.

Satz, P., and Sparrow, S. 1970. "Specific developmental dyslexia; a theoretical formulation," in Bakker, D. J., and Satz, P. (eds.), *Specific reading disability.* Rotterdam, The Netherlands: University of Rotterdam Press.

Schuell, T. J., and Keppel, G. 1970. Learning ability and retention. *Journal of Educational Psychology* 61: 59–65.

Sidman, M., and Kirk, B. 1974. Letter reversals in naming, writing, and matching to sample. *Child Development* 45: 616–25.

Simon, H. A. 1967. Motivational and emotional controls of cognition. *Psychological Review* 74: 29–39.

Singer, H. 1970. "Theoretical models of reading: Implications for teaching and research," in Singer, H., and Ruddell, R. B. (eds.), *Theoretical models and processes of reading.* Newark, Delaware: International Reading Association, 147–82.

Smith, F. 1971. *Understanding reading,* New York: Holt, Rinehart, and Winston.

Stein, N. L., and Mandler, J. M. 1974. Children's recognition of reversals of geometric figures. *Child development* 45: 604–15.

Suchman, R. G. 1967. New look at young children's perceptual skills. Proceedings of the 75th Annual American Psychological Association Convention, pp. 157–58.

Sutherland, N. S. 1961. Shape discrimination by animals. *Experimental Psychological Society Monograph,* I.

Tenney, J. 1973. Development of cognitive organization in children. Doctoral dissertation, Cornell University.

Venezky, R. L., and Calfee, R. C. 1970. "The reading competency model," in Singer, H., and Ruddell, R. B. (eds.), *Theoretical models and processes of reading.* Newark, Delaware: International Reading Association, pp. 273–91.

Vurpillot, E. 1968. The development of scanning strategies and their relation to visual differentiation. *Journal of Experimental Child Psychology* 6: 632–50.

Warrington, E. K., James, M., and Kinsbourne, M. 1966. Drawing disability in relation to laterality of cerebral lesions. *Brain* 89: 53–82.

White, S. H. 1965. "Evidence for a hierarchical arrangement of learning processes," in Lipsitt, L. P., and Spiker, C. C. (eds.), *Advances in child development and behavior,* 2, New York: Academic Press.

Williams, J. P. 1969. Training kindergarten children to discriminate letterlike forms. *American Educational Research Journal* 6: 501–14.

_____. 1971. "Learning to read: A review of theories and models," in Davis, F. B. (eds.), *The literature of research in reading with emphasis on models.* New Brunswick, N.J.: The State University at Rutgers.

Williams, J. P., and Ackerman, M. 1971. Simultaneous and successive discrimination of similar letters. *Journal of Educational Psychology* 62: 132–37.

Zeaman, D., and House, B. J. 1967. "The relation of I.Q. and learning," in Gagne, P. M. (ed.), *Learning and individual differences.* Columbus, Ohio: Charles E. Merrill.

6

S. Jay Samuels

Hierarchical Subskills in the Reading Acquisition Process

> Not to know the past is to repeat history many times over.
> *"Do not fear to repeat what has been said. Men need the truth
> dinned into their ears many times and from all sides. The first
> rumor makes them prick up their ears, the second registers, and
> the third enters."*
>
> Rene Laennec
> *Professor of Medicine*
> *Collège de France*

HISTORICAL PERSPECTIVE

All of us are aware of the extent to which men have fractionated themselves. We have compartmentalized ourselves into nations and nations into political factions. The World Almanac lists eighty-one major religious bodies in the United States. Reading has not escaped this trend, and it, too, has its denominations and variegated approaches to a problem like reading instruction.

The current debate going on in educational circles as to whether reading should be introduced more or less as an holistic process, with an emphasis on meaning and comprehension, or whether it should be taught by means of a subskill approach, is not an entirely new problem. In fact, the controversy goes back some one hundred years and has raged on two continents. The alphabetic method of teaching reading, which was used almost universally in Greece and Rome and in European countries

Support for this paper was provided by the Minnesota Reading Research Project (National Institutes of Child Health and Human Development Grant #HD-06730-01), by the Center for Research in Human Learning (National Science Foundation Grant #GB-17590), and by the Research, Development, and Demonstration Center for the Handicapped (Bureau of Education for the Handicapped).

generally until well into the nineteenth century, was the most common method used in America to teach reading until about 1870.

In the alphabetic method of reading instruction as practiced in Europe and on this continent, the child learned to name letters before learning to read words. After mastering the names of letters, nonsense syllables such as ab, ib, and ob were introduced. The student first spelled each letter and then pronounced the syllable. He progressed to three-letter nonsense syllables, short words, and finally sentences; naming the letters generally preceded pronouncing the syllables or words.

In 1840 Bumstead commented that the practice of drilling the child month after month on letter names was irksome to the student and teacher. The chief criticism of the alphabet method was that spelling the word before pronouncing it interfered with comprehension. As an alternative the whole word method was suggested. During the 1840s, in our country, the controversy in reading was not over phonic versus whole-word methods but over the alphabet method versus the whole-word method. By 1870 this conflict appeared to be settled in favor of the whole-word method. This method remained dominant until Rudolf Flesch published his widely read book, *Why Johnny Can't Read* (1955). In his book Flesch argued that children who were taught by the whole-word method had difficulty because of their failure to acquire word analysis skills. Flesch's criticism led to a growing emphasis on phonics as part of the initial reading method.

This brief historical sketch of reading methods used on this continent indicates the slow pendulum swing between whole and part approaches to instruction in reading. This state of flux was found in Europe just as it was on our own continent. In trying to bring the philosophical principle of "naturalness" to the reading act, Friedrich Gedike (1754–1803), one of the most influential Prussian educators of his day, was of the opinion that a book was the logical whole with which to begin instruction. He thought that the synthetic method, that is, going from parts to the whole, was reserved for God. Man had to be content with going from the whole to its parts. Other reading methods were developed in Europe based on the principle of wholeness and naturalness, where either the sentence or the word was used as the whole unit. Instruction then proceeded from the larger to the smaller units (Mathews 1966).

From a historical stance, the controversy which has been presented is not so much a "whole" or "part" dichotomy, but a question of "when," that is, when to introduce a particular size unit. Part methods started with relatively small units (letters or words) and advanced to larger units (words, sentences or long passages) while the whole methods began with larger units and advanced to smaller units. The real controversy, then, appeared to be over the size of the unit with which to begin instruction, in essence a sequencing problem. As we shall see shortly this is similar to the controversy with regard to teaching the alphabet we are encountering today. As Venezky (1972) pointed out, "almost all methods for teaching reading include letter-sound learning somewhere in the teaching sequence, although the amount and exact placement of this training account for the central disagreement between methods."

The current debate on holistic versus a subskill approach is not a simple either/or dichotomy but one of focus, emphasis, and sequence. The problem, then, between those who advocate starting reading instruction with large meaningful units and those who advocate a subskill approach, may be overdrawn in the sense that regardless which size unit one uses for beginning reading, one must also include for instructional purposes units at the other end of the scale. This view was expressed in a recent article (Singer, Samuels, & Spiroff 1974), which stated: "While this study has demonstrated that for the purpose of teaching children to identify a word it is best to present that word in isolation . . . we also recognize the need for the child to get ample practice reading meaningful and interesting material in context so that he will develop strategies for using semantic and syntactic constraints in passages as aids in word recognition" (p. 566).

Another aspect of the problem we are encountering today relates to who determines which subskills should be taught and when they should be introduced. One school of thought suggests that when the student encounters a problem, the teacher should analyze the nature of the difficulty and remedy it. This approach places the teacher in the role of a "trouble shooter." Thus, the particular subskills that are taught are determined by the student, that is, by an analysis of the student's weaknesses, and the skills are introduced after the problem is uncovered. The other school of thought suggests certain subskills must be mastered in the reading acquisition process, and these skills can be taught routinely before the student shows signs of having a problem. Thus, with this approach, it is the teacher or curriculum expert who determines a priori which skills are to be taught and when. However, it would be fair to say that there are certain similarities between these two approaches, and in the last section of this paper, these will be discussed.

CRITICS OF SUBSKILL APPROACHES

To bring this discussion up to date, the current debate in reading is centered about the question of what is the most efficient way to get children to read well. According to one authority, the best way to get children to read well in school is to stop trying to teach them how. At the

40th Annual Claremont Reading Conference, Dr. Malcolm Douglas, professor of education at the Claremont Graduate School, expressed the viewpoint that the ability to read is not enhanced by teaching about reading. Douglas contends that devoting more time to the teaching about mechanics of letters and words may be accomplishing just the opposite of our intent. According to Douglas, reading is something that must be learned indirectly as a personal, private sort of experience. The most effective way to get children to read is to surround them with a variety of reading materials and to stimulate their thinking about ideas. Then practice will provide good readers in nearly all cases.

Children, Douglas pointed out, learn to speak and listen without formal instruction; reading is a natural outgrowth of listening and talking, he said, and it is a mystery why educators think this progressive line of development should stop with oral language and then require formal instruction with written words. He contends that learning to read develops naturally in children and grows through practice and not from direct instruction from teachers.

Douglas is not alone in condemning direct instruction in reading. Perhaps the most influential critics of fractionating reading into subskills and the sequencing of these subskills are Dr. Kenneth Goodman and Dr. Frank Smith. In order to present their views on selected topics, such as teaching reading, subskills, and sequencing, excerpts from their published writings are listed below:

Teaching reading. We have been teaching reading as a set of skills to be learned rather than as a language process to be mastered (Goodman 1972*b*, p. 506).

Universal literacy will be achieved only when we have understood enough about the reading process and its acquisition to stop interfering with learners in the name of helping them (Goodman 1972*b*, p. 505).

The teacher is not so much a source of wisdom in sound reading instruction as a guide and aid, monitoring the learner's progress, offering help when a hang-up is detected, stimulating interest in reading, helping him find relevant, worthwhile materials to read, and offering continuous encouragement (Goodman, monograph, p. 4).

Children learn to read only by reading. Therefore the only way to facilitate their learning to read is to make reading easy for them. This means continuously making critical and insightful decisions—not forcing a child to read for words when he is, or should be, reading for meaning; not forcing him to slow down when he should speed up; not requiring caution when he should be taking chances; not worrying about speech when the topic is reading; not discouraging errors (Smith 1973, p. 195).

The skill of riding a bicycle comes with riding a bicycle (Smith 1973, p. 195).

Meaning must always be the immediate as well as the ultimate goal in reading. Instruction must be comprehension centered. This must be foremost in the mind of both the teacher and the learner. Every instructional activity must be organized around a search for meaning (Goodman 1970, p. 24).

Subskills. Language systems are interdependent and hence language is indivisible. Fractionating language for instructional purposes into words and word parts destroys its essential nature (Goodman 1970, p. 25).

Language cannot be broken into pieces without changing it to a set of abstractions: sounds, letters, words (Goodman, 1972*b*, p. 507).

Such research treats language as a string of sounds, letters or words; it assumes that language is like a salami that you can slice as thin as you want, each slice still retaining the characteristics of the whole. That simply is not true. Language can't be broken into pieces without qualitatively changing it (Goodman 1972*a*, p. 1259).

And teaching kids to match letters to sounds is not related to the end which is comprehension. Teaching them to read nonsense is as bad because they can't tell when they're done, whether they've been successful since what they read makes no sense (Goodman 1972*a*, p. 1261).

One need not be able to pronounce a word to get its meaning. Most proficient readers have many words in their reading vocabularies they do not use or have not heard used orally (Goodman, monograph, p. 6).

We have ignored the language structure and in the name of teaching, fed children strings of letters or strings of words (Goodman 1972*b*, p. 506).

Phonics isn't necessary to the reading process. In fact in a proficient reader any kind of going from print to oral language to meaning is an extremely ineffective and inefficient strategy. By inefficient is meant that it's not the best way to do it and by ineffective is meant that the reader doesn't get the results that he's after (Goodman 1972*a*, p. 1261).

The question, of course, is whether in beginning stages of acquisition phonics has any function. This writer believes that excessive concern for phonics induces short circuits in reading. Instead of teaching the processing of language to get to meaning, phonics instruction teaches the processing of language to get to sounds or to get to words (Goodman 1972*a*, p. 1261).

Learning hierarchies and sequencing reading skills. There is no possible sequencing of skills in reading instruction since all systems must be used interdependently in the reading process even in the first attempts at learning to read (Goodman 1970, p. 25).

Frequently sequential skill instruction will interfere with comprehension since the learner's attention is diverted from meaning.

Programmed learning is another example of what happens with a narrow base. Programmed learning forces everything through the narrow bottleneck of highly systematic sequencing. It elevates sequencing to the primary consideration and then says, "Let's find something we can sequence" (Goodman 1972*a*, p. 1254).

The part-whole relationship is certainly distorted, perhaps destroyed in that kind of programming. Questions relating to whether, in fact, language can be learned sequentially are ignored (Goodman 1972*a*, p. 1257).

SPEECH AND READING ACQUISITION COMPARED

Before discussing other issues, it might be advantageous to examine Douglas's claim that learning to read should be as easily and naturally acquired as learning to speak. It should be recognized that first language acquisition, with its speaking and listening components, is a unique human experience and different in important ways from other kinds of learning, such as learning to read. New theories concerning the nature of language and the modes of its analysis have raised strong doubts as to whether traditional, associationistic, learning theoretic accounts of language are tenable. There are a number of arguments to support the belief that the child's learning a language involves innate, genetically determined mechanisms operating on information about the structure of language that a child gets from listening to the speech of adults. First, linguistic universals, such as phonetic systems and syntax, are common to all languages; second, historical investigations of languages reveal that although spoken languages change, at no time does one find evidence of human speech that can be described as aphonemic or ungrammatical. Third, specific language disability, characterized by delayed speech onset, poor articulation, and marked reading disability, in which general intelligence remains unaffected appears to be inherited. Fourth, the developmental schedule of language acquisition follows a fixed sequence, so that even if the entire schedule is retarded, the order of attainment of linguistic skills remains constant. Finally, comparisons of children learning non-Indo-European language with children learning English indicate a high degree of concordance between the milestones of speech and motor development.

While it is true that speech acquisition appears to proceed easily and naturally, it is not at all apparent that learning to read need necessarily proceed in as easy a manner. The primary reason for this difference is that whereas speech acquisition seems to be a genetically determined behavior common to all people, reading does not follow this pattern. Speech acquisition appears to be natural to humans, much like walking, but reading is not a natural behavior indigenous to our species. Whereas all humans, regardless of the culture in which they are found, have developed language systems, not all societies are literate.

Interesting comparisons can be made between the acquisition of speech and learning to read. Generally, learning to speak is accomplished with little difficulty, whereas learning to read requires considerably more effort. According to Staats (1963) although the process of speech acquisition is gradual, beginning at infancy and extending for a considerable period of time, the introduction to reading is much more abrupt and less gradual. Second, there are strong sources of reinforcement involved with speech acquisition, while in the typical classroom, sources of reinforcement for reading appear to be much less forceful. Those strong reinforcers that are applied in speech acquisition seem to be applied almost immediately following appropriate speech behaviors, while in the learning-to-read process, the much weaker reinforcers are often delayed or may be nonexistent. According to Staats, perhaps the most important difference between speech acquisition and learning to read is that in learning to read there are intensive periods of concentration required that may easily take on aversive characteristics.

To summarize the differences between speech and reading, it is indeed accurate to say that for nearly all people first language acquisition appears to be easily mastered, but for a sizable number of people literacy is achieved only with difficulty, if at all. It is important to differentiate, however, between language acquired early in one's life and language acquired later, generally following the period of puberty with the accompanying cerebral lateralization (Lenneberg 1967). Students learning foreign languages in high school and college generally find it to be difficult. Thus, while language has the hallmarks of a species specific, genetically determined behavior that seems to be easily and naturally acquired, it is limited to languages acquired early in life and not later. Reading, on the other hand, is not a behavior common to all men and its acquisition frequently requires the expenditure of considerable time and effort.

ROLE OF SUBSKILLS IN LEARNING

Psychologists have known for a considerable length of time that in learning complex skills, mastery of subordinate units must precede final goal attainment. In investigating the learning curves of students taking a course in telegraphy, Bryan and Harter (1897) observed that the mastery of this complex task required the simultaneous learning of several components. They noted that there were plateaus in the learning curves during which practice did not lead to improvement. These plateaus, they thought, indicated temporary periods devoted to the organization of component skills into larger units or the learning of particularly difficult parts of the larger task. It is interesting to note that three-quarters of a century ago Bryan and Harter (1899) used a term like the "Acquisition of a Hierarchy of Habits" in the title of one of their articles, and today the role of learning hierarchies in reading is one of the issues of central importance.

While Hilgard and Marquis (1961) wrote that most learning is complex and requires the simultaneous learning of several components, questions remain about simple learning, such as associational learning. Is the formation of simple associations influenced by subsystems?

Historically, associational learning was believed to be a simple, single-stage process, but as psychologists continued to investigate the nature of associational learning they discovered that stimulus-response learning was anything but a simple, single-stage process. Research in associational learning over the past twenty-five years has revealed that there are stimulus-learning stages, response-learning stages, and associational stages. In fact, these stages are influenced by other factors, such as overt attention, perceptual learning, memory, and mediational strategies. Thus, even the so-called simple learning tasks have their complex aspects, and fractionating a simple association task into subskills can facilitate the learning process.

Even in so simple an associational task as learning a letter name, it appears that breaking the task into subskills facilitates learning (Samuels 1973). In one experiment, an experimental group received visual discrimination training on noting distinctive features of letters. Following perceptual training, they learned the letter names. A control group was taught using a holistic approach; this group did not get perceptual pretraining. They were shown the letters and were told to learn their names. The experimental group that got subskill training learned in significantly fewer trials and the savings were enough to make a practical difference as well.

There are a number of examples from the psychomotor domain that can be used to illustrate how a subskill approach can facilitate goal attainment. To support the notion that one learns to read by reading meaningful material, Smith (1973, p. 195) mentioned that one learns to ride a bicycle by getting practice riding the bike. However, it should be pointed out that children often go through a graded series of experiences of increasing difficulty before they learn to ride a large-frame, two-wheel bike. They frequently practice first on a tricycle, then graduate to a two-wheeler with a small frame, and practice getting their balance on the small-frame bike before they use the pedals on the two-wheeler.

One might inquire into the most desirable method to use in teaching a child to ride a bicycle. Would it be preferable simply to place the child on a two-wheeler or to allow the child to gather experience on a graded series of activities, each somewhat more difficult, before encountering the two-wheel bicycle?

Today, the methodology of teaching down-hill skiing has advanced to the point where advanced skills can be taught in significantly less time than was previously required. First, a subskill approach is used. More complex skills are built upon less difficult skills. But perhaps the most significant recent advance has been with the GLM, graduated length method. The beginning skier uses short skis to practice his basic moves and then advances to longer skis as skill develops.

The sport of wrestling is similar in many ways to the game of chess. For every move there is a countermove, and countermoves to countermoves. However, unlike chess, in wrestling the athlete has little time to think, and the one who is fastest and most automatic in his moves has the advantage. Every move in wrestling is broken down into its parts and the athlete practices these parts prior to putting them together to form a move that has fluid motion. When a move is finally mastered, combinations of moves are worked together to form larger units or patterns of moves.

Much the same can be said about learning dance steps. In watching skilled dancers, we are observing combinations and variations of steps that are strung together. The trick in learning a new dance step without the aid of a teacher is to try to identify the basic move from which the variations originate. What the teacher does to simplify learning a dance is to select the basic step and to teach the subskills that comprise the basic step. Years ago the Arthur Murray system used this procedure to introduce people to social dancing. Their basic step was called the box step and was used to introduce a number of dances as well as their variations.

Leaving the psychomotor domain, one can find examples from perception and reading to illustrate the principle that smaller units are mastered prior to mastering the larger units. The model of perceptual learning developed by LaBerge and Samuels (1974) is a hierarchical model and shows the sequence and progression of learning from distinctive features, to letters, to letter clusters, and on to words. In the process of learning to recognize a letter, the student must first identify the features that comprise the letter. For the lower-case letters b, d, p, and q, the features are vertical line and a circle in a particular relationship to each other; that is, the circle may be high or low and to the left or right side of the vertical line. Having identified the parts and after an extended series of exposure to the letters, the learner sees it as a unit. In other words, the parts are perceptually unitized. There is evidence recently gathered at our laboratory that skilled readers appear to have perceptually unitized—or chunked—digraphs such as th, ch, and sh. These are not processed as t + h, c + h, or s + h, but as a single unit. Other evidence gathered elsewhere (Gibson & Guinet 1971) indicates that units longer than the letter, such as affixes -ed, -ing, can become perceptually unitized. These findings from different laboratories suggest that perceptual learning seems to follow a pattern from smaller to larger units.

At one time, following the suggestions found in Gestalt psychology, there was a belief that when a beginning reader encountered a word, the perceptual unit was the whole word. Research by Marchbanks and Levin (1965) and Samuels and Jeffrey (1966) indicated that children tended to use a single letter rather than the whole word as the cue for word recognition. In fact, it is not until the tenth grade that it appears that a single eye fixation suffices to take in the whole word at once (Taylor et al. 1960).

Still other examples are available to illustrate the point that subskill mastery is necessary prior to achieving skill in reading. The purpose of a recent study by Shankweiler and Liberman (1972) was to investigate whether the main source of difficulty in beginning reading is at the word level or at the level of reading connected text. In other words, how well could one predict a child's fluency in oral reading of paragraph material from his performance on selected words presented in tests? The average correlation was 0.70 between reading individual words on a list and reading connected discourse. Thus, roughly 50% of the variability in oral reading of connected words is associated with how well one can read these words in isolation. The authors concluded: "These correlations suggest that the child may encounter his major difficulty at the level of the word—his reading of connected text tends to be only as good or poor as his reading of individual words" (p. 298).

A similar conclusion was reached by a classroom teacher with perceptive insights into problems children have with reading. She wrote:

. . . there has been great emphasis put on developing the child's comprehension ability. It is true that poor readers in the upper grades wrestle with comprehension problems. I have found this problem stems mainly from the student's lack of word-decoding skill. The comprehension cannot improve until the reading process becomes automatic, a development that takes place after the conscious analysis skills have been mastered. Therefore, though you want the child to understand the story he is learning to read, his ability will not be perfected until the child actually learns to read accurately (Stevenson 1974, p. 20).

Before leaving this section, two laboratory studies should be described that investigated a problem of some importance to reading. This problem dealt with the question of what type of initial training in reading—phonics versus the whole-word approach—provides the best basis for transfer to reading new words. One of the studies was done with children who were nonreaders (Jeffrey & Samuels 1967) and the other used adults who had to read using an artificial alphabet (Bishop 1964). Both studies came to the same conclusion, that specific training on letter-sound correspondences was superior to whole-word training for transfer to recognizing new words.

This section on the role of subskills in learning has looked at complex cognitive skills such as learning telegraphy, and transfer tasks in reading, "simple" cognitive tasks such as associational learning of letter-names, perceptual learning, and psychomotor learning. What psychologists have learned from these tasks is that they are comprised of lower-order skills, mastery of the higher-order skill may be contingent on mastery of lower-order skills, and that successful attainment of the final task may be facilitated by helping the student to master the lower-order units.

VALIDATING LEARNING HIERARCHIES

White and Gagné (1974, p. 19) have written that ". . . the validity of hierarchies should now be considered virtually at an end because of the increased support for hierarchies provided by the evidence of recent studies." Athey's (1974) National Institutes of Education position statement for essential reading skills states:

Every system of teaching reading presupposes some kind of hierarchy, explicitly or implicitly, as a condition of proceeding toward some goal in a rational manner. One possible reason for this is that the concept of a hierarchy has an inherent appeal in that it appears to present a logical and rational method to approach the instructional process.

Historically, the curricula that teachers have used regardless of the method employed, have been organized on the basis of some preconceived hierarchy. This procedure has received some theoretical support in the concept of developmental stages and the associated concept of readiness.

On the other hand, hierarchical systems appear to have some basis in the behavioristic approach as exemplified in programmed instruction, in which a terminal task is analyzed into small steps of progressive difficulty and the student is moved through the individual steps at his own pace. The underlying assumption is that learning will progress maximally if the task is broken down into small steps through which the child progresses in an orderly sequence at his own pace.

Learning hierarchies have been described as patterns of learning tasks that lead to a terminal skill: each subordinate task can be considered a prerequisite for the task above it, the subordinate prerequisite skills providing transfer to the terminal behavior (White & Gagné 1974). Gagné (1974, p. 12) wrote:

The tasks that people are expected to do must be analyzed into trainable components. First, each task must be broken down into behavior capabilities that are not themselves the task, but are *contributors* to the performance of the task. Second, these contributors must be further classified, if possible, into types that serve to identify different optimal conditions for their learning (and thus for the instruction that supports learning). Without such analysis and categorization, all one can say about optimal instruction is to apply general rules such as "motivate the learner," "use the principle of contiguity," and "arrange the contingencies of reinforcement." The unquestioned validity of these principles is not enough. With task analysis, one can begin to deal directly with the planning of instruction for different kinds of learning outcomes.

Task analysis, then, was conceived as a technique which could be brought to bear upon the problem of how to get from known human tasks to designed optimal conditions of instruction which would yield competence in those tasks. Of course, there are some tasks for normal human adults which need no instruction —such as "closes the door," or "makes a check mark," or "counts the number of people in a room." There are still others which require a minimum of instruction, and which therefore need no instructional design, such as "to energize the starter, turn key to right," or "to turn on the lights, push the switch upwards." But in many other instances, people cannot perform the tasks competently without a measurable period of learning, often accompanied by instruction. Task analysis was proposed as a method of identifying and classifying the behavioral contributors to task competence, for which differential instructional design was possible and desirable.

Despite claims by White, Gagné, and Athey that learning hierarchies do exist, there are contrary claims. To determine the subskills in reading comprehension, factor analysis has been used to study this problem. Davis's analysis (1944) identified nine subskills, of which six were significant. However, a refactorization of Davis's data by Thurstone (1946) suggested that, except for word knowledge, the reading skills were not separately distinguishable. The most recent refactorization of the Davis data by Spearritt (1973), using a different technique, has in fact revealed that word knowledge and three other skills were shown to be separately identifiable, but the latter three skills were highly correlated and could be measuring a single skill.

Perhaps the major methodological weakness of those factor-analytic studies attempting to identify subskills in reading, aside from the fact that the tests that have been used were not designed to reveal subskills, is the failure to differentiate between good and poor readers in the analysis. The fluent reader has mastered the subskills, combined them into higher units, so that the intercorrelations among subskills should be high, thus making reading seem to be but one skill—called reading. On the other hand, the beginning reader has not mastered the subskills, has not combined these skills into higher units, and so the intercorrelations among the subskills should be low. Guthrie (1973) designed special tests and analyzed the intercorrelations separately for the good and poor readers. As predicted, he found with the good readers the intercorrelations were highly significant, suggesting lack of subskills, and that reading had become but one skill. With poor readers, the opposite was found, and the low intercorrelation suggested separate subskills. Guthrie concluded that interfacilitation among subskills was necessary for good reading and that one source of disability among poor readers was the lack of mastery of subskills, with subsequent interfacilitation of subskills into higher-order units.

LEARNING HIERARCHIES IN READING

Despite the fact that learning hierarchies have a logical appeal, that we have known about them for at least three-quarters of a century, and that commercial reading series, with their scope and sequence charts, order the reading tasks as if we did know the nature of the learning hierarchy in reading, the sad truth is that the task is so complex that a validated reading hierarchy does not exist. Athey (1974)) has said: "The mere construction of hierarchies through logical means has not always proven to lead to a valid hierarchy. Until valid hierarchies have been established and proven to be efficient means of indicating instructional sequencing, the use of hierarchies to determine instruction remains based on an unproven assumption."

Part of the reason for the state of ferment and confusion about reading hierarchies is that educators have approached this problem as if there were one hierarchy and one way to sequence these subskills. Important distinctions between subskill sequence, teaching-learning sequence, and performance sequence have not been made. To illustrate how these distinctions can be useful, assume an objective upon which a task analysis will be performed. The objective (terminal behavior) is, "When shown a new word, the student will be able to pronounce it." Three subskills are essential for successful completion of this objective: (a) a left-to-right visual scan; (b) letter-sound knowledge; and (c) ability to blend the sounds to form the word (see Fig. 6).

One decision that must be made is in which order the subskills should be introduced. Actually, it makes no difference to the final outcome in which order they are introduced. Another decision that must be made is what the most efficient teaching-learning sequence might be in introducing a particular subskill. Recent research indicates that a particular sequence is most desirable. For example, in learning letter-sound correspondences, the perceptual learning phase should be separated from and precede the response hook-up phase. Furthermore, in order to help the student learn the distinctive features of each letter, the visual discrimination training should be on high-similarity letters (b, d, p, q). Simultaneous discrimination training should be given prior to successive training, since it is during the simultaneous phase that the features are most easily noted, while during the successive discrimination phase these features can get chunked in memory. Following perceptual training, the response hook-up phase can be introduced. Each training phase should go beyond accuracy to automaticity (Samuels 1973; LaBerge & Samuels 1974). Once the three subskills have been mastered, the student is ready to attempt the objective.

In performing the terminal behavior, it is imperative that the subskills be performed in the order of A, B, and C. First, the reader must scan the letters from left to right. Second, the letters must be sounded. Third, the letter-sounds must be blended to form the word. This particular example illustrates that for certain objectives it may make no difference in which

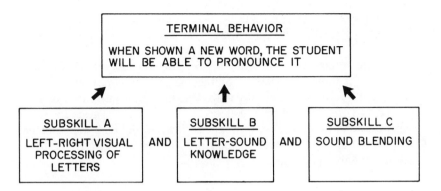

TEACHING - LEARNING SEQUENCE
1. PERCEPTUAL TRAINING
   a. SIMULTANEOUS DISCRIMINATION
   b. SUCCESSIVE DISCRIMINATION
2. STIMULUS - RESPONSE HOOK-UP

SUBSKILL SEQUENCE : SUBSKILLS CAN BE INTRODUCED IN ANY ORDER

PERFORMANCE SEQUENCE: IN PERFORMING THE TERMINAL BEHAVIOR,
   THE SUBSKILLS MUST BE DONE IN FIXED SEQUENCE A, B, C.

Fig. 6.1. Subskills that must be mastered in order to achieve the terminal behavior.

order the subskills are introduced, that there is a preferred teaching-learning sequence for a particular subskill, and that in order to perform the terminal behavior, a particular sequence may be essential.

As mentioned earlier, different kinds of hierarchies may exist in reading, depending upon the terminal behavior to be taught. The different types of hierarchies are outlined below (Athey 1974):

1. Contingency Relationship. Successive skills each of which is necessary to the mastery of the next step (e.g., A is necessary to B).

    C
    B
    A

1a. Conjunctive Contingent Relationship. Successive skills in which more than one skill is necessary to the mastery of the next step (e.g., A and B necessary to C).

    C
    A and B

1b. Disjunctive Contingent Relationship. Successive skills in which there is a necessary relationship of skills, but alternate routes may lead to the goal.

    C
    A or B

2. Supportive Relationship. No skill is necessary to the next step but the skill may facilitate acquisition in the sense of pro-

viding positive transfer (e.g., learning sets, learning-to-learn, acquisition of algorithmic approaches to a problem).

Different approaches are available for the purpose of determining hierarchies. To mention several of the methods that have been used Gagné (1962) took a terminal behavior, fractionated it into subskills that were ranked from lower to higher order, and developed tests for each level. He found that students who failed a lower-order task, were unable to pass a test at a higher level. In addition, Airasian and Bart (1974) have used tree theory to determine hierarchies.

IMPLICATIONS FOR READING INSTRUCTION

A major point made by critics of the subskill approach is that fractionating the reading process interferes with the essential characteristic of reading, which is comprehension. This point is well taken. Many teachers who use the subskill approach have lost sight of the fact that it is simply a means to an end. What has happened in many classrooms is that goal displacement has occurred and the means have become ends in themselves. In using the subskill approach, care must be taken to prevent the subskills from becoming the focal point of instruction. Once again, perhaps, this point should be made, that it is important for the child to get ample practice, reading meaningful and interesting material in context.

While agreeing with the critics of the subskill approach, that too much emphasis can be placed on these subordinate skills, the critics probably are in error in failing to recognize the importance of subskills in the developmental sequence of skill attainment. Just because fluent readers are able to access the meaning in a printed page is no reason to believe that beginning readers can do the same or that we can transfer the sophisticated strategies of the fluent reader to the beginning reader. While it is true that sophisticated strategies can be taught to the less sophisticated, these transfers of skills have been accomplished by doing a task analysis of the sophisticated strategies and teaching these subskills to the beginner.

As the advocates of the holistic approach point out, the essential element of reading—deriving meaning—is destroyed by taking a whole and breaking it down. However, current research suggests that before one deals with wholes, smaller aspects have to be mastered first. For example, before one can visually process letter clusters as a unit, individual letters have to be unitized. The controversy between letter-by-letter and whole-word processing in word recognition seems somewhat resolved now that we have evidence to indicate that familiar words can be processed by fluent readers as a unit, while unfamiliar words tend to get processed letter-by-letter.

Many critics of the subskill approach suggest that meaningful reading material should be given to a child and subskills should be taught when the student asks for help or shows evidence of needing particular skills. This approach has shortcomings when one realizes the logistical and managerial problems facing the teacher with a large group.

With regard to this last point, it is important to consider that many students do not know what kind of help to request and many teachers are not sufficiently trained to diagnose and pin-point the cause of the student's difficulty. Even when the teacher is able to diagnose the cause of the problem with accuracy, the managerial problems of giving individual help as needed loom so large as to make the system difficult to operate, if not unworkable. It would seem more manageable to assume on a priori grounds that there are certain subskills beginning readers require. These skills would be taught routinely to students. For those students who fail to master these skills, additional time could be allocated and different methods could be tried.

Earlier in this paper the point was made that the adverse relationship between holistic and subskill approaches may not exist. Both approaches recognize there are subskills. Subskill approaches start with smaller units and move to larger and more complex units. On the other hand, the holistic approach begins with the larger unit and moves to smaller units. One of the important factors differentiating the two approaches is that of sequencing. In considering this factor, we must think about which tasks and which unit size one would use to start instruction and how one would program the sequence of skills to be taught as the student progresses in skill? Another similarity between the two approaches is that both recognize the importance of diagnosis of difficulty in reading and the need to remedy the problem. The subskill approach, however, attempts to reduce the number of students who will experience difficulty with reading by teaching the prerequisite skills before a problem appears.

Although at the present time we do not have validated learning hierarchies in reading, we do have a fairly good idea of what the necessary subskills may be. We need to continue our work on validating a minimal set of subskills and on determining their optimal sequence.

REFERENCES

Airasian, P., and Bart, W. 1973. Ordering theory: A new and useful measurement model. *Educational Technology* 13: 56–60.

Athey, I. 1974. Essential skills and skills hierarchies in reading comprehension and decoding instruction. Paper presented at conference of the National Institute of Education.

Bishop, C. H. 1964. Transfer effects of word and letter training in reading. *Journal of Verbal Learning and Verbal Behavior* 3: 215–21.

Bryan, W. L., and Harter, N. 1897. Studies in the physiology and psychology of the telegraphic language. *Psychological Review* 4: 27–53.

———. 1899. Studies on the telegraphic language. The acquisition of a hierarchy of habits. *Psychological Review* 6: 345–75.

Bumstead, J. 1934. Cited in Nila B. Smith, *American Reading Instruction.* New York: Silver, Burdett and Company.

Davis, F. B. 1944. Fundamental factors of comprehension in reading. *Psychometrika* 9: 185–97.

Flesch, R. 1955. *Why Johnny can't read.* New York: Harper Brothers.

Gagné, R. M. 1962. The acquisition of knowledge. *Psychological Review* 69: 355–65.

———. 1974. Task analysis—its relation to content analysis. *Educational Psychologist* 11: 11–18.

Gedike, F. 1779. *Aristoteles und Basedow oder Fragmente über Erziehung und Schulwesen bei den Alten und Neuren.* Berlin und Leipzig.

Gibson, E. J., and Guinet, L. 1971. Perception of inflections in brief visual presentations of words. *Journal of Verbal Learning and Verbal Behavior* 10: 182–89.

Goodman, K. S. 1970. The reading process: Theory and practice. Paper presented at the annual meeting of the International Reading Association, Anaheim, California, May 1970.

———. 1972a. Orthography in a theory of reading instruction. *Elementary English* (December): 1254–61.

———. 1972b. Reading: The key is in the children's language. *The Reading Teacher* (March): 505–08.

———. [no date] Strategies for increasing comprehension in reading. *Scott, Foresman Monograph.* Palo Alto, Calif.: Scott, Foresman and Company.

Guthrie, J. T. 1973. Models of reading and reading disability. *Journal of Educational Psychology* 65: 9–18.

Hilgard, E. R., and Marquis, D. G. 1961. *Conditioning and learning.* New York: Appleton-Century-Crofts.

Jeffrey, W., and Samuels, S. J. 1967. Effect of method of reading training on initial learning and transfer, *Journal of Verbal Learning and Verbal Behavior* 6: 354–58.

LaBerge, D., and Samuels, S. J. 1974. Toward a theory of automatic information processing in reading. *Cognitive Psychology* 6: 293–323.

Lenneberg, F. 1967. *Biological foundations of language.* New York: Wiley and Sons.

Marchbanks, G., and Levin, H. 1965. Cues by which children recognize words. *Journal of Educational Psychology* 56: 57–61.

Mathews, M. M. 1966. *Teaching to read, historically considered.* Chicago: University of Chicago Press.

Samuels, S. J. 1973. Effect of distinctive feature training on paired-associate learning. *Journal of Educational Psychology* 64: 164–70.

Samuels, S. J., and Jeffrey, W. F. 1966. Initial discriminability of words and its effect on transfer in learning to read. *Journal of Educational Psychology* 57: 337–40.

Shankweiler, D., and Liberman, I. 1972. "Misreading: A search for causes," in J. F. Kavanagh and I. G. Mattingly (eds.), *Language by ear and by eye: The relationships between speech and reading.* Cambridge: The M.I.T. Press.

Singer, H. 1970. Theories, models and strategies for learning to read. Paper presented at the National Reading Conference, St. Petersburg, Florida, December 1970.

Singer, H., Samuels, S. J., and Spiroff, J. 1974. Effect of pictures and contextual conditions on learning to read. *Reading Research Quarterly* 9: 555–56.

Smith, F. 1973. *Psycholinguistics and reading.* New York: Holt, Rinehart and Winston.

Spearritt, D. 1972. Identification of subskills of reading comprehension by maximum likelihood factor analysis. *Reading Research Quarterly* 8: 92–111.

Staats, A. W., and Staats, C. K. 1963. *Complex human behavior.* New York: Holt, Rinehart and Winston.

Stevenson, N. 1974. *The natural way to reading: A how-to method for parents of slow learners, dyslexic and learning disabled children.* Boston: Little, Brown & Co.

Taylor, S. E., Frackenpohl, H., and Pettee, J. L. 1960. Grade level norms for components of the fundamental reading skill. Huntington, N. Y.: Educational Developmental Laboratories.

Thurstone, L. L. 1946. Note on a reanalysis of Davis' reading tests. *Psychometrika* 11: 185–88.

Venezky, Richard L. 1972. Language and cognition in reading. Technical Report No. 188, Wisconsin University, Madison, Office of Education (DHEW), Washington, D. C.

White, R. T. 1973. Research into learning hierarchies. *Review of Educational Research* 43: 361–75.

White, R. T., and Gagné, R. M. 1974. Past and future research on learning hierarchies. *Educational Psychologist* 11: 19–28.

7

Lauren B. Resnick
Isabel L. Beck

Designing Instruction in Reading: Interaction of Theory and Practice

This paper is about reading. It is also, more generally, about instructional design strategies and the relationship between psychological theory and its applications in education. A common conception concerning this relationship between theory and practice is that there exists a linear, one-way communication. According to this view, scientists offer their knowledge and principles for others to apply, but they continue to draw their research questions almost exclusively from within the "basic" science community. We take a different point of view here. We consider it to be more fruitful for both parties if application and science maintain an interactive communication; a communication in which scientists direct their attention, in part, to questions that are posed by social needs and in which application experts—in the present case, instructional designers —become active partners in the generation and testing of theory. (See Resnick 1974, for a more general discussion of the relationship between basic science and instructional design.)

As colleagues, we represent, in a quite personal way, the kind of interaction about which we are speaking. We are a psychologist (Resnick) and a reading specialist (Beck), who work in a unique institutional environment (the Learning Research and Development Center at the University of Pittsburgh) that not only accepts but also actively encourages collaboration across disciplinary boundaries. We will, in this paper, refer extensively to a primary grade reading program whose development,

The preparation of this paper was supported by the Learning Research and Development Center supported in part as a research and development center by funds from the National Institute of Education, Department of Health, Education, and Welfare. The opinions expressed in the paper do not necessarily reflect the position or policy of the Office of Education and no official endorsement should be inferred.

under Beck's direction, exemplifies the kind of interaction between scientists and practitioners, psychologists and instructional designers, that we would like to see become more widespread.* During our discussion here, we will allude to certain segments of the program, but no attempt will be made to describe it fully. Rather, we will describe particular portions of the program that will help to illustrate the points we are making about the content and form of early reading instruction and their relation to an emerging theory of instruction.

The term "instruction" is used here in its most general sense. It refers to any set of environmental conditions that are deliberately arranged to foster increases in competence. Thus, instruction includes demonstrating, telling, and explaining; but it also includes physical arrangements, structure of presented material, sequences of task demands, and responses to the learner's actions. A theory of instruction, therefore, must concern itself with the relationship between any modifications in the learning environment and the resultant changes in competence. When we are concerned with intellectual competence, the development of a theory of instruction requires a means of describing states of intellectual competence in psychological terms and, ultimately, a means of relating manipulations of the learning environment to changes in these states.

Task analysis plays a central role in the development of a theory of instruction for intellectual or "cognitive" domains such as reading. By task analysis we mean the translation of "subject-matter" descriptions into psychological descriptions that take into account such basic psychological processes as attention, perception, memory, and linguistic processing. Such analysis links the complex tasks of education to the constructs developed in the laboratory and provides psychologically sound descriptions of the content of instruction. With the content thus described, it becomes possible to apply psychological principles of learning and performance to the design of interventions that will facilitate the acquisition of competence and the maintenance of desirable levels of performance.

In this paper, we shall attempt to illustrate the role of information-processing task analysis in linking psychological theory to instructional practice. We begin by taking a limited part of the reading domain—decoding. We propose a pair of detailed information-processing models of word-attack behavior and show how psychological considerations suggest

---

*The program is designed to teach primary grades reading in a school environment that is committed to adaptation to individual differences. The early portions of the program have been used in trial versions with several hundred kindergarten and first-grade children. Tests of the more advanced levels are just now beginning. The program is a complex one, using multiple resources—teacher and cassette-led instruction, self-instructional materials, games, free reading activities, and the like. (See Beck & Mitroff 1972, for a full rationale and description of the system.)

the superiority of one model over the other as a basis for instruction. We then examine actual instructional procedures for teaching the model selected and relate these procedures to certain general principles of instructional design. We also discuss research questions that are stimulated by the existence of instructional programs—thus completing the communication cycle between practice and science.

In a later section, we return to the larger domain of reading comprehension and consider the kinds of analyses that will be needed to bring psychological theory to bear on instruction in the more complex skills involved in reading comprehension. We will propose a general psychological "map" of reading comprehension and will consider its implications for both research and instruction. Throughout this paper we will be drawing attention to the "problem-solving" character of reading behavior, particularly its character of successive reduction of uncertainty, and the potential fruitfulness of attempting to build formal models of these processes of problem-solving and search for meaning.

INITIAL READING

Choosing a Basic Approach

Over the years there has been substantial debate concerning appropriate strategies for initial reading instruction. Without reviewing the "great debate" (Chall 1967) over decoding as opposed to "whole-word" approaches to reading, it may be useful to point out a set of hidden assumptions that underlies the differences of opinion. Proponents of various whole-word approaches—basal reading, language experience, etc.—usually assume that good initial reading should match skilled reading performance as closely as possible. In other words, since skilled readers process units such as words and sentences, so should beginning readers—even if they can manage only a few words and sentences. Similarly, since skilled readers interpret and apply what they are reading, so should beginning readers. By contrast, a decoding emphasis in early reading assumes that the initial job is to learn the most generative form of the reading process—a form that is relatively easy to learn and that allows the learner to later approximate the performance of skilled readers. In other words, code-breaking implies teaching the basic structure of print-to-sound mapping, which is the core "subject-matter" of very initial reading.

We adopt here a code-breaking approach to initial reading. In doing so we are agreeing with the large majority of scholars—both psychologists and linguists—who argue that a fundamental task of initial reading is learning the structural relationships between written and spoken language—i.e., the grapheme-phoneme mapping that characterizes the language (Chall 1967; Diederick 1973). While virtually all scholars concerned with reading now agree that early and regular instruction in some type of code-breaking is needed, there still exist competing theories about how code-breaking itself should be taught. There are two major approaches, the "analytic" and the "synthetic." The "analytic" approach attempts to teach grapheme-phoneme correspondences to the child by having him examine displays of words that share and contrast major spelling patterns. The "synthetic" approach teaches grapheme-phoneme correspondences directly by having the child assemble words from phonemes. The main point of difference between the two approaches concerns whether or not learners should ever be asked to pronounce individual phonemes outside of the auditory context of the entire word. Proponents of the analytic approach argue that, since isolated phonemes do not occur in natural speech, the blending process of the synthetic approach unnecessarily and unnaturally burdens the child and magnifies the difficulties of his learning task.

We agree that the analytic method of teaching decoding might indeed avoid the problem of pronouncing isolated phonemes and of blending them. However, it introduces another problem that may be even more difficult for the child. Analytic decoding methods do not eliminate the need to abstract phonemes from the speech stream; in fact, they require that the child independently extract the phonemes. For at least some children, this detection of phonemes requires very extensive skills in auditory analysis and in general concept attainment strategy. By contrast, the synthetic approach provides direct help by indicating the units with which the child must deal. The child's attention is directed to the grapheme, and the phoneme is sounded; he need not discover the relationship independently. Furthermore, a natural feedback system is inherent in the process. Since phonemes do indeed normally occur in the environment of other phonemes rather than in isolation, the child can test his own verbal production (the result of blending) against what "sounds right." For example, having blended /k/ /a/ /t/ to produce *cat*, he can test to see whether he has pronounced a word that is in his aural vocabulary.

For these general reasons, we came to favor a synthetic approach to decoding instruction. However, since one of the primary pedagogic objections to this approach has been the difficulty of learning the process of blending, we sought to determine whether there was any way of simplifying or making more explicit the process of putting sounds together. For this purpose, we began with an analysis of two possible strategies of blending, one which is commonly used in initial teaching, and one which we developed while working with children who were having initial difficulty in learning.

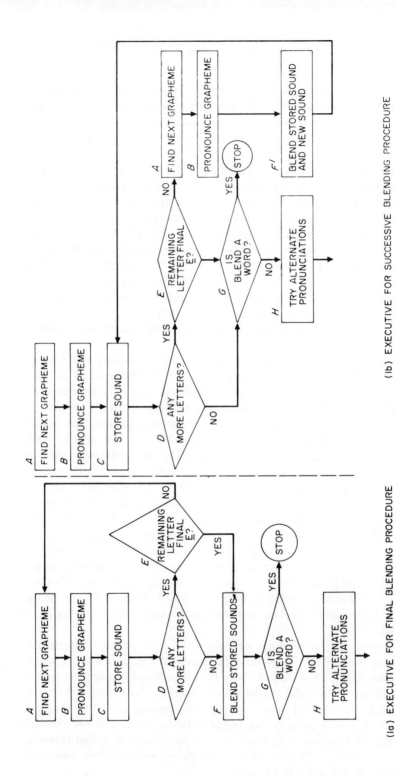

(Ia) EXECUTIVE FOR FINAL BLENDING PROCEDURE

(Ib) EXECUTIVE FOR SUCCESSIVE BLENDING PROCEDURE

Fig. 7.1. Executive routines for synthetic decoding.

Analysis of the Decoding Process

Two Blending Procedures

Figure 7.1 shows the general structure of the two blending routines that we examined. In each case, the routine is capable of decoding single syllable, regularly spelled words—the typical vocabulary of a beginning phonics program. At the left (Fig. 7.1a), the procedure depicted is one in which the sound of each grapheme is given and stored; the synthesis occurs only after the final phoneme has been pronounced. We call this the "final blending" procedure, since blending is postponed until the very last step. Figure 7.1b, at the right, calls for successive blending. As soon as two sounds are produced, they are blended and successive phonemes are incorporated in the blend as they are pronounced.

The final blending and the successive blending routines call upon the same set of decisions and actions: finding graphemes in sequence (Component A); pronouncing identified graphemes (Component B); "storing" (remembering) pronounced sounds (Component C); deciding whether more graphemes remain to be sounded (Components D and E); blending (Component F); and, finally, in each case, matching the produced "word" against one's linguistic knowledge to determine whether the word generated is an acceptable decoding. The two routines differ only in the organization of these components, a difference in "executive" that appears to have important consequences concerning the ease of learning and of performing the decoding act.

To illustrate the differences between the two blending routines, let us use the word *cats* as an example and analyze the exact respects in which the two routines differ. The child who uses the final blending routine would proceed as follows: /k/ /a/ /t/ /s/ *cats*. The child who uses the second system would proceed thusly: /k/ /a/ /ka/ /t/ /kat/ /s/ /kats/ *cats*.

Consider the contrast between the two procedures. According to the final blending routine, each grapheme's sound is given, and the full set of phonemes in the word must be held in memory until the entire word has been "sounded out"; only then does any blending occur. But in the successive blending routine, blending occurs sequentially at each stage at which a new phoneme is pronounced. At no time must more than two sounds be held in memory (the sound immediately produced and the one that directly precedes it); and at no time must more than two sound units be blended. Thus, the routines differ in two respects: (1) in the maximum number of sound units to be held in memory during the course of decoding, and (2) in the maximum number of units to be blended during a given attempt. The standard routine on the left requires remembering each of the separate units that the reader identifies as graphemes. The routine on the right never requires remembering more than two units.

It would seem, at first glance, that while the two routines might produce very different levels of difficulty for the pronunciation of long or complex words, they would be approximately equally difficult for the pronunciation of shorter words (words of no more than three or four graphemes), which compose the beginning reading vocabulary of any phonically oriented instruction. After all, first-grade children normally have a memory span that can easily encompass three elements (as shown, for example, by the digit-span test of the Stanford–Binet, which expects memory of three digits at age three; five at age seven).

Tests such as the digit span, however, require only that items be held in memory. Items need not be generated, and no competing processing interferes with retention. This, however, is not the case during decoding. A substantial amount of other processing must occur simultaneously with the retention of the phoneme elements. Assuming a limited working space or "working memory" (as is common in virtually all current information processing theories), this additional processing is likely to interfere with remembering the sounds; or, rehearsal of the sounds may interfere with other processing (cf. Baddeley & Hitch 1974; Posner & Rossman 1965). In either case, decoding will not succeed.

The Find Next Grapheme Subroutine

The complexity of the competing processing tasks can best be appreciated by considering some of the subroutines involved in the two blending procedures. Figure 7.2 shows an analysis for the subroutine of Find Next Grapheme (Subroutine A). This subroutine is required because of a small but significant number of cases in which graphemes consist of pairs of letters that carry one single sound. Such graphemes are digraphs (e.g., ch, ea) or diphthongs (e.g., oy). If the reader neglects to "look ahead" in order to detect the presence of a digraph or a diphthong, then the word cannot be correctly decoded. The first step (A1) is to find the leftmost letter not yet sounded and then, if more letters remain (A2), to find the next letter after that (A3). Embedded in these simple statements, but not explicitly broken out as a program, is a complex set of requirements that involves maintaining left-to-right encoding during reading, and keeping track spatially of one's position within a word and within a line of text. This spatial information must be maintained despite the interruptions of sounding. Thus, these two simple steps may involve considerable demands upon a beginning reader, demands that compete for processing space with the retention of the sounded-out phonemes.

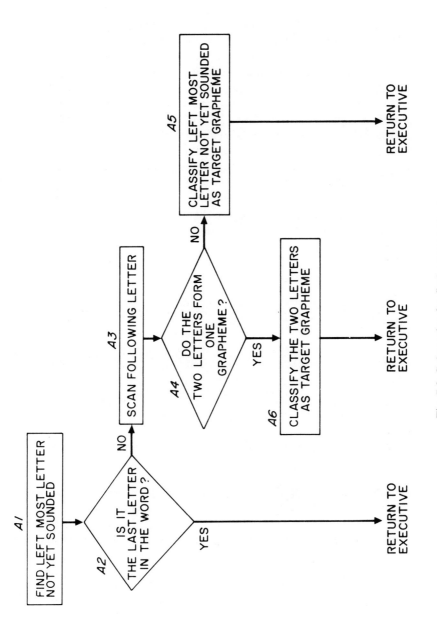

Fig. 7.2. Subroutine for find next grapheme.

Having focused upon two successive letters, the reader must decide whether they form a single digraph or a diphthong (A4). This decision assumes that the individual has in memory a list of digraphs and diphthongs with which the current letter sequence is matched. Presumably, this list is gradually compiled during the course of learning to read and becomes longer and longer as the acquisition of reading ability progresses. If two letters form a digraph or diphthong, they are classified jointly as a grapheme (the "target") (A6), and control of behavior is now returned to the executive program (Fig. 7.1). If the two letters do not form a single grapheme, attention is returned to the first letter identified in the subroutine, and that letter is classified as a grapheme (the "target") (A5). Control is then returned to the executive. The return of control signifies completion of the subroutine; the executive will now move to the next subroutine indicated. In both the final blending and the successive blending executives, the next subroutine is pronouncing the grapheme (Subroutine B of Figure 7.1).

The Pronounce Grapheme Subroutine

Figure 7.3 shows the subroutine for the pronunciation of graphemes. This subroutine assumes that a grapheme (the "target") has been identified. The pronunciation routine depends upon whether the target grapheme is a consonant or a vowel unit (B1). If it is a consonant, the grapheme must be matched against a stored list that classifies consonants as variant or invariant in pronunciation (B2). If it is variant (e.g., the letter c), then the next letter is scanned (B3) for information regarding the appropriate pronunciation of the target (e.g., hard sound if an *a* follows; soft sound if an *i* follows). On the basis of the next letter, the target grapheme is pronounced (B4). Control then returns, as it does after any pronunciation, to the executive program. If the target grapheme is classified as a vowel (B5), it can be either a single vowel (B6) or a vowel digraph or diphthong. If it is a digraph or diphthong, then that vowel combination is pronounced (B7) without further scanning, since the succeeding context will not typically determine pronunciation in regular words. If the target is a single vowel, the decoder looks at the remaining letters (B8) and decides whether they are all consonants (B9) (e.g., *nt* in *ant,* or *tch* in *stretch*). If so, then the target grapheme is pronounced with the short vowel sound (B10). If the remaining letters are not all consonants, the decoder notes the final e (B11), which is the only nonconsonant ending possible in regular single-syllable words, and the target vowel is pronounced with the long vowel sound (B12).

This subroutine for pronouncing graphemes will succeed in a large but nevertheless limited set of word environments. It assumes single-syllable

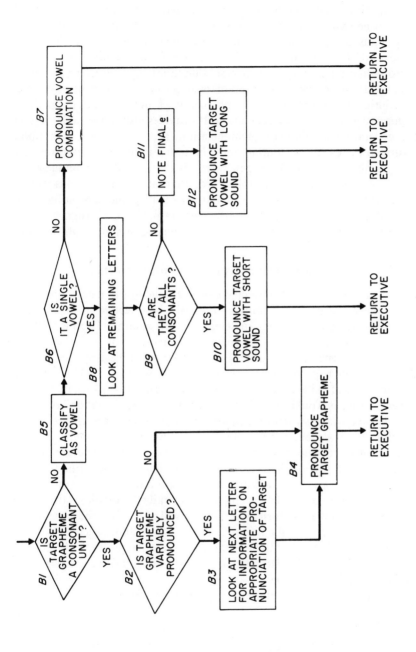

Fig. 7.3. Subroutine for pronounce grapheme.

words, with regular grapheme-phoneme mappings. The routine would have to be expanded substantially to cope with certain words that have very unusual grapheme-phoneme structures. Nevertheless, the basic patterns of decisions, and classifications that are based upon scanning the surrounding graphemic context would undoubtedly characterize such an expanded routine. A further point is important to keep in mind; the subroutine for pronouncing graphemes does not—*cannot* in English——guarantee a correct pronunciation. It provides only a workable routine for generating a candidate pronunciation, a pronunciation that, upon return to the executive routine, must be tested in order to determine if a recognizable word has been generated. If the candidate pronunciation does not produce a recognizable word, alternate pronunciations will be tried. Thus, the total program, including executive and subroutines, can be characterized as a generate-and-test program, a type of program that is heuristic in nature and that iteratively gathers and organizes information.

The Task Analyses as Routines for Instruction

The task analyses just presented can be thought of as detailed hypotheses concerning decoding routines that will be effective in instruction. Several criteria are relevant in selecting such routines (Resnick 1975). These criteria derive from a general consideration of the relationship between the structure of a task as defined by the subject-matter and the ease with which particular routines can be learned or taught, and the performance of skilled individuals on a task. To put the case in its most general form, it would seem useful to think of a "triangulation" relationship between task structure, acquisition, and skilled performance. This relationship is schematized in Figure 7.4. As indicated there, a good instructional routine must be clearly related to the structure of the subject-matter (the A–B relationship). The instructional routine, once acquired, must also put the learner in a position to move to more skilled or fluent performance such as characterizes skilled individuals (the B–C) relationship. Skilled performance, in turn, will also reflect the structure of the subject-matter, but at a different level; it will include efficiencies based on the elimination of redundant steps, the use of larger units of information, etc. This set of relationships suggests the following criteria for a good instructional routine:

1) The routine must embody a good representation of the subject-matter structure.

2) The routine must be teachable with relative ease.

3) The routine as taught must be transformable into the more efficient routines of the skilled individual.

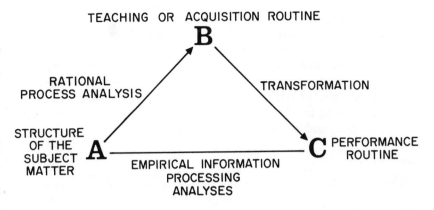

Fig. 7.4. Relations between teaching routines, performance routines, and structure of subject matter.

Let us elaborate somewhat on each of these criteria, suggesting how the present analyses meet them and describing how the analyses have influenced instructional decisions.

Representation of Subject-Matter

The decoding routines shown here represent the subject-matter of grapheme-phoneme correspondences in the form of an "idealized" performance. The routines include a representation of the grapheme, as opposed to single-letter structure of English (as in the "Find next grapheme" subroutine). They show the way that the surrounding graphemic context affects the pronunciation of any given grapheme (in the "Pronounce grapheme" subroutine). In fact, the explicitness of these representations leads quite directly to certain decisions concerning the order in which specific symbol/sound correspondences are introduced in instruction; this is a central decision in the design of any decoding-oriented program. Two criteria are traditionally used: (a) the ease with which a given symbol/sound correspondence can be learned, and (b) the utility of a grapheme, in conjunction with other graphemes, in generating meaningful and possibly pictureable words. The first criterion in particular suggests that highly "regular" and simple graphemes should dominate the early phases of instruction. This would usually mean invariantly pronounced consonants and only a single, usually the short, vowel sound. It would also mean single letters as opposed to digraphs. The analyses of the "Finding and pronouncing grapheme" routines (Figs. 7.2 and 7.3), however, suggest that this strategy might hinder a child's subsequent reading progress by discouraging the scanning ahead to identify graphemes and their pronunciations; behavior that is characteristic to both routines. In our curriculum, therefore, examples of consonant and vowel digraphs are included early in the graphemic sequence, as are both short and long single vowel pronunciation patterns. Thus, even when exposed to a relatively limited and regularly patterned corpus of words, the child learns that reading involves a searching ahead for information and that it cannot be performed as merely a chain of responses.

Teachability

Our comparison of the final and successive blending procedures, we believe, strongly suggests the advantages of the successive procedure. The advantage lies essentially in the reduction of memory load, which for many children may make the difference between a learnable and an unlearnable word-attack routine. For this reason the successive blending routine is systematically taught in our program.

Transformability

Skilled readers do not often go through a decoding process as detailed as the one we have shown. They do not usually read in letter or graphemic units. In fact, the speed at which normal skilled reading occurs suggests that for much reading there may not be a full intervening translation into an auditory form. Even when they encounter difficult words, skilled readers are likely to analyze the words in terms of syllabic or morphemic units rather than graphemes.

Although the units change, it seems reasonable to suggest that basic flow of generating and combining sounds is probably the same for more advanced as for beginning readers. Returning to Figure 7.1 for example, it would be simple to rewrite it substituting the more general term "unit" for "grapheme" and "letter." Thus, subroutine A would read "Find next unit"; B would read "Pronounce unit"; D would read "Any more units?" (E, the check for final *e* would perhaps drop out). Storing sounds, blending them, and testing them against aural vocabulary would proceed much as shown in Figure 7.1. The emergence of the larger units need not be left wholly to chance. Several instructional strategies can assist learners in early expansion of their units of analysis. One strategy is to use spelling pattern and syllable recognition exercises. A second is the gradual build-up of a demand for faster reading, thus encouraging children to process in larger, and therefore fewer, units. A third is an early focus upon reading for comprehension, even of very simple, single-line texts so that the child's attention is focused on finding units that cue meaning. All of these techniques are woven into the earliest units of our program.

What is crucial to the eventual evolution of reading fluency is the development of a large and easily accessed word recognition vocabulary. To encourage this development, explicit attention is paid in our program to moving words that have been initially learned through the sounding and blending procedure into the recognition vocabulary. Immediately after a new phonemic element has been learned, words containing that element are used in the texts with special frequency. This high frequency of occurrence leads most children to begin to recognize the words without calling upon any word-attack routines. A few children need special help in building recognition vocabulary, and this is offered via games and additional simple texts.

Testing the Validity of Instructional Hypotheses

We have said that the analyses presented here constitute hypotheses, expressed as information-processing routines, for effective instruction. How would one go about testing these hypotheses, i.e., validating the routines for instructional use?

We have already tried to show that the routines presented embody a reasonable representation of the grapheme-phoneme correspondences that constitute the subject-matter of initial reading. Thus, the first criterion for a good instructional routine (see p. 13) has been met—at least to the degree that our earlier discussion has been convincing. The next requirement for validation would be to establish the teachability of the routines (our second criterion) by teaching them to a variety of different kinds of learners. The third criterion for an effective instructional routine requires that it be transformable into a more skilled and automatic performance. This criterion demands a more complex approach to validation, combining controlled instruction in decoding with systematic observation and simulation of decoding behavior of individuals over time. The strategy we propose includes the following steps:

1. Teach the hypothesized routines in a highly controlled way, in order to insure that the routines used by the child at the outset of instruction are the ones shown in our analyses. As part of this instruction we would require overt performance of the decoding routines. Simultaneously, write computer simulation programs for the hypothesized instructional routines. At this stage, we would expect a close match between computer outputs in reading words and the performance of children in the instructional program. That is, they should make similar errors and, to the extent they are measurable, require similar latencies.

2. Gradually loosen our demands on the child for overt decoding performance in order to allow the "transformation" process to begin to take place—i.e., larger units and direct word recognition to emerge. As

these transformations occur, we would expect the match between the computer's and the child's performance to decline, since the computer would still be performing the initial instructional routine.

3. Next we would try to vary parameters of the simulation programs in an attempt to regain the match between human and program performance, preferably for individual children. We might, for example, introduce a larger number of possible pronunciations for certain graphemes. We might change the "unit" of decoding from graphemes to spelling patterns (e.g., ing, ate, etc.). We might input a larger aural recognition vocabulary or a larger sight recognition word list. The aim of this model adjustment is to produce as detailed as possible descriptions of performance at different stages of the learning process.

A research program of this kind would constitute a series of tests of reading models based on reading instruction of a particular kind. We believe the simulation models can be built, although we do not yet have them in running (i.e., "sufficient") form. We do already have, however, the controlled teaching strategies required.

The Instructional Strategies

We can describe briefly these instructional strategies, really just to give their flavor and to show the likelihood that children experiencing them will indeed learn the routines taught. We will describe two of the initial teaching strategies included in our program. Each is designed for teacher-led small group instruction and uses a series of steps to guide the child from imitation of the teacher to independent performance. Both programs are described below.

Teaching the Grapheme/Phoneme Correspondences

In this sequence, teachers are trained to give simple, direct statements to children and to control additional cueing or prompting in order to fade prompts deliberately and systematically.

Techniques for teaching symbol/sound correspondences are as follows:
1. the teacher models the isolated sound;
2. the children imitate the model;
3. the teacher models the sound again, this time pointing to the symbol (the letter on a printed card);
4. the children imitate the model sound, while looking at the symbol. Concurrent with the children's imitation, the teacher mouths the sound silently. In doing this, she consciously establishes a cue or prompt;
5. the children produce the sound to match the symbol, without the spoken model, but with the silent mouthing cue;

6. the teacher fades the silent mouthing cue as the children produce the sound;

7. the children produce the symbol/sound correspondence independently.

Compare the directness of the above with the indirectness and miscueing of the following procedure observed in a traditional classroom of an experienced teacher. The teacher held up a card with *m* printed on it and said, "This is an *m*. The name of the letter is *m* but the sound is /m/, as in '*mmmm*ountain.' I want to hear everyone say it." One child said *em*, two said /m/, another said "*mmmm*ountain." The teacher said, "No, I want you to say the sound. Listen: /m/ as in '*mmmm*ountain,' '*mmmm*other,' '*mmmm*onkey.' Who can think of another /m/ word?" Hands went up. One child said, "'*Mm*ary' like my name." Teacher: "Good, *Mm*ary. Any others?" A second child said, "We went to the mountains once. It was our vacation and we slept in a tent." With so many concepts floating about, only the most sophisticated child could extract the relevant information from the lesson. Training in the techniques of programmed teaching as described above can enable a teacher to instruct children in the basic skills with more precision.

Teaching Blending

Once five symbol/sound correspondences are established they are immediately used to blend real words. A precise program for teaching the blending routine has been prepared for this purpose. You will perhaps have noted that our task analyses did not include a detailed subroutine for blending. This is because we know of no reasonably elaborated theory for how humans manage to recognize the equivalence of the single sound (e.g., /ka/) and the separate phonemes (e.g., /k/ and /a/). We know only that the equivalence is a difficult one, and that the ability to recognize it, and therefore to produce a blend, becomes greater with greater experience. In the absence of a strong hypothesis concerning the cognitive processes involved, a visual/motor analogue of the blending operation helps to organize the process for the child. We have, therefore, developed a rather ritualized procedure for blending, in which motor acts accompany the oral blending. These motor acts provide a kind of external representation of what goes on during the blending process.

For example, in the case of the word *cat*, the child who was performing the blending procedure independently would:

1. Point to the c and say /k/.
2. Point to the a and say /a/.
3. Slowly slide his finger under the ca and say /ka/ slowly.

4. Quickly slide his finger under the ca and say / ka/ quickly.
5. Point to the t and say /t/.
6. Slowly slide his finger under cat and say /kat/ slowly.
7. Circle the word with his finger and say, "The word is *cat*."

The techniques for teaching the blending procedure include a series of steps that lead the child from imitating the procedure toward performing it independently. Essentially, the teacher repeats the linking and blending of sounds three times. At each repetition, the teacher systematically fades out of the process and gives greater responsibility to the child. At the end of the sequence, the child demonstrates the procedure by himself. More specifically:

1. The teacher models the blending procedure. She models the sounds and the blends and uses finger-pointing procedures and intermittent verbal directions.

2. The children imitate the model while the teacher repeats both the verbal cues and the finger cues to assist them.

3. The teacher repeats the procedure, but this time does not model the sounds or the blends. She gives only the verbal cues and the finger cues to assist.

4. The procedure is repeated. This time, the teacher drops the verbal cues. She gives only finger cues (i.e., the prompts are faded).

5. The child performs the pointing, sounding, and blending steps independently.

A strong advantage for the teacher of this blending procedure is the precise information available for locating an error. If a child makes an error while performing the procedure, the teacher knows exactly where the error is, that is, which link in the process is incorrect. With this kind of precise information, the teacher can give him a direct prompt. For example, if the child's inability to pronounce a word was caused by a substituted or omitted phoneme, the teacher would point to the letter and ask the child to say its sound. If he hesitated, she would prompt him with a silent mouthing cue. If necessary, she would model the sound. If the error was in a blend (e.g., the *ca* in cat), she would run her finger under the *ca* and ask the child to say the blend, she would cue the blend if the child hesitated, and if necessary she would model the blend. The availability of this kind of precise information enables the teacher to adapt her behavior to the particular needs of the individual child.

Context and Comprehension in Early Reading

We will turn in a moment to consideration of general processes of reading comprehension. But it is important, before terminating our discussion of early reading, to consider the role of comprehension in early reading behavior. Learning to read is not a matter of learning to recognize words then learning to comprehend. Rather, it is a matter of learning to recognize words in order to comprehend. We have already suggested that in initial decoding word recognition and some level of comprehension are closely interdependent. Part of the decoding process involves testing a blended word against one's existing aural recognition vocabulary. Decoding of nonsense words would be quite another matter. A simple extension, one we will discuss more fully in a moment, is that the candidate word is tested for suitability to the immediate context. This testing in fact forms an integral part of the word attack process, although we have not shown it in the models yet. Many children—perhaps most—appear to engage in this testing naturally, once they recognize that printed language is a schematic map of the spoken language they already know. The process can be assisted, however, by instruction that at a very early stage draws attention explicitly to context—for example, by requiring the child to choose the "best fitting" of two words for a given context, or by requiring him to indicate which specific segments of a text provide clues to a word's meaning. A variety of activities of this kind are included in our program from virtually the initial lessons. In addition, as the lessons progress and as increasing vocabulary and fluency are developed, a few simple comprehension activities are introduced, such as selecting the best fitting picture for a text of several lines, or following directions of several sentences' length. These activities are not intended to teach comprehension systematically. Rather, they help the reader to keep alert to the details of the text and to maintain a meaning-detection rather than a word-recognition orientation toward the process of reading.

Reading Comprehension: Mapping the Domain

We turn now to the possibilities for creating models of reading comprehension processes themselves. We cannot offer any models as detailed as those we proposed for decoding, although we can point with some optimism to work elsewhere that may provide deeper understanding of language comprehension in general and, thus, a basis for models of text comprehension. Such work includes artificial intelligence efforts on sentence processing (e.g., Winograd 1972), and story comprehension (Charniak 1972), simulation models of the understanding of verbal instructions (Hayes & Simon 1974), and increasing empirical work on natural language and text processing.

What we can offer here is not a formal model, but a general map of the reading comprehension domain, a description that can direct our atten-

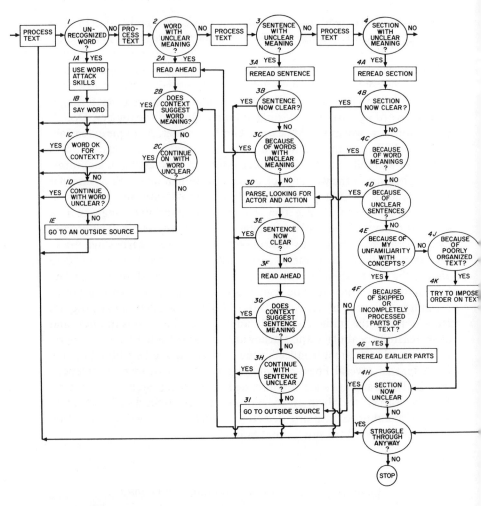

Fig. 7.5. A schematic model of the reading comprehension process.

tion to some of the most important psychological and instructional issues that need to be addressed. Figure 7.5 is such a map. It represents the hypothesized flow of behavior for an effective reader performing the complex behavior of reading a moderately difficult text. The reader might be a third-grader reading a social studies text dealing with prehistoric animals or a college student reading this paper.

Although at a much less specific level than the models shown earlier, Figure 7.5 retains the flow diagram format, because of the usefulness of this format in displaying the decision-making sequences that we assumed to be characteristic of comprehension activity. Like the earlier analyses, Figure 7.5 contains two kinds of statements: direction statements (rectangular boxes) and queries (diamonds). Using the computer program analogy, the direction statements can be considered as subprograms that can be activated by the more general "Reading" program. The queries are decision points, points at which the program assesses its own state and "decides" whether to continue or to enter a correction loop in which more information is sought. These decisions are not necessarily conscious but, rather, they represent points at which the reader recognizes that deeper processing is needed for comprehension purposes. The top line of the figure describes the flow of processing and self-monitoring for a reader who encounters no difficulties at all in the course of reading. This is a rare occasion, of course. Most frequently readers will encounter occasional difficulties in recognizing words or in interpreting meaning; these difficulties require readers to search for further information. These searches are described, in quite general terms, in the sequences shown below Queries 1 through 4.

An ongoing text-processing activity is assumed (the "process text" boxes in the top line). This processing activity is interrupted by occasions on which the reader decides he has inadequate information and initiates a search for just enough information to satisfy his own demands for an adequate level of comprehension. The first such interruption is for an unrecognized word (Query 1). It is important to note that a skilled reader will probably not interrupt reading for every unrecognized word, nor may he even attend to every separate word in the text (cf., Goodman 1970). However, a certain "adequate" level of word recognition is required, and even skilled readers will occasionally encounter unrecognized words that are significant to the general meaning of the text and that necessitate the use of word attack skills to "decode" the word. The word-attack strand as shown here is a very condensed statement of the decoding routines discussed in the first part of the paper. Boxes 1A and 1B are summaries of all of the material in Figures 7.1–7.3. Decision 1C represents a check for the pronounced word's semantic and syntactic suitability for the context. If an acceptable word has been found, the reader returns to the main text-processing flow; otherwise, the reader must decide whether to continue reading with the word still unclear (1D) or to seek information from an outside source. The "outside source" for a decoding problem is likely to be another person, although finding the same word in another context sometimes solves the problem.

The second interruption indicated occurs when a word is sounded that has an unclear meaning and that appears important enough to comprehension to warrant further information search (Query 2). We assume that the most frequent first response under these conditions is to read ahead a little, searching for context that will suggest a meaning (2A). The success of this context search is tested at 2B. Success sends the reader back into the main processing strand, while failure gives him the same choices as before: to continue reading with the word unclear, or to utilize an outside source. Now, dictionaries, glossaries, etc. are available as outside sources as well as other people, although other people may remain the preferred "least effort" source. We will see in a moment that the decision to continue with words unclarified may effect subsequent processing. Nevertheless, it is often a good choice in reading—depending upon the depth of comprehension required for a particular task, and upon the degree of informational redundancy.

At Query 3, processing is interrupted by awareness of a sentence or clause whose meaning is not completely clear. The reader's first action is probably to reread the sentence and to test for success in gaining meaning (3A and 3B). If simple rereading fails, a next reasonable test would be to determine whether individual words—perhaps those deliberately left unclear in early decisions—are the source of difficulty (3C); if this is so, then the word-meaning strand is entered. If individual words are not the problem, attention must next be focused upon the syntactic and semantic structure of the sentence. The sentence must be parsed to reveal its basic structure (3D). This is a complex and still incompletely understood process, although some current models for sentence parsing (e.g., Winograd 1972) may offer a basis for understanding this aspect of reading behavior. If parsing is successful in revealing meaning (3E), then the reader reenters the main processing strand; if parsing fails, then a set of decisions similar to those for individual words probably occurs. The reader may decide to proceed with the sentence (temporarily) unclear (3H), or he may turn to an outside source (3I).

We come finally, at Query 4, to a situation in which an entire section (paragraph, chapter, whatever) is seen as unclear. As for sentences, the first likely act is rereading (4A). Next unclear words (4C) or unclear sentences (4D) may be the source of difficulty. If so, the reader returns to the word-meaning or sentence-meaning strands. If neither of these seems to be the cause of difficulty, an interesting set of further tests may occur. The reader may try to decide whether the present difficulty is due to his own unfamiliarity with the concepts discussed in the text (4E). If this seems a likely cause, perhaps it is due to incomplete processing of earlier parts of the text; (4F) in which case rereading the earlier parts (4G) may help. If the difficulties do not appear to reside in the reader's unfamiliarity with the concepts (a "no" answer at 4E), then the skilled reader may begin to wonder whether the text itself is so poorly written that it is the cause of the problem (4J). He may then try to impose order on the text (4K). If all of these tests and actions fail to produce clarification ("no" answer at 4J and 4H), a fundamental decision must finally be made—whether to struggle ahead anyway. We suspect that many children in school do struggle through, with very little comprehension, simply because they have been told to read something. People reading independently will rarely do this, nor would we reasonably expect them to.

The model we have presented here, as we stated at the outset, represents only a general mapping of reading processes. It suggests in broad terms the probable major components of the reading process and how these components might interact; it does not attempt to describe the processes in detail. Some simplifying assumptions have been made. For example, we assume a highly motivated reader—it's impossible to stop following this route map until an entire section is found unclear! Second, we have assumed the availability of an outside source for help—an assumption that is not always fulfilled in real reading situations. Further, we have depicted deliberate "decisions" for situations in which choices are probably normally made much less explicitly. Nevertheless, even in this simplified outline state, we believe the model as presented helps to make evident certain important features of reading. Perhaps the most important feature is the indeterminacy of the process, its trial and error character. Reading is not an algorithmic process in which straightforward application of a set of rules or procedures will invariably yield comprehension of a text. Rather, it is a kind of interaction with a text, an interaction in which information is sought at various levels of specificity and in which a gradual reduction in "unknowns" is sought as more and more of the text is processed.

One general suggestion for reading instruction that emerges from this characterization is that readers be explicitly taught some of the self-monitoring strategies implied by the model. Even if we are still unable to specify the details for some of the processes outlined, it seems likely that alerting readers to the kinds of difficulty that may be encountered and to some broad strategies for dealing with the difficulties may be very powerful. Recent work in mathematical problem-solving suggests that self-consciousness about goals and overt planning activity increase success (e.g., Resnick & Glaser 1975; Greeno 1973). Some of the same principles are probably applicable to reading. What the present model outlines are some of the strategies for conducting the interaction, and it shows the strategies to be heuristic—that is, to depend on the reader's judgment along the way concerning how well he is gathering and interpreting the necessary information.

The model also suggests that reading is a very context-bound activity—i.e., that the characteristics of the text will have a great effect upon what constitutes effective reading strategy. Thus, there is no single sure-fire way to read well. Even the most skilled of readers will sometimes encounter texts that are not processed without considerable search activity. Further, success in reading is partly knowledge-bound. Much depends upon the knowledge the reader brings to the text. Not only must words be in the auditory vocabulary, but, similarly, unfamiliarity with the subject-matter concepts is often a cause of difficulty in comprehension, unless the text is explicitly designed to introduce the reader to some subject-matter. The instructional implication of this is that reading comprehension may best be taught in the context of other subject-matters rather than as a separate discipline, in order to allow the acquisition of a broad range of knowledge as the basis for effective reading.

NEXT STEPS

We have in this paper offered a general proposal about the relationship between psychological theory—especially information-processing descriptions of complex tasks—and the design of instruction. We have described a process in which rational analyses of reading were developed in response to questions raised by problems of instruction, and we have shown some of the ways in which these models have guided the design of a reading program. The models we have presented must be regarded as hypotheses for the moment, since we have not offered firm evidence of their validity as descriptions of how people read, but we have suggested a strategy for testing them.

The strategy proposed is an iterative one: model building and refinement, based on instructional efforts. We believe that attention to modeling the reading process will become increasingly important as instructional efforts in reading shift focus from decoding to the syntactic and semantic processes involved in comprehension. In this paper we have attempted to show that even the relatively simple skills of word attack involve complex heuristics of judgment and self-monitoring. Such is even more strongly the case for comprehension skills, and for this reason careful theory-generation and testing is especially required for these skills. Our current capacity to describe what is to be taught in the way of comprehension abilities is extremely limited. The best we now have are taxonomies, lists of classes of stimuli and classes of responses, sometimes ordered according to relative difficulty or complexity. Until we "look inside" to find out what processes mediate the behaviors we call comprehension, we can expect little progress beyond the exercises that now fill children's intermediate and middle school days and that seem to fail so many children so badly.

At the risk of prediction made too soon, we would like to suggest that instruction based on models of language comprehension, such as are now beginning to emerge from both experimental cognitive work and related computer modeling is likely to differ significantly from what we now know in reading comprehension. First, we are likely to focus heavily on helping children to build extensive bodies of knowledge that will help them to interpret new materials that they encounter in written texts; this will mean less reliance on collections of brief, unrelated reading selections in favor of extended reading and related experiences in a few areas of interest. Second, we are likely to teach children general strategies of reasoning and thinking, since it appears unlikely that comprehension of written material will involve totally different processes than comprehension of oral language. Third, we will probably teach children more explicit mediational strategies for organizing and remembering what they read (strategies such as visual imaging, self-questioning, regrouping of information, etc.). Fourth, we are likely to try to help children to become aware of their language processes and to call deliberately on their most effective strategies. We will seek, in other words, to establish what might be called a system of "meta-comprehension" by which children can monitor and organize their own comprehension processes.

Such are our predictions. Our prescription for next steps is to get to work on testing these predictions by beginning for complex comprehension skills the iterative process of model building, instructional design, and experimental testing that is now well begun for initial reading.

REFERENCES

Baddeley, A. D., and Hitch, G. 1974. "Working memory," in G. H. Bower (ed.), *The psychology of learning and motivation* (vol. 8). New York: Academic Press.

Beck, I. L., and Mitroff, D. D. 1972. The rationale and design of a primary grades reading system for an individualized classroom. Pittsburgh: University of Pittsburgh, Learning Research and Development Center (Publication No. 1972/4).

Chall, J. 1967. *Learning to read: The great debate.* New York: McGraw-Hill.

Charniak, E. 1972. *Toward a model of children's story comprehension.* Cambridge, Mass.: Massachusetts Institute of Technology, Artificial Intelligence Laboratory (Al TR-266).

Diederich, P. B. 1973. II. Research 1960–70 on methods and materials in reading. TM Report 22, ERIC Clearinghouse on Tests, Measurement, and Evaluation. Princeton: Educational Testing Service, January 1973.

Goodman, K. S. 1970. "Reading: A psycholinguistic guessing game," in H. Singer and R. B. Ruddell (eds.), *Theoretical models and processes of reading.* Newark, Del.: International Reading Association.

Greeno, J. G. 1973. "The structure of memory and the process of solving problems," in R. L. Solso (ed.), *Contemporary issues in cognitive psychology.* Washington, D.C., V. H. Winston.

Hayes, J. R., and Simon, H. A. 1974. "Understanding written problem instructions," in L. W. Gregg (ed.), *Knowledge and cognition.* Potomac, Md.: Lawrence Erlbaum Associates.

Posner, M. I., and Rossman, E. 1965. Effect of size and location of informational transforms upon short-term retention. *Journal of Experimental Psychology* 70: 496–505.

Resnick, L. B. 1975. "The science and art of curriculum design," in D. Hampson and J. Schaffarzick (eds.), *Strategies for curriculum development.* Berkeley, Calif.: McCutchan Pub. Co., in press.

―――. "Task analysis in instructional design: Some cases from mathematics," in D. Klahr (ed.), *Cognition and instruction.* Hillsdale, N.J.: Lawrence Erlbaum Associates, in press.

Resnick, L. B., and Glaser, R. "Problem solving and intelligence," in L. B. Resnick (ed.), *The nature of intelligence.* Hillsdale, N.J.: Lawrence Erlbaum Associates, in press.

Winograd, T. 1972. Understanding natural language. *Cognitive Psychology* 3: 1–191.

8
Joanna Williams

Commentary on
Research in
Reading Acquisition

We may well look back on the 1970s as a landmark decade the field of reading. The current focus within academic psychology on cognition and the current vigor of the field of linguistics have led to an enormous amount of interest in basic research on reading. The emphasis on literacy as a key national goal, of course, has provided another strong impetus to both theoretical and applied work in the field. We do seem to be making important progress in understanding the complexities of the processes of reading, and, in addition, there have been substantial contributions to the design of effective instruction in reading.

The papers presented at this symposium attest to the vitality of the field. The participants, from a number of diverse disciplines, have dealt with a wide range of relevant issues. In this paper I shall review some of the highlights of the presentations and try to put in a general perspective some of the major ideas and issues that were discussed.

Benson's contribution provides us with a fascinating description of some neurological aspects of reading. Education has leaned on neurology for many years. The so-called "medical model," which attributes certain learning and behavioral difficulties to central nervous system damage, has greatly influenced the educational treatment of disabled readers (and other disabled children, of course) over the years. Many instructional programs, most of which have heavily emphasized perceptual-motor skills, have been justified on the grounds that there was neurological impairment to be overcome. However, the model has rarely, if ever, been evaluated directly. Children are categorized not on the basis of any actual signs of neurological impairment but rather on the basis of inferences from behavior—and the educational treatments designed on the basis of these assumptions have not fulfilled their promise. Up to now, rather little increase in our understanding of the disabled child has resulted from advances in neurology. Benson's discussion, however, leads us to speculate rather optimistically about the prospects for the future.

Benson identified three distinctly different types of alexia, which is an acquired incapacity, produced by a cerebral lesion, in the comprehension of written material. His classification is derived from the correlations that can now be found between specific types of pathology and certain highly specified behavior patterns. Of course, there are many cases where the clinical pattern must be described as "mixed" and where the pattern of brain damage does not neatly fit into the boundaries of the described categories. But a substantial proportion of cases can indeed be categorized according to the taxonomy, and that is truly impressive.

There is no doubt that great strides are being made in the understanding of the relationship between brain and behavior. How can this research help us understand the process of reading, and how, ultimately, will it help children learn to read?

Benson has told us that his work does not offer any direct answers to these questions, but that it can provide some useful guidelines. Let us consider what this means and what would be required to get more direct answers to our questions. The data that Benson has presented are based on observation of adult patients. An adult is different from a child; his nervous system has gone through its developmental sequence and is, as they say, "well committed." If a child's nervous system is altered before it is fully organized by experience, the consequences may be different from those that would be seen in an adult who suffers neurological damage. It is possible, because the nervous system is so plastic early in life, that there will be no deficit at all; compensatory structures will take over all the functions that the damaged portion of the system took care of previously. On the other hand, if the damage is severe enough, the whole system may go out, leading to generalized retardation rather than to a more specific deficit, such as that of language and speech functions. Even the statement I just made may be too strong and definite to represent adequately the state of our knowledge; the important point is that we cannot easily generalize from adult to child. Since the effects of a lesion may also change with time, because of continued development of the individual or of different recovery rates, the matter becomes very complicated. A great deal of study is needed on the relationship between lesion type and behavioral pattern as a function of the age of the individual at the time of the damage. Obviously, such data are hard to come by. However, we may speculate that in the future we shall have taxonomies just as carefully outlined as the one presented here by Benson, indicating, for different age levels, a clear linking of specific areas of the brain with specific losses of functioning. (It may turn out, of course, that neurological damage to children simply leads to more diffuse effects than does damage to adults.)

In addition, the consequences of neurological damage for people who functioned normally prior to their brain injury may well be different from cases in which the abilities had not developed before the trauma. The development of reading proficiency continues over the course of several years. As skill increases, more and more of the lower-order components——like letter-recognition or basic decoding skills—become highly automatic. Often, evidently, there is relatively good recovery after brain injury of such automatized functions, but there might not be any recovery of these abilities in children who had not reached an automatic level before the injury was sustained.

How might this type of information be utilized in the development of educational strategies? At present, we can ask the question meaningfully only about the training of adults. If we knew that certain neural pathways had been knocked out and that certain functions were blocked, for example, we could explore the ways in which the still-intact structures might compensate. That is, what functions does the person still have that could be used to retrain what he has lost? The questions are simple, but the answers will not be easily attained. Careful observation of patients leads to highly delineated descriptions of specific tasks that can or cannot be performed. It is risky to try to describe a clinical syndrome in terms of more general functions, and yet, more general categorizations would certainly be much more useful as a basis for devising educational strategies. Obviously, we cannot yet meaningfully pursue the question of educational strategies in children; and this means that, for the most part, concerns about beginning reading instruction cannot yet be tackled.

In summary, we are quite far at present from being able to use neurological knowledge in the development of reading instruction. The most direct application of this challenging work is, possibly, in the increased understanding of the components of a complex skill and how they are put together. Luria (1966), for example, has suggested that the process of breaking down a skill into its most simple elements, analyzing each step of the operation, and creating new and different procedures to restructure the steps that can be learned with still-intact cortical areas, will move forward our general understanding of the psychological processes involved in reading. He quotes Pavlov: "Pathology permits one to highlight that which is normally hidden, and to analyze that which normally forms an integral whole." The Resnick and Beck paper and the Samuels paper have addressed this same issue and, in my opinion, have outlined more direct and probably more fruitful ways of analyzing complex skills. It is certainly true, however, that important insights could well come out of clinical neurology. In any event, we shall have to wait patiently for implications and applications from this field; but they will come, and they are likely to revolutionize our thinking.

While it is true that we do not have good enough answers at present to the question of how to make instructional materials and methods maximally effective and efficient, we do know that special, intensive, individualized remedial help is useful. We may not succeed with all children, of course, but at least there is enough gain in skill in enough children who are given remediation so that we remain confident. Indeed, the problem is really one of identifying those children who should be given special treatment. It is a difficult problem. Standardized tests of intelligence or readiness tests seem to offer little help. One complication is that the course of reading acquisition over the first few school years can be quite uneven. Some children have no trouble at any stage. Others perform badly during their first year of instruction, and, as one would expect, continue to do badly later on. But there is a sizable group of children who, after performing badly during the first year, catch up and make normal progress. DeHirsch, Jansky, and Langford (1966) found that of a group of children scoring low in reading at the end of first grade, half improved in the second year ("slow starters") and half continued to fail. Thus, first-grade achievement did not predict future growth completely.

Because of this problem, there is a widespread reluctance to begin remedial training too early. This "waiting" policy would be perfectly reasonable if, after the remediation were administered, we could be sure that children would be able to read. But the relatively few studies available suggest that reading skill has been improved to a considerably greater extent in cases where the intervention was begun early. Moreover, the failure that a child experiences during the years when he, unlike his classmates, cannot make gains in reading often leads to a real aversion for the task. So it behooves us to try harder to develop a procedure for early detection of problem readers.

Satz seeks to do just this. His longitudinal study is not yet completed, but the report of his progress suggests a variety of critical issues that deserve our consideration. Satz hopes to develop a test battery that will identify the precursors of specific reading disability several years before the disorder is clinically evident. His test battery should be administered before the child begins formal reading, when, presumably, he would be more responsive to remediation attempts. The model is one of maturational lag: different skills are in primary ascendancy at different ages, and children who have specific reading disability will show a changing pattern of poor performance. Specifically, at an early age, these children will be depressed in sensori-perceptual-motor-mnemonic skills, on which they will later catch up to children who are developing normally. They then might lag behind on the cognitive-linguistic skills, which have a slower and later development. Satz reports success in predicting from his kindergarten assessment to first-, second-, and third-grade reading achievement in between 70% and 85% of the cases, when they have been categorized into four groups: severe disability, mild disability, average reader, and superior reader. This is promising, but the fact that one can call it promising reveals just how unsatisfactory today's assessment procedures really are.

Satz is interested in specific reading disability, but his sample consists of the total white male population enrolled in twenty schools. I should think that there would also be cases in this group of a more general learning disability or of other specific types of disability. It is true that it is quite difficult to categorize children into one or another of these groupings, syndromes being generally so diffuse; but, presumably, there are a few relatively discrete categories. For example, certain disorders are characterized primarily by hyperactivity and distractibility; others, by difficulty with all school subjects dominated by language content (including reading); others are restricted specifically to (a) reading and spelling, (b) coordinative skills—athletics, handwriting, or (c) arithmetic.

If there is any true differentiation to these categories or to any categorization within the general learning-disabled classification, it would seem that the lag in development of certain underlying skills ought to vary among them. That is, children who manifest the hyperactivity-impulsivity syndrome or the arithmetic disorder should perhaps not show the same lag that is hypothesized for the reading-disabled children, i.e., in tests that tap the sensori-perceptual-motor-mnemonic factor early and tests that tap the cognitive-linguistic factor later. Rather, they should show different maturational patterns that reflect the task structure in arithmetic, let us say, and the changes in that task structure that occur over the first few school grades. It would be very interesting indeed to examine the achievement of Satz's subjects in areas other than reading, especially in arithmetic.

We certainly need a valid technique for identifying those children who may become problem readers. Perhaps Satz's battery will provide one for us, and perhaps it will also provide evidence for the maturational lag theory. It is too bad that the study will have to go on for so long before sufficient data is collected to evaluate the hypotheses, but that is the nature of longitudinal research.

Kinsbourne is also interested in the problem of identifying the disabled reader. Acknowledging the same difficulties in long-term prediction that Satz discussed, Kinsbourne chooses a different approach. He has developed a battery of tests that cover the visual, auditory, and associative components encompassed in beginning reading, and he proposes that the battery not be used for predicting future performance, but rather that it serve as an immediate guide to teachers. The test results could pinpoint just what component skills were giving a child problems and thereby indicate the proper remedial instruction. This proposal makes good sense; it appears that Kinsbourne's tests do indeed assess the appropriate skills and that they might well hold promise in terms of diagnosing what is giving a child trouble. However, there is one difficulty: at present, there are few instructional programs that would be suitable as remediation. I can think of a few current research and development efforts that make sense in this context. If the child scores poorly on Kinsbourne's easy tests, Richard Venezky's pre-reading program, Jerome Rosner's perceptual skills curriculum, or the auditory-skills-oriented decoding program that we are developing at Teachers College might be used. Children who score relatively high on Kinsbourne's battery might well be placed effectively in Resnick's and Beck's reading program. I expect that in the near future there will be a greater number of process-oriented curricula, so that Kinsbourne's test battery would be more generally useful.

Let us turn now to Menyuk's discussion of the acquisition of oral language and its relationship to the acquisition of reading. Menyuk's analysis of the ways in which oral and written language are similar and also how they differ is illuminating, and it points up the myriad possibilities that must be considered in developing a model of reading. Obviously, there are many parallels between oral and written language: babbling and scribbling; segmenting via pauses and via white spaces; distinctive features of phonemes and of letters; and so forth. The differences are more provocative; the differences in segmentation hierarchies strike me as particularly interesting. Menyuk suggests that the processing strategies in speech perception start at the level of meaning. Only later does the child make distinctions at more analytic or smaller-unit levels. That is, the child first responds to sentences, marked by intonation and stress patterns, and then to words and/or to syllables. Presumably, he never has to differentiate isolated phonemes, though of course he responds on the phoneme level—he can distinguish *bag* from *bat, can* from *cat.* In written language, on the other hand, there is a different sequence. Analysis comes first, and the child now for the first time must become conscious of phonemic segments, for he must learn how they map to orthographic representations. While successful readers appear to move on to a consideration of superordinate structures (such as phrase and sentence) fairly rapidly, this transition is difficult for some children. Sometimes, in fact, children never reach the final stage of reading for meaning.

Presumably, the sequence in written language comprehension would vary somewhat with the method of instruction used. For example, it is sometimes claimed that if you simply read a story over and over again to a child, letting him follow along on the printed page, he will gradually pick up the salient features of correspondence between oral and written representation, and he will learn how to read. It would seem to me that people who argue for this instructional approach must assume that the child picks up superordinate units first and then works through the hierarchy in the same way as he does in oral language comprehension. Samuels has mentioned in his paper some people who would presumably endorse such a procedure. I myself do not; I think that while a child might learn in this way, it would be a terribly inefficient procedure. I think that it would be difficult for all but the most able children to make all the inductions on their own, especially at the level of the relationship between grapheme and phoneme. So I agree with Menyuk that the difference between the sequence in oral comprehension and in written comprehension, while not logically necessary, is, in almost all cases and for all practical purposes, a genuine one and a very useful one. Incidentally, I am pleased to see that Menyuk has focused on the beginning reader; most analyses of the relationship between written and oral language have been done with a focus on the proficient adult (Williams 1970). While many important insights for the understanding of language in general may come out of such studies, focusing on the adult does not appear to be the most profitable course one could take if he were interested in the understanding of reading acquisition and how to teach reading. Menyuk's analysis, on the other hand, delineates distinctions at the right level, which should be most valuable for those considering instructional strategies.

Most of the emphasis in this paper is on phonology. She presents evidence of an ordering in the development of perceptual speech-sound distinctions. She discusses the organization of production in terms of syllable features. She cites Reed's data on the phonological generalizations that children develop before formal instruction, data of Shankweiler and Liberman demonstrating the great difference between reading errors and listening errors, and data from her own laboratory that indicates differences in phonological coding between normal children and those who suffer from different language disorders.

It is true, as she points out, that much of the work comparing the oral language of good and poor readers has focused on matters of phonology. But that seems to be changing, and differentiations can certainly be made between good and poor readers in other aspects of oral language. For example, there is a limited amount of evidence that in both receptive and expressive speech, children with reading problems are less fluent and know fewer words. They also give less mature definitions; that is, poor readers give more descriptive definitions (e.g., a bicycle has wheels) and fewer categorical definitions (e.g., a bicycle is a vehicle). Problem readers also do not perform as well in processing grammatical structure; they respond word-by-word, ignoring prior context (e.g., Steiner, Weiner, & Cromer 1971). Other studies also demonstrate the greater influence of linguistic organization on good readers.

Menyuk is properly cautious about the kinds of implications we might draw from the limited work that has been done, and she suggests that it might be informative to make an evaluation of successful children's strategies before formal reading instruction is begun. These data would be extremely valuable, and I think that such an approach would be more promising than another research approach that seems likely at this point, that is, continuing to make comparisons on all aspects of oral language between good and poor readers. Not that the information we would gain from the latter approach would not be significant; it surely would. But as I reflect on the enormous quantity of data collected in the past on the correlations between various perceptual-motor tasks and reading achievement, and the overall failure of the remediation attempts based on perceptual-motor training that inevitably, if illogically, were promoted by those data, I can only hope that the same thing doesn't happen again. To date the data do suggest that it might be of some value to design remediation focused on improving the language skills of poor readers. However, it is too early to predict exactly what types of remediation might be useful. We must be very careful. It would be wasteful and indeed unfortunate if people now started to declare that training in language skills was "the answer," without taking the time for proper evaluation.

Menyuk is too wise to claim that language factors are responsible for all reading failure, even though in these days psycholinguistics seems to be one field that is very likely to yield answers to some of our most important questions. Indeed, she points out that motivation and the attitudes of peers and teachers play very important roles. Let us turn now to a consideration of the social context of reading and to Entwisle's paper.

We all know that social variables influence reading. The substantial differences in achievement between the sexes and among various subcultures cannot be understood without recourse to explanations involving social factors. Everyone acknowledges that a child's attitude toward a task will affect his acquisition and his performance of that task; that one of the teacher's most important jobs is to instill and/or maintain appropriate motivation; and that early home envirvnment provides such a powerful set of lessons that it is very difficult for later influences to succeed in modifying a child's basic value system. But while we pay lip-service to these ideas, not much research is undertaken in the area, probably because it is such a difficult area in which to work (and possibly also because intervention attempts that are likely to be successful are so complicated and difficult to implement).

Entwisle must be congratulated for taking on the challenge. In her paper, she has described a longitudinal observational study of the expectations of elementary school children. What kinds of aspirations do children really have, and do they expect to achieve their goals? How do their expectations influence their achievement, and what effects do other people's expectations have?

The difficulty of carrying out a research plan in this field is striking. All of one's skills and sensitivities are tested in even such seemingly simple matters as persuading parents to participate in the study. Ensuring that the questions asked of the children will be understandable, so that the assessment of their expectation will be a valid assessment, is another tricky problem. Entwisle's arguments for the validity of her measures are convincing, especially the fact that there is a negative correlation between expectation in reading and expectation in arithmetic. However, it appears that in the classroom the children seem to get heavy doses of positive feedback about their performance, and perhaps what happens on a daily basis is more salient than a once-in-a-blue-moon report card. Perhaps, in future cohorts to be studied, the focus could be broadened, so that an assessment of a child's expectations is based in some way on more than just the report card.

The issues involved are complex. For example, some research suggests that the potency of reinforcers varies as a function of social class. One study by Zigler and Kanzer (1962) found that "tangibles are more effective reinforcers for lower-class children and that teachers' approval is more effective for middle-class children." These differences make it difficult to compare feedback in the different schools studied. As the research progresses and more data are collected, careful analysis will have to be made of such factors.

What the actual effects of grading practices are is an important question, and Entwisle's study should give us valuable insights. The two schools that she describes have widely diverging philosophies about grades; one grades according to the individual child's ability and the other on an absolute standard. How clearly do the different contingencies really come through to the child? The delicate question of what kind of feedback should be given to a child becomes an interesting ethical issue. What are the implications of providing heavily positive reinforcement—in the form of grades, every-day comments in the classroom, or whatever—in order to promote maximal academic achievement, if it also will lead the child to make an unrealistically high appraisal of himself vis-à-vis the world outside the classroom? Or, if we have to make the choice, can we decide that a healthy self-image is more crucial than high achievement and engineer the reward-structure accordingly? These matters will have to be explored fully.

Samuels' paper presents an issue that provokes a good deal of controversy among some educational researchers. If the question were only of academic interest, there would not be so much argument, but the answer to the question presumably leads directly to instructional application—unlike many questions discussed by educational researchers.

Can a complex skill like reading be analyzed into component skills arranged in a hierarchy? Should the development of instructional programs be guided by such an analysis? Samuels points out clearly the conflicts between this approach and a more holistic approach, which argues that complex processes cannot be fractionated without being changed qualitatively and which obviously leads to quite different instructional methodology. He has made a good case for the hierarchy approach. He cites early studies, including the classic study by Bryan and Harter on learning telegraphy, and more recent studies of his own and of others that demonstrate that even very simple paradigms like that of associative learning can be analyzed into component parts. He has also outlined an instructional sequence for teaching letter-sound correspondences, identifying the subskills—left-right visual scan, letter-sound knowledge, and sound-blending—and demonstrating that in this particular case instruction can proceed effectively in the subskills in any order, as long as all the skills are provided.

The approach is certainly reasonable, and it seems to be well justified in terms of a number of goals. First of all, it fits in with today's ideal of individualized instruction, for it allows the progress of students to be charted very precisely. Generally speaking, curriculum development should be improved by the availability of valid skill-hierarchies.

As Samuels has pointed, out, validated hierarchies of subskills have not been established yet. Robert Gagné (1970) proposed the notion of "hierarchy" in his theory of complex human learning in the early sixties, and the first hierarchies that were developed, both by Gagné and others, were in basic mathematics. It is not difficult to see why this is so: component tasks in arithmetic and their prerequisites are fairly easy to describe and to sequence. But reading is a different matter, for it is not a process that is easily analyzed. To be sure, the process of decoding is amenable to such an analysis; and both the Samuels paper and the paper by Resnick and Beck have offered nice analyses of certain aspects of the decoding process. But I am not convinced at present that the study of reading comprehension will make much progress using this approach.

How are skill hierarchies validated? Psychometric procedures are often used. A battery of tests assessing the various skills in the presumed hierarchy is developed, and relationships among test scores are evaluated by scalogram analysis or other such procedures. If passing one test reliably predicts whether or not another test is passed, then those tests are hierarchically organized. From this type of validation, one can evaluate a hypothesized sequence of skill acquisition, but the sequence is inferred and not tested directly.

Experimental studies provide another more powerful way of validating a hierarchy. For example, one might compare the effects of teaching two or more tasks (a) in the order predicted by the hierarchy, or (b) in another order. Is the predicted sequence most efficient in terms of learning time? Does the learning of a skill specified as a prerequisite lead to the acquisition not only of the terminal task but also of transfer tasks? This type of work will lead to strong validation of the hierarchy and to the design of optimal instructional sequences. But this sort of research, of course, is painstakingly slow, and so we don't have very much of it.

It is worth pointing out that such carefully sequenced instruction is probably not necessary for all pupils. But this does not invalidate hierarchical analysis or component-skills theory. What it does do, however, is make one stop to think before he invests in large-scale development and validation of a skills hierarchy as a basis for developing instructional programs. Some children, especially the more able ones, do well with instruction that is organized more grossly. One must therefore evaluate the hierarchy approach in terms of the type of pupil he hopes to reach.

Samuels ends his paper with a recommendation that should be underlined. He points out that taking a subskills approach does not mean that beginning instruction in reading cannot be made meaningful. There is no reason why such educational procedures cannot be utilized alongside a well-analyzed and -sequenced skills-oriented instructional program.

Resnick and Beck begin where Samuels leaves off. That is, they are thoroughly committed to task analysis, the development of hierarchies of reading skills, and the teaching of component skills, so that they take for granted what Samuels has justified for us. They point up the continued need for links between theory and educational practice, and they propose a loosely defined process model from which can be derived general instructional principles and subskills for further analysis. The goal, a detailed, valid and useful model of reading, is, of course, a long way off, but the steps required are laid out nicely. The authors have proposed that reading comprehension as well as lower-order skills be studied within their framework; of course, this aspect of the model-building will take considerably longer, since at present development in this area is at such a preliminary stage.

Using a computer analogy, the authors delineate the processing engaged in by a skilled reader. I do not know of any other paper with an information-processing point of view like Resnick and Beck's that presents such an explicit, detailed set of steps outlining the complex behavior of a proficient reader.

An important contribution of this paper is the detailed analysis of two different strategies for teaching blending. In one case, each grapheme is pronounced and stored separately, and not until all individual graphemes are thus processed is there an attempt to blend the stored phonemes. In the other strategy, blending occurs sequentially at each stage at which a new phoneme is pronounced. Thus two is the maximum number of units that are blended at any one time. The authors hypothesize that this decreases the memory load of the learner because the number of sound units that must be held in memory is presumably smaller. Because of this difference, the successive, blending procedure should be superior.

At this point, the models are offered only as hypotheses; they have not been validated. Even at the present stage, where they have been developed strictly by rational analysis, the models ought to help in instructional design, in the sense that they identify what processes should be taught and in which order they should be presented. Successful empirical validation will probably involve several different methodologies. First of all, the behavior of children taught by means of an instructional program derived from the model should be examined to determine whether the strategies used were indeed the ones that had been taught, as well as whether the strategies were successful. The authors point out that it must be determined that those processes that are taught are in fact the ones used; otherwise, no conclusions about a process model are possible. All of this makes excellent sense.

Another validation strategy proposed is computer simulation. Inputting a child's memory and entering knowledge, the program should output a good match to the actual performance of the child. Successive iterations will lead to refinements and a better match. After an initial stage of decoding in a fairly simple step-by-step manner, the child will presumably start using other cues like context, or he may start organizing by units larger than simple grapheme-phoneme correspondences. This means that the child's processing will diverge from the computer model, which will have to be changed accordingly (e.g., by readjusting the units utilized, increasing the oral recognition vocabulary, or increasing the memory capacity). If any of these adjustments involves comprehension—and they will, very early, because children start very early to use context, for example—the model that Resnick and Beck are working with will have to be elaborated further.

There seem to me to be several special considerations in simulating reading acquisition. For one thing, it must be determined that the instructional program is, in fact, successful in the real world with real children. This is not as simple as it might sound. Can a well-structured sequence of instructional steps, presented in a much less flexible way than the way the typical teacher would present the instruction, actually teach blending? Laboratory analogs similar to what would be presented have not been notably successful to date.

My concern is that if a real instructional situation cannot be demonstrated as effective, or if the results of simulation do not square with a couple of simple variations in either instructional procedure or the child's entering knowledge, there will not be much point to the formalization of the model by computer simulation. A model such as this must have psychological validity. Simulation is time-consuming and costly, and only after an extended period of work can one expect to achieve any significant results at all. Given this, such a research program should not be undertaken lightly, but should be preceded by intensive study of its likely outcomes.

Taken together, these papers represent rather well our current concerns and emphases. Well-conceived basic research in most instances now has some genuine theoretical underpinning, and serious applications to real educational problems are now being influenced heavily by the results of conceptual and empirical analyses. The Symposium has demonstrated the fruitfulness of multidisciplinary discussions of common problems.

REFERENCES

DeHirsch, K., Jansky, J., and Langford, W. 1966. *Predicting reading failure.* New York: Harper & Row.

Gagné, R. M. 1970. *The conditions of learning* (2nd ed.). New York: Holt, Rinehart, and Winston.

Luria, A. R. 1966. *Human brain and psychological processes.* New York: Harper & Row.

Steiner, R., Weiner, M., and Cromer. W. 1971. Comprehension training and identification of good and poor readers. *Journal of Educational Psychology* 62: 506–13.

Williams, J. P. 1970. "From basic research on reading to educational practice," in Levin, H., and Williams, J. P. (eds.), *Basic studies on reading.* New York: Basic Books.

Zigler, E., and Kanzer, P. 1962. The effectiveness of two classes of verbal reinforcers on the performance of middle- and lower-class subjects. *Journal of Personality* 30: 157–63.

Index of Names